The
Assertive
Woman

The Assertive Woman

A New Look

Stanlee Phelps
and
Nancy Austin

Arlington Books
King St, St James's
London

THE ASSERTIVE WOMAN
First published in Great Britain 1988 by
Arlington Books (Publishers) Ltd
15–17 King St, St James's
London SW1

© 1975, 1987 by Stanlee Phelps and Nancy Austin
Published by arrangement with Impact Publishers
San Luis Obispo, CA93406, USA

Specified selections on pages 30, 55, 156, 157, 175 from The Search for
Signs of Intelligent Life in The Universe by Jane Wagner. Copyright ©
1986 by Jane Wagner, Inc. Reprinted by permission of Harper & Row,
Publishers, Inc.

Learning Assertive Behavior with PALS, by Sharon A. Bower, © 1974.
Used by permission of the author.
'Chart of Three Fellows We All Know,' by Gerald W. Piaget, Ph.D.,
Behavior Therapy Associates, Los Altos, CA, presented at the
Orthopsychiatric Convention in San Francisco, April, 1974. Used by
permission of the author.

British Library Cataloguing-in-Publication Data

Phelps, Stanlee
The assertive woman
1. Self assertion. Manuals — For women
I. Title   II. Austin, Nancy
158'.1

ISBN 0–85140–731–5

Typeset by Inforum, Portsmouth
Printed and bound by
Billing & Sons Ltd, Worcester

Table of Contents

Chapter 1

Introduction

. . . the thought we would like to leave with you is that becoming an assertive woman is a giant step toward personal freedom and growth. We urge you to take this first step – and let us hear from you. Good luck, patience, perseverance, assertiveness, and love.

The Assertive Woman (1975)

That's the way we ended the first edition of this book.

In 1975, *The Assertive Woman* was the product of a sea of change in America. For the first time, women began to realize that they had clout and the options that go with it. Gone were the days when women's rights could fit on the back of an envelope – few civil and personal liberties required little space! Women of all ages, economic standings, political bents, and occupations were powerfully attracted to the idea that they could stand up for themselves, that they didn't have to apologize, that they could leave guilt behind. It was an immense relief.

Since the women's movement peaks of the 1970's, many feminist issues have been confronted and resolved, partially or wholly through assertive communication and action. The status quo was shaken as new alternatives for women were born, and courageous women – and men – began to write new scripts for their lives. The basic assertiveness skills we described in the first edition of this book are no longer enough.

What started with the assertiveness 'basics' – saying no, expressing anger, recognizing the Compassion Trap, shedding the need for approval, giving up excessive apology – soon grew into a movement that literally swept America. Everywhere, women were learning how to be more assertive on the job and at home. The changes were astonishing.

The best news was that individual women could express themselves assertively and uniquely: there was no such thing as a perfect ten in the Assertiveness Olympics! Differences in character, personality, background, interests, talents, and goals could all be forged into an assertive approach. Assertiveness could be happily blended into special, interesting lives. The skill became an identity, and assertiveness now goes hand in glove with maturity.

You may be reading this book because you are seeking for the first time to enhance your self-confidence and self-expression. This new edition of *The Assertive Woman* offers answers based on a dozen years of practice and the experience of hundreds of thousands who have gone before.

If you are an old friend, reading this edition for our 'New Look,' you'll not be disappointed. So much has changed in the past decade!

Our personal accounts of finding the assertive woman in each of us show that our paths are both alike and very different – beyond the obvious contrasts of place, time, or people. This book reflects those differences, and more. We've moved in new directions professionally, philosophically, geographically. Chapter Two describes our personal experiences in some detail, but we want to say a little more about them here.

As you read this book, you might come across a section that sounds 'more like Stanlee' or 'more like Nancy.' You may be right! We want to enhance, not blur, our individual strengths. One of the most exciting social experiments over the last ten years is the astonishing variety of new options women have chosen. Gone is the 'typical Western woman' we used to hear about, and in her place is a strong, talented individual who wants to be judged on her own merits. Some artificial limits have been discarded, others added, but clearly, there is no 'standard' way to be assertive anymore.

Though our perspectives differ, one thing has not changed since the first edition was completed: we still feel a thrill of pride in each other's accomplishments. That pride binds, supports, and makes room for our own voices in this book. Here's a brief introduction to each voice:

Stanlee
My own natural curiosity has put me in pursuit of new frontiers, and not just for myself: I want to share everything I've learned. It's my goal to assist people in knowing and loving themselves and in manifesting their dreams and vision. Although I work primarily as a business consultant and seminar leader, I've discovered valuable information in fields outside of the traditional business world.

Breakthroughs in alternative health care, psychology, metaphysics and education have opened up new possibilities. There is a higher consciousness on our planet, brought about by many people seeking their own spirituality. There's also an increased need to understand humanity so that we are able to work and play together in peace.

The applications of New Age philosophy fascinate me. I use them in all of my work and personal life. For me, spirituality and business are no longer mutually exclusive. In fact, I observe a transformation taking place in business as people are being nurtured more by their work. It isn't just an emphasis on productivity, excellence and profitability; it is now the freedom of expression – internal and external – that is producing happy, hopeful human beings.

Nancy
Most of my time is spent writing and speaking about organizations that perform exceptionally well – often far better than the closest competitor – even in forgotten, embattled corners of the American market. Many of these outstanding performers are small or medium sized companies, not enormous giants. Yet they share an amazing dedication to serving their customers better than anyone else, speeding up the development and delivery of new products or services, and above all, making things that work! The surprise is, of course, how rare that is in late-twentieth-century America.

The best-kept secret is that the winners achieve their results by granting extraordinary elbow-room to the people they employ. Sure, they make good use of technology, but the heart of the matter is commitment, pride, and ownership – three things we didn't pay much attention to when I was a business student.

Inside every employee – secretary, shipping clerk, accountant, lawyer, manager – is a talented, thoughtful contributor. The challenge, well into the next century, is whether we will listen to and rely on their good sense. More than one company has failed due to out-of-touch management. I hope this book encourages everyone who reads it to step out and make themselves heard, and that it helps to guide the efforts of those whose job it is to listen.

How to Use This Book as a Workbook

Throughout this book, exercises have been included for you to complete. Some of the exercises require only a written response, and others involve actually performing new behaviours. We have used all of the exercises in our workshops and found them to be most effective aids to learning assertive behaviour.

We suggest that you complete each exercise in the order in which it is presented. Some of the exercises are designed for you to complete alone. Others are intended to be completed with a friend, and several work best when used as group exercises.

The exercise pages may be copied for use in groups or workshops, provided they are not sold commercially, and that credit is given. Please refer to the copyright notice, page ii.

Do You Know Your AQ?

You may ask yourself, 'What do I really hope to gain by reading *The Assertive Woman?*' Test your assertiveness quotient (AQ) by completing the following questionnaire. Use the scale below to indicate how comfortable you are with each item:

    1 – makes me very uncomfortable
    2 – I feel moderately comfortable
    3 – I am very comfortable with this

There may be some situations which are not relevant to you nor to your particular lifestyle; in such cases, try to imagine how comfortable you might feel if you were involved in the situation.

Some of our workshops have included men, who have found it interesting to test their own assertiveness and to relate their responses to their own experiences or those of women they know. Thus, the AQ Survey can be a non-threatening way to initiate discussions between women and men.

Becoming Assertive

- Speaking up and asking questions at a meeting. _____
- Commenting about being interrupted by a male directly to him at the moment he interrupts you. _____
- Stating your views to a male authority figure, (e.g., minister, boss, father). _____
- Attempting to offer solutions and elaborating on them when there are men present. _____

The Inner Game of Assertiveness

- Using your inner wisdom to guide you in making clear decisions vs. doing what others think you should do in an effort to meet with their approval. _____
- Going out with a group of friends when you are the only one without a 'date.' _____
- Being especially competent, using your authority
  - and/or power without labelling yourself as 'bitchy, impolite, bossy, aggressive, castrating, or parental.' _____
- Requesting expected service when you haven't received it (e.g. in a restaurant or a shop). _____

Obstacles on the Path to Assertiveness

- Laughing at or ignoring the negative chatter in your head that reinforces old beliefs and prevents you from taking assertive risks. _____

Compassion Trap

- Choosing to do what is right for you without guilt, in spite of another's manipulations. _____
- Respecting your own needs as much as or more than others do their needs. _____

Empowering Yourself to be Assertive

- Taking time every day to work on increasing your power and confidence, with specific methods that work for you. _____
- Being expected to apologize for something and *not* apologizing since you feel you are right. _____
- Requesting the return of borrowed items without being apologetic. _____

Expression of Assertion

- Confidently using assertive expression that fits your own unique style and personality – not aiming for 'perfection.' _____
- Recognizing the difference between genuine assertiveness and its imitations: Pollyanna Assertion, Fraudulent Assertion, and Reckless Assertion. _____
- Respecting the limits of assertion and preventing the Superwoman Syndrome. _____

You're Worth It

- Talking about your talents and triumphs openly without embarrassment. _____
- Looking in the mirror with a genuine smile and saying to yourself out loud, 'I really like you. You're O.K. in my book.' _____

Assertive Body Image

- Entering and exiting a room where men are present. _____
- Speaking in front of a group. _____
- Maintaining eye contact, keeping your head upright, and leaning forward when in a personal conversation. _____

Compliments, Criticism, and Rejection

- Receiving a compliment by saying something assertive to acknowledge that you agree with the person complimenting you. _____
- Accepting a rejection. _____

- Not getting the *approval* of the most significant male in your life and/or of *any* male. _____
- Discussing another person's criticism of you openly with that person. _____
- Telling someone that she/he is doing something that is bothering you. _____

Saying 'No'

- Refusing to get coffee or to take notes at a meeting where you are chosen to do so because you are a female _____
- Saying 'no' – refusing to do a favour when you really don't feel like it. _____
- Turning down a request for a meeting or date. _____

Manipulation

- Telling a person when you think she/he is manipulating you. _____
- Commenting to a male who has made a patronizing remark to you (e.g., 'you have a good job *for a woman*'; 'you're not flightly, emotional, stupid or hysterical *like most women*'). _____

Sensuality

- Telling a prospective lover about your physical attraction to him/her before any such statements are made to you. _____
- Initiating sex with your partner. _____
- Showing physical enjoyment of an art show or concert in spite of others' reactions. _____
- Asking to be caressed and/or telling your lover what feels good to you. _____
- Negotiating with a prospective lover for 'safe sex' that insures against sexually-transmitted diseases. _____

Anger

- Expressing anger directly and honestly when you feel angry. _____
- Arguing with another person. _____

Humour

- Telling a joke. _____
- Listening to a friend tell a story about something embarrassing, but funny, that you have done. _____
- Responding with humour to someone's put-down of you. _____

Friends and Lovers

- Speaking and making a request for emotional support and understanding from a friend. _____
- Letting go of old friends and making new friends when it is appropriate to do so. _____
- Risking rejection, feeling foolish and exploring the unknown in a romantic relationship. _____
- Taking positive action to face fear and conflict in your relationships. _____

Family Relationships

- Approaching your relationship with your parents more honestly and openly. _____
- Disciplining your own children. _____
- Disciplining others' children. _____
- Explaining the facts of life or your divorce to your child. _____

Assertiveness on the Job

- Initiating a discussion with your boss about a rise or opportunity for promotion. _____
- Refusing to do your boss's personal errands or shopping _____
- Accepting performance feedback from your boss, especially when it concerns the need to improve in some area. _____
- Pushing for employer-sponsored day care programmes. _____

The Mythology of the Working Woman

- Debunking the most common myths about working women: they are too emotional, too insecure, not professional enough. _____
- Knowing the difference between a Superwoman and a super woman. _____
- Speaking up when you or another woman is accused of being 'too emotional' to be effective. _____
- Being able to say no when asked to take on one more extra project 'for the sake of your career.' _____

The Hardy Spirit

- Accepting a challenge and sticking with it.
- Picking up that hobby or special interest which was abandoned earlier in life.
- Taking a courageous stand, either personally or politically.

Though our 'AQ Survey' is not a validated psychological scale or test, you can use it to help you discover in what ways you are not assertive. If you have 1's and 2's under a particular heading, be sure to give special attention to the corresponding chapter. If you have more 1's and 2's throughout the AQ Survey than you do 3's, *The Assertive Woman* can help you to express yourself more spontaneously and honestly. For those of you who have fifty or more 3's – congratulations! You already are an assertive woman. We especially recommend reading Chapter 24, 'Freedom,' and putting your assertiveness to work for yourself and others.

Although our book is intended to be read in sequence, you may choose to concentrate on some areas that relate more to your individual needs, as highlighted by your AQ score. After reading *The Assertive Woman* and completing the exercises, test your AQ again to see how much your responses have changed.

We've included suggested readings for most chapters and lots of examples of situations calling for assertiveness. You may find some of them unrealistic; we recognize that life does not always go as smoothly and neatly as presented in the pages of a book. We hope you'll recognize the limitations of space and forgive us if the situations seem too easily resolved. They are included not as models of 'how to succeed at assertion without really trying,' but as illustrations of how the process can be applied. When another person leaps off the printed page and confronts you for real, you may need to persist longer and remain firmer. When your assertiveness is wholeheartedly welcomed, you may find it to be a piece of cake. Part of the process is the experience of each.

Chapter 2

Our Personal Journeys

Stanlee Phelps

> *You teach best what you most need to learn.*
> – Richard Bach, *Illusions*

The Assertive Woman was first published in 1975. Since then I have had an opportunity to wrestle with the realities of being an assertive woman. Initially, assertiveness was a revolutionary concept for me. Now it has become an evolutionary process. It reaches well beyond the mastery of behaviour skills and consciousness-raising devices. Being assertive has come to mean much more.

Alberti and Emmons have managed to describe the complex and diverse dimensions of assertion in their most recent edition of *Your Perfect Right:*

> *Assertive behavior promotes equality in human relationships, enabling us to act in our own best interests, to stand up for ourselves without undue anxiety, to express feelings honestly and comfortably, to exercise personal rights without denying the rights of others.*

This definition takes into account elements of emotion, personal power, intellect, decision-making capabilities, intuition, logic, behaviour, justice, social conscience, relationships and self-esteem. These elements comprise the fabric of a life long process.

Quite early in this process of becoming assertive I wondered what my life would be like. For the most part my personal journey as an assertive woman has been exhilarating and rewarding. I have succeeded in establishing more freedom and flow in my life. Yet, identifying and creating assertive choices has been difficult too. The price I paid for keeping my options alive was not always worth it. And, being an assertion expert did not help! I felt pressure to live up to what I had put into print. I wanted to be a model for others. Indeed, there were times when I could actually do that. At other times I pretended in Mary Poppins-like fashion while I disintegrated inside. Much later I learned it was O.K. not to be assertive sometimes. Yes, sometimes I did not *want* to be assertive. I did not want to decide anything. However, I did decide that there is a qualitative difference between being Superwoman, or the 'Type E Woman' (who tries to be *E*verything to *E*verybody), and being an assertive woman. I began to explore other possibilities. For example, if I chose not to choose – to be passive – or if I chose to be aggressive, the act of *choosing* was still assertive. Choosing more honestly and responsibly helped me to feel freer. In this way I was not locked into assertiveness as just another oppressive 'should' or 'must.' This approach had some extraordinary advantages. I could be human instead of an assertiveness robot!

Probably the single most motivating reason for my attraction to assertiveness was wanting to escape from powerlessness. I wanted power.

Thus, I began my journey using assertiveness as a tool to bring about the necessary changes in my life. It worked. I began to experience mini-triumphs – returning damaged merchandise, saying 'no' to salespeople, public speaking, delegating more instead of assuming every burden, speaking up around men, accepting compliments and other things I could proudly label 'assertive.'

Something I began to notice, however, was that it was not as smooth and easy asserting myself with significant people in my life, or in situations in which I felt a threat to my security. It was not apparent to me that many of my significant encounters were power struggles. This was hard to see. I had always considered myself an easy going and a very 'nice' person. I underestimated my fear of domination and dependency. And I usually denied the *level* of my anger. I used assertive skills to cover up these realities – a form of fraudulent assertion.

My inner journey consisted of a string of promises I was making to myself – sort of an insurance policy against future pain. The promises all sounded like, 'I'll never . . . again,' or, 'It will be a long time before . . ,' and, 'I'll do what I please; I'll show him.' I was re-acting – not pro-acting. My intellectual insights lacked emotional integration. Having clearly defined assertion for myself and other women through my speaking and writing did not immediately enable me to master the process of assertion. What a humbling discovery!

It became increasingly evident to me that real assertion began first with creating an assertive woman inside of me. I had to learn to play my own inner game of assertion instead of making unrealistic promises to myself. My goal was to clarify my values, my likes and dislikes, and most of all – to become comfortable with my inner self.

My earliest attempts at assertion were based on a textbook approach. I was trying out ideas of what assertion should be without examining more deeply how these ideas fit with what I really wanted. Acting assertively was easier once I started playing my inner game. First, I would assess a situation using my intuition instead of ready-made logical answers. My inner wisdom was uncluttered by bad habits of non-assertion. The assertive woman inside of me simply knew what to do. I only had to be truly *open* to what she was telling me.

To play the inner game I needed some preparation. I needed to empower myself. I told myself over and over that it was OK to be open, that I could trust myself. I used some 'New Age' tools like meditation, affirmations and treasure mapping to assist me. These along with other tools I've used are described in the following chapters. This process enabled me to build a more solid foundation for real assertion. I was experiencing a new spirit of assertion, which we've labelled 'the hardy spirit.'

Besides growing confidence how did I know this process was working? I needed to test it outwardly in the laboratory of my life. The changes in my career and personal relationships presented me with many opportunities.

For example, after the publication of *The Assertive Woman* I started my public speaking and corporate consulting career. I didn't let go of counselling or teaching right away. Anxiety in trying something new and letting go of financial security along with established professional credibility made this a slow, gradual process. It took courage to risk stepping out into the unknown.

While Nancy went on to UCLA to get her Masters degree, I pursued the world of business through trial and error. If any mistakes could be made, I made them all. Transitioning from salaried positions at hospitals, mental health centres and universities to being an entrepreneur in business was a giant roller coaster ride. Imagine 'buckling up for safety' and screaming on the downhill slides! This period of my professional career I fondly and humorously refer to as 'my Masters in experience.' The curriculum was quite different!

What was significant for me at this turning point was that it was marked with a deep sense of dignity and honour in making my new choices. Mostly I recognized that not only was I fully capable of making a commitment, I was sincerely committed to what was right for me. I sought quality time with my friends and in my work, instead of maintaining a Superwoman pace. I spent time alone.

During the last decade my personal relationships were transformed as well. Through implementing an inner process of assertion, the quality of my interactions with people improved. As I learned to be more true to myself, I created more genuine, healthy relationships. The time I spent going inward did not induce a selfish 'me oriented' person as I feared. Instead the self-compassion I discovered gave me a stronger way to connect with others: non-judgemental vs. defensive, responsible vs. reckless and impulsive, comfortable vs. fearful and anxious, and with humour vs. heaviness.

Relationships have always presented the most challenging vehicles for me to be assertive. After I let go of trying to be ideally assertive and began making choices out of my inner awareness, I was able to implement a more solid style of assertive expression. Trusting myself gave me room to grow. Focusing on inner harmony gave me the peace and motivation to pursue more balanced relationships. The inner and outer assertive woman fused into a whole person at last!

There are many examples of how this integrated assertive style has contributed very positively to my relationships in recent years. I stopped colluding with my mother in her self-destructive path of alcoholism. In confronting with her what we both feared, I was able to overcome helplessness. She stopped her pattern a few years ago. She has found a way to enjoy life. And we have found a new friendship based on love, respect and freedom.

In my relationships with men I have achieved increased compatibility. I move more freely and easily in the business world, relating to men realistically. I enjoy relating to assertive men who appreciate assertive women. I employ compassion and confrontation with those who don't.

My friendships with men have changed. In platonic relationships I am able to give and receive affection and vulnerability without it becoming a sexual threat. In romantic relationships I have courageously communicated who I am. As a single woman I wanted to understand men and finally feel safe with a man. I have steadfastly held a vision of creating a committed primary relationship with a man with whom I can share mutuality, love, friendship, intimacy, passion and creativity. I see evidence that I am succeeding.

Although a career-oriented single woman, I have created two very special relationships with a young woman and a young man which combine elements of parenting and friendship. Sometimes they've known me better than I've known myself. And in many ways we've grown up together.

More fulfilling than ever, my relationships with women continue to blossom personally and professionally. Much of my life's work is aimed at contributing to the unfoldment and advancement of quality lives for all women and, of course, the men and children in their lives. On a personal level I have deepened and expanded my individual friendships with women. Some are single; some are married; some are workmates, playmates, or both. One of the most powerful and unique ways I have been in relationship is through participating in an ongoing women's support group, comprised of essentially the same women, for the last 15 years. We've shared career changes, divorces, marriages, triumphs, turmoil and even the year-and-a-half battle with cancer and eventual death of one of us.

Finally, no less cherished is my relationship with you, dear reader. The feedback and encouragement we've received from you already, or may receive from you in the future, has contributed a great deal to our personal journeys and the ability to write about what life has been like for assertive women in general.

Having embarked upon this journey of assertion sixteen years ago, how do I measure my progress?

The most meaningful yardstick I have today is how assertive I am feeling inside from moment to moment. It is not contingent upon what anyone else thinks is assertive for me, including many of the women's magazines and self-help books. There is no *absolute* standard. Successful assertion for me occurs when I am clear that I have made my own choice using my inner guide. This choice is made in the spirit of sincerity, dignity and love. With this choice I put forth my best effort to apply the assertive skills I know to bring about a responsible result. It is this blend of attitude, behaviour and skills that produces my feeling of mastery.

Letting go of unsuccessful assertions, impossible situations or impossible people has become easier. It is less threatening to let go now that I know I will always have myself. The patterns and cycles seem to shift more gently and quickly as they become more apparent to me.

Sometimes late at night when I'm thinking or writing in my journal, I open up a bag of Chinese fortune cookies to munch. Once in a while a fortune is worth saving . . .

*'If you take a wrong direction, make corrections,
don't try to save face.'*

Nancy K. Austin

> *I have come to a strange land. I do not understand the language.*
> *The customs are peculiar.*
> *At home I didn't have to think which path to take. One foot*
> *simply followed the other out into an average expectable en-*
> *vironment to which I had a built-in adaptability. The unex-*
> *pected could happen but remained the exception. Unthinking*
> *reactions had a natural fit with the way things were. In this land*
> *fixed attributes of life have fallen loose and slanted. Familiar*
> *things are slightly twisted, have entered another dimension,*
> *and, no spontaneous reaction of mine fits with anything. I must*
> *stay alert. I can never sleep. I have a terrible longing for home.*
>
> – Allen Wheelis
> *On Not Knowing How To Live*

The year Stanlee and I wrote *The Assertive Woman,* we knew who she was: an honest, direct, courageous woman who could make her own choices, return faulty goods to a department store without feeling compelled to apologize for her wanton misuse of their perfect product, say 'no' to unreasonable requests, express love and affection (and be loved back) without self-consciousness, never let her job and/or her family walk all over her – and she did it all without sweaty palms, and without trespassing on the rights of those around her. It is, a decade later, an attractive image. Yet for me the promise of being an assertive woman provoked its own difficult questions, and there were no easy answers.

Since our book's publication, particularly during times of person-al challenge (starting graduate school, handing a confrontational meeting, learning how to be a stepmother), I've reread it. *The Assertive Woman* makes me want to keep going when I'd rather give up. It has had, at times, the noble capacity to encourage ('to stimulate by assistance or approval,' according to the dictionary), to push me toward what is best confronted squarely. Even if it is only getting out of bed when the alarm goes, it seems a courageous act against an assertive landscape. Sometimes, that is enough.

But unlike the book, my own life has refused to proceed neatly, step by step. Against our own advice, I haven't mastered the easy stuff before testing my mettle on really big events. It's been a game of stops and starts, of having to begin new things without feeling ready – hardly conducive to a fresh-caught skill, one that seems to flourish with time, care, and order. So along the way I have often wondered how 'real' assertive women do it. Where do they get their nerve?

One of my first clues came when I decided to apply to graduate business school after spending four good years in the mental health field. I was one of a handful of people who had staffed a study group to evaluate the relative effectiveness of various therapies. Assertiveness training surfaced as a new, little-known technique, one of several we researched. I was drawn to it. Demand for our assertiveness training workshops took off. We started writing things down. *The Assertive Woman* was published two months before I entered UCLA's Graduate School of Management as a first-year MBA candidate, in the autumn of 1975.

I was well acquainted with student life, not that it helped. Each day was the first day of school – replayed over and over for three long months of my first academic quarter. My previous work experience (which, according to the Admissions people, came highly prized) seemed flatly irrelevant in the business school classroom. Insecurities flourished in all of us newcomers. We were scared. I could name that tune: so what if I co-authored a book? So what if I'd always been a good student? So what if I could be proud of my career so far? That was then. When asked why I changed direction and applied to business school, I never had trouble explaining that I knew what I didn't want to do, but just what I did want (and how an MBA might help me find it) resisted definition. I wondered if I could handle the coursework, if going to graduate school was the right decision, if I could keep up with the rest of the students. Since women comprised only about 30% of the student body, I felt additional pressure to prove that the school's investment in me was not misplaed. I identified with Woody Allen, who could not but doubt the wisdom of any group that would have him as a member.

The other women students and I felt extra pressure to prove

ourselves worthy of our chosen career paths. So did the men, no doubt; but no one pestered them with questions about how they planned to achieve 'balance' in their lives. A good offence, we reasoned, was the best defence, and so we took advantage of each tiny opportunity to demonstrate, beyond any possible doubt, our commitment to our careers. In this spirit, a second year veteran presented me with a symbol: a Pentel mechanical pencil like the one she always used. The product of impeccable engineering and sporting an improbable .5 millimeter lead, it represented a rite of passage. I loved mine and used it for everything from figuring financial performance ratios to crosswords. I still use such a pencil, truth be told, but of course then it was much, much more than just a writing instrument. It was one of many (I hoped) little indicators that I couldn't be brushed off as one of those squishy emotional types who were temperamentally unsuited to management. Combined with my strong academic record, I believed such small symbols of serious commitment would overcome any sceptic's doubts that I, for one, could cut it.

What I struggled with, I later understood, was an old dilemma: while I was in school, women were determined to show that they could compete just as successfully as the men who dominated the playing fields of commerce. We wanted to prove that we, too, could break into, and thrive in, the rough and tumble business world, even if it meant matching our male predecessors step for step. We lacked the confidence in ourselves and in our employers to believe we would be valued for our own unique contributions. Demonstrating that we were as good as everybody else was much more urgent than standing up for our differences.

I wanted to be assertive, and as the co-author of *The Assertive Woman*, my ability to live up to it was often tested in business. Some higher-ups were put off by the 'assertive woman' label, and it took extra time and care to build those working relationships. More often, though, business associates (and bosses) were surprised to discover that assertiveness didn't mean aggressiveness, and that an assertive manager didn't mean an uncooperative one. There were those meetings when I was so afraid of being thought aggressive that I kept a lower profile than was actually constructive – but no one could say I was bitchy! Gradually, I began to develop a sense of humour about my role as an assertive woman, a real test of my confidence. When a man with whom I worked shoulder-to-shoulder for four years joked that my next book should be *The Assertive Woman's Cookbook*, I really thought it was funny – coming from Ray, that is, whose genuine respect for me and my work came through loud and clear every day we collaborated.

I see that I have neglected to mention that those two years of graduate school went by fast, without benefit of much inner reflection on my part. It was a sloppy process. My motto (which, incidentally, was shared by a lot of us students) was 'hurry up as often as you can.' I kept no personal journal. I attended no self-help classes. The only books I read were marketing, finance, or texts. I didn't have time for anything else. Fortunately, every day presented ample opportunity to flirt with my future, and little, real life experiments were often helpful. I could go talk with the Dean of the school and thus learn how it might feel to look the boss in the eye. I could sign up for a 'Day on the Job' excursion, where a few students spend a real day in a real company with real employees and real inventory. I could think about why I clashed with that particular professor, because I could bet my student loan balance that I'd clash that way again with somebody else! I could try on one or two assertive approaches and find out that some situations (and people) are immune to assertiveness. The only way to learn was to put one foot in front of the other and speedwalk.

Some experiences on this particular fast track were standouts. Straight A's, for one. Auditioning for and winning a role in a musical production produced and directed by MBA's who concentrated in Arts Management, for another. Meeting the man I would marry. He was not a fellow student, but the Placement Director, the one who convinces employers to recruit new employees from the programme's graduates and who counsels students about their career plans. I began my second year of business school with a husband, a house, and an eight-year-old son.

We've been married over ten years now, and the eight-year-old kid is a University student. Since completing my MBA degree, I've worked for a multi-billion dollar high-tech company (and loved it), a Big Eight accounting firm (a mistake), a tiny consulting firm (another mistake). The companies I co-founded several years ago are doing fine, as is the product of my second writing partnership. *A Passion for Excellence*. I'm now president of my own tiny company, Bill is vice president, and working together agrees with us. These days I can be found a) on an airplane, or b) talking to business leaders in every imaginable industry (in every imaginable location) about building excellence.

I've put 350,000 miles on one frequent flier programme alone over the last twelve months, on my way to or from one of those presentations. Occasionally, Bill travels with me, but mostly I am the only woman sitting up there in the first-class section among the equally weary business travellers. Their conversations run along traditional themes: why a deal went bad, planned acquisitions, next week's budget meeting, weekend plans. One thing is clear. Most of these travellers have, as I do, a spouse who manages the details of life on the ground – like taking the car for the service and taking the dogs and cats to the vet and the clothes to the cleaners. Not to mention grocery shopping and cooking. Unless you have help like that, you can't be away from home this much and still have a home to come back to.

As I write this, I am once again the solo woman in the packed first class section of my favourite airline. When I arrive in Kansas City tonight, I'll call home and hear what I've missed. Yesterday afternoon Bill signed the vast paperwork which made the purchase of our new home official. Last night, our 19-year-old university student called from his university digs in Eugene, Oregon. And through the day there were cat stories and dog adventures and unplanned meetings with our soon-to-be neighbours. Today is Halloween. Five days ago I turned thirty-seven. I was at home for my birthday, owing to a cancelled engagement. Bill and I spent that day meandering through a spectacular new shopping centre. What I wanted was an ordinary day – no room service, no airports, no big dinner out. It was heaven.

One thing you learn from constant travel: a thick skin helps. Women who travel alone are perceived differently. The thing I worry most about is when, and how much, to tip. Women are reputed to be stingy in such matters and so I always express my thanks generously. Does assertiveness help on the road? Sort of. You can't assert your way out of a too-low tip, I find. And I learned my limits: I will not go to the trouble to locate the best restaurant in the city I happen to be in, just so I can go have a peaceful dinner by myself. I won't make someone's acquaintance just to insure a dinner companion, either. For me, it's room service, every time.

The reason is simple. There is this constant pressure to prove myself, not only on stage, but in anonymous airports and hotels. I have learned to take it, as much as possible, on my own terms. Which means that if I happen to be seated next to a party animal on some flight, assertiveness has helped me learn to say I don't want to talk. Saying no has got a lot easier; there usually isn't time to waiver. And, at the same time, I've met some very interesting and talented people, though they are acquaintances, not 'relationships,' because relationships depend on contact and I'm never anywhere long enough to qualify.

Almost all of what I've learned about being assertive I've learned in real time. You can't spend four years employed by a 75,000-person company and not learn how to get things done as part of a group. I am especially thankful for the mistakes I've made and the wrong turns I've taken. Without those, it would have taken a lot longer to figure out what I really could do well, though it's an effort to think of some of those whoppers as educational experiences and not dismal failures.

The November, 1986 issue of *Working Woman* magazine, which I have with me, trumpets this message on its cover: 'How Working Women Have Changed America.' They are 'America's Secret Weapon,' announces the magazine, and six such secret weapons are honoured in this tenth anniversary issue. Each of the women are described in two word labels: discount broker, television executive, management consultant, broadcast executive, catalogue retailer – and Lucille Ball, in a class by herself. The article suggests that these half dozen share one particular trait despite their many differences, and they politely call it 'perseverance,' until they flat out admit it's 'pigheadedness.' Of that, I have no doubt. I've never seen anything good come from anyone who wasn't. You have to be stubborn and

strong to persist against long odds! And that, I believe, is the
essence of assertiveness: at its best, it stimulates commitment to
break out of somebody else's idea of what you should be so you can
go and be who you want, with the sort of life you want. And even if
you don't get quite the life you planned, you can be proud of the
journey.

That's what it's done for me. It hasn't been especially easy. I fail
all the time. But I am learning in the real world, on all kinds of
playing fields. There are things I want to change, like time on
planes. But the point of real assertiveness is that it comes from the
inside, from your own ability and interests. One size definitely does
not fit all. You move under your own power, in a direction of your
own choosing. Despite the barriers and the struggles and the
disappointments, it is still the best idea we ever had.

Chapter 3

Will the Real Assertive Woman Please Stand Up?

The most important section of The Assertive Woman *was the exercise where you asked me to look in the mirror and list 10 positive things about myself. I had an incredible feeling – 'I really don't know myself!'*

– a female educational administrator,
mid 30's and married.

In the 1970's the assertive woman's task was to discover her own uniqueness and make the 'right' assertive choices.

Many never understood the meaning of assertiveness in the first place: they believed, and still do, that it is just a slick cover-up for aggression. Some think that assertiveness is just a milder, 'nicer' form of aggressiveness. Yet the two are entirely distinct sets of behaviours with different objectives and motivations. They are different in kind – like apples and spinach – not degree, like big apples and little apples.

From reading hundreds of letters and listening to thousands of seminar participants, we know that *real* assertiveness doesn't happen overnight. We're keenly aware of the frustration experienced by people who sincerely want to become assertive. We know that assertiveness is not born in a textbook, seminar, or self-help book. Real assertiveness is born within. (That's not to say, 'You either have it or you don't.' Rather, 'If you want it, it must start with you.')

Ideal vs. Real Assertiveness
We need to balance the very orderly, rational process we read and write about with the chaotic, disorderly process we frequently face

in day to day life. We need to distinguish between 'ideal' and 'real' in order to choose attitudes and motivations that produce happy, successful results. The following chart spells out some differences between ideal and real assertiveness:

IDEAL	vs.	REAL
I need to be perfectly assertive.		I'll do my best; it may not be perfect.
She/he must respond to my assertions assertively.		She/he may be passive or aggressive in response to my assertiveness.
Others must appreciate my assertions.		Others may not like my assertions.
My assertions must always achieve the desired result.		I may not always get what I want.
I must want to be always assertive.		Sometimes I won't want or care to be assertive.
I need to know what is the most assertive response at all times and implement it immediately with ease and comfort.		Sometimes I'll be confused about what's assertive, afraid, or just plain forget and revert back to old patterns.
If I blow it, I won't have another chance.		I can always try again.

A New Look at Four Women We All Know
As you begin your journey toward greater effectiveness in self-expression and relationships with others, it will help to have a framework for comparing the way you usually behave with the style you'd like to develop.

Generally, there are three ways people behave in any given situation: passive, aggressive, and assertive. As each is described, you will probably find yourself identifying with all of them. We have added a fourth general classification by treating aggressive behaviour in two parts: direct and indirect. We feel that this distinction is helpful because women frequently attempt to hide or mask their aggressiveness. Being indirect is a culturally-approved choice

FOUR WOMEN WE ALL KNOW [AND THEIR MALE COUNTERPARTS]

	DORIS DOORMAT (DONALD DOORMAT)	AGATHA AGGRESSIVE (HUGH THE HORRIBLE)	IRIS INDIRECT (IAN INDIRECT)	APRIL ASSERTIVE (AL ASSERTIVE)
Basic Attitude	I'm not okay.	You're not okay.	You're not okay, but I'll let you think you are.	I'm okay and you're okay, too!
Power	Feels helpless, turns power over to others, uses guilt to control.	Substitutes control and domination for power.	Uses manipulation and deceit to gain control.	Has personal power and shares power easily. Can be vulnerable.
Decision Making	Lets others choose for her.	Chooses for others whether they like it or not.	Is sneaky or deceitful in choosing for others.	Plays the inner game; chooses for herself and supports others in making their own decisions.
Potential Traps	Compassion trap. Pollyanna assertion.	Reckless assertion; super assertion; aggression trap.	Fraudulent assertion.	Superwoman trap.
Feedback from others	Guilt, anger, frustration, lack of respect, abuse.	Fear, defensiveness, humiliation, hurt.	Suspicion, confusion, frustration; feels manipulated.	Respect, love, support, inspiration, acceptance, comfort.
Sense of Humour	Is often cruelly teased, colludes with put-downs about herself; lets others be funny.	Caustic wit, put-downs, can't laugh at herself.	Sarcasm and cynicism.	Playful, loving humour; can laugh at herself; risks being funny.
Courage	Fearful, withdraws, does not stand up for her convictions; tries to get sympathy.	Attacks and blames others to cover up her fear and insecurity. Talks "tough" and takes unwise risks.	Uses trickery and feigns other emotions (e.g. love, sadness, anger) to cover up her fear.	Is willing to deal with difficulty and pain; has the strength of her convictions; takes calculated risks.
Gains/Payoffs	Attention, sympathy, protection, doted on.	Controls people and situations; wants authority and to be right.	Sometimes seen as cute and clever; has fun playing games.	Self-respect, integrity, responsibility, freedom, intimacy.
Price Tags Paid	Loss of freedom, self-respect and creativity.	Loss of love, friendship and teamwork.	Is not trusted; is the victim of retaliation and vengeance.	Unrealistic expectations from self and others to be "perfectly" assertive.
Burnout Potential	Very high — usually depletes herself; can't say no.	Very high — overwork competition, often superachievers with physical health problems.	Very high — takes more and more energy to cover-up deceits and games.	Very high — can become too competent and accomplished from not discriminating her choices and setting limits.
Career Profile	Does what she thinks she should do — even if it makes her unhappy.	Often an unhappy overachiever, who may be a financial success and a person of status.	Once her untrustworthiness is discovered, her career takes a nosedive.	Usually happy and successful, she feels she can do anything she desires.
End Results	Life is a chore for the martyr.	Loneliness and bitterness.	Loss of identity, trust, and respect.	Love, happiness and peace of mind.

for women, while being overtly aggressive has been reserved for men. Other authors have chosen to refer to indirect aggression as 'covert aggression' or 'passive-aggressive' behaviour. We chose not to use 'covert' since the word has an almost insidious connotation that may make women appear to have preconceived, evil intentions. We do not feel this is true, but that, in fact, women have been given little opportunity to behave in a more direct way. When one is oppressed, one learns to be subtle. Nor do we use the term 'passive-aggressive,' because it recalls a Freudian concept, and gives an inaccurate image of the behaviour we are describing.

Perhaps you wanted to read this book in order to learn how to act differently in some situations where you feel trapped by your own habit patterns. As the four behaviours are presented, it would be helpful to imagine which seem most suited to you and which you see as difficult. Most woman identify with passive or indirectly aggressive behaviours more than the aggressive or assertive. How do you see yourself?

Passive or Non-Assertive

In the accompanying chart, we refer to the passive woman as *Doris Doormat*. When Doris is non-assertive, she allows other people to make her decisions for her, even though she may later resent it.

She feels helpless, powerless, inhibited, nervous, and anxious. She rarely expresses her feelings and has little self-confidence. She does best when following others and may be fearful of taking the initiative in any situation. She feels sorry for herself to the point of martyrdom, and wonders why others cannot rescue her from her plight. When a woman *only* relates to the world passively and fails to turn to others, she frequently turns to alcoholism, drugs, physical complaints, or eating disorders to escape her misery.

Aggressive

On the other hand, *Agatha Aggressive*, is very expressive, to the extent that she humiliates and deprecates others. You could call her obnoxious, vicious, or egocentric. No matter what you label her, she has the same destructive effect on you; you feel devastated by an encounter with her. Her message to you is that she's OK and you definitely are not. In our society, it takes a lot of courage for a woman to be aggressive, especially since this style of behaviour has been viewed as totally non-feminine. So, the price the aggressive woman pays is usually alienation from almost everybody.

Indirectly Aggressive

Because of the reaction accorded to the aggressive woman and the misery experienced by the passive woman, many women develop the ability to get what they want by indirect means. In our chart, *Iris Indirect* illustrate this type of behaviour. Iris has learned her lesson well; in order to achieve her goal she may use trickery, seduction, or manipulation. Iris has learned that a woman is expected to use her 'womanly wiles' to get what she wants. Therefore, Iris is seen as 'cute and coy.' However, when she is angry, she is likely to use sneaky ways to get revenge. She can be so indirect that the person with whom she is angry may never know.

Assertive

There is another way to respond to people and situations: *assertively*. In our chart, *April Assertive,* like Agatha, is expressive with her feelings, but without obnoxiousness. She is able to state her views and desires directly, spontaneously, and honestly. She feels good about herself and about others too; she respects the feelings and rights of other people. April can evaluate a situation, decide how to act, and then act without reservation. The most important thing to April is that she is true to herself. Winning or losing seem unimportant compared to the value of expressing herself and choosing for herself. She may not always achieve her goals, but the resolution isn't always as meaningful to her as the actual process of asserting herself. Regardless of whether April has something positive or negative to say to you, she says it in such a way that you are left with your dignity intact and with good feelings about what was said.

When our four fictional female characters were first introduced in *The Assertive Woman*, they were instantly recognized. Workshop participants and readers alike identified themselves in two or more of the characters. They wanted, perhaps, to tone down their Doris Doormat behaviour, and make way for the emerging April Assertive.

As time went on, the cartoon faces were added to match each communication and personality style. Not long after, we heard from men who also identified with the styles and wanted masculine character identities too. Both men and women seemed able to face their non-assertiveness more readily when it was associated with funny cartoon characters.

It is quite rare to be similar to only one character, and natural to see a little of yourself in all four. It may be instructive to allocate percentages next to each character, to represent how much that approach captures your communication style. For example, your own approach might be expressed as 20% passive (Doris), 5% aggressive (Agatha), 35% indirect (Iris), and 40% assertive (April). In other words, about 75% of the time you rely on indirect or assertive behaviour. If you want to change those percentages, write your goal percentage nearby as an incentive.

'Can I be assertive and feminine too?'
Because this is still such a popular concern, we give special attention to 'feminine assertiveness,' which simply means that *a woman* may incorporate her new assertive skills comfortably into her own style of being *a woman*. She may *choose* to retain some ways of acting, speaking, or dressing which would still be part of the traditional concept of femininity. As long as she is doing this by choice, we feel she is being assertive.

The following list exemplifies assertive choices that may also be considered traditionally feminine:
● Choosing to cook and do housework.
● Choosing to shave her legs because she likes the way they feel.
● Choosing to wear a dress when others may be in trousers.
● Choosing to go into a 'woman's profession,' such as teaching, nursing, or social work because it really does appeal to her more than becoming an executive, doctor, or lawyer.
● Choosing to remain soft-spoken instead of trying to develop a tougher voice than necessary to be heard.

- Choosing to wear some make-up without feeling inferior if she doesn't have 'her face on.'
- Choosing to allow someone to open a door for her or to carry something heavy.
- Choosing to be compassionate and nurturing without feeling obligated to do so.

Women must feel free to make any of these choices. *Having to* conform to 'new' standards can be just as oppressive as having to conform to 'old' standards. Let's keep our options alive!

Situational Examples

How each woman responds to given situations reveals a lot about her behaviour patterns. Examine these situations and find yours.

What's for Dinner?

Situation: A man and a woman, each with a full-time job, live together. The woman has her share of housework and cooking, and the man has his share of the domestic chores. She returns from work one evening quite tired, and finds her mate in the study reading.

Passive: Doris sighs as she enters the study. She felt like going out to dinner and is really too tired to cook, but doesn't say so. She 'puts a smile on her face' and asks sweetly, 'What would you like for dinner?' She quietly goes off and prepares dinner, feeling all the while like a martyr. Her mother phones while she's cooking, and Doris complains bitterly that she has to do *all* the work.

Aggressive: Agatha moans about what a hard day she's had. She shouts at her mate, 'If you think I'm going to cook when I feel this bad, you're mad!' She threatens to leave him if he doesn't do something about the messy house and at least take her out to a nice restaurant. She calls him a 'lazy slob' and belittles him for not caring about her feelings. He responds by offering to help, promising to take her out, or going out alone, slamming the door behind him.

Indirectly Aggressive: Iris steps lightly into the study and asks, 'What would you like to do about dinner?' She wants him to suggest going out or at least helping her cook, but he's candid and says, 'I'm tired, would you mind preparing dinner tonight?' Iris makes an attempt to look even more tired and bedraggled, hoping again that he will take the hint. He doesn't. So, she agrees to prepare dinner and proceeds to the kitchen, banging pots and pans furiously, preparing something she knows he hates, and burning it besides.

Assertive: April finds her mate in the study and asks that they talk for a minute about plans for dinner. She tells him that she had a hard day and is feeling quite tired, and asks how he's feeling. She suggests that they either prepare dinner together or go out to eat, since he said he was feeling tired too. She understands his feelings, but does not cheat herself by hiding her own. They reach a compromise: neither feels like a martyr or put down. They enjoy dinner together in a relaxed atmosphere.

'You're Not Interested in My Work!'

Situation: A husband and wife are struggling to achieve success and security in related fields. The man complains that his wife is not interested in *his* work because she doesn't take an active and enthusiastic role in finding out more about what he does and why he does it. She isn't usually available to accompany him on business-related trips. He feels she should make a greater effort to be gracious and to entertain his work associates.

Passive: Doris feels guilty. She is convinced that her husband's success or failure depends on how much responsibility she takes in playing an auxiliary role in his job. She vows to find a way to please him. She minimizes her own needs regarding *her* work and its limitations and demands. To keep peace, she gives in and puts his interests first.

Aggressive: Instantly Agatha's defences flare up. She argues with her husband, recounting instances when she has supported him and he hasn't appreciated it. Then she launches an attack about the times when she needed him, and he obviously didn't care at all. They both feel alienated, misunderstood and hurt. The problem is sure to flare up again.

Indirectly Aggressive: The last thing Iris wants to do is take any responsibility for her husband's accusations. Even if she were guilty of sabotaging his work (typical for Iris), she would never admit it.

She tries to manipulate him by bemoaning how her work 'forces' her to be less supportive of him. She is dishonest about 'feeling terrible' for him and in her own sweet-but-back-stabbing way, she puts him down for being 'weak' and unable to stand on his own 'like a man.' She doesn't seem to recognize she would feel differently if the tables were turned and she needed his support. She feels self-righteous; he feels threatened and alone.

Assertive: April listens to her husband's complaints. She encourages him to express how he feels about the situation: his anger, frustration, hurt, and aloneness. Then she shares with him how she really feels about the issue. She is able to understand his need for support and recognizes the legitimacy of that need within him as well as within herself. April then asserts that there may be some things that each can do to be mutually supportive. She explores alternatives with him, for example, by suggesting that they spend an hour or a day at each other's place of work once in a while, that they set aside a certain time every day (perhaps after dinner) to talk together about their feelings, that together they plan some social occasions with each other's work associates. They both feel better due to April's assertiveness.

In this chapter we have presented the four major ways to behave in any situation – passive, aggressive, indirectly aggressive, and assertive. By discovering how you behave, you will be able to recognize situations you could handle more assertively.

Learn as much as you can about which experiences bring out the Doris, Agatha, Iris or April in you. Carefully examine your relationships with other people: your spouse, flatmate, friends, children, parents, brothers or sisters, employer, employees, neighbours, colleagues, teachers, and others. Whose wishes usually prevail?

This self-examination is an important step toward identifying your own preferences and 'comfort zones' with regard to enhancing assertiveness. Although we recognize that your body and your mind work together, we suggest that you follow this analysis with two separate approaches to becoming assertive: awareness of your body's image and consciousness of your mind's patterns.

Chapter 4

Becoming Assertive

One's philosophy is not best expressed in words, it is expressed in the choices one makes . . . In the long run, we shape our lives and we shape ourselves. The process never ends until we die. And the choices we make are ultimately our responsibility.
— Eleanor Roosevelt

Acquiring new assertive behaviours involves becoming more aware of your own attitudes, actions and reactions, and understanding those that will promote your assertion and those which delay it. It also involves becoming more aware of the possible consequences of choosing to be assertive.

For example, as you begin to behave more assertively, you may find that you are working against old, non-assertive behaviour patterns that you learned years before. Applying some basic learning principles will help you to develop and maintain assertive behaviour as you combat old behaviour patterns. Using the guidelines in this chapter will prepare the way for your continued success in becoming assertive.

Social behaviours are learned and practiced over time. You become assertive by paying attention to your attitudes as well as to specific behaviours. Whether or not the environment will support your newly-adopted behaviours is also an important consideration.

Attitudes
Knowing how you feel about yourself is the first step toward learning assertive behaviours. From childhood you may have developed attitudes that inhibit learning assertiveness. Some

possibilities are listed below. Which did you grow up with?
- Women should be seen and not heard.
- I am helpless when it comes to taking action that promotes change.
- Risking frightens me, so I don't enjoy taking risks.
- I'd rather let somebody else be the leader. I'm a good follower.
- What other people think is more important than what I think.
- It's better to put up with things than rock the boat.
- If I ask for what I want people will think I'm selfish.
- It's better to be liked than speak up and be seen as a trouble-maker.
- Girls who assert themselves are being aggressive.
- A woman who is too competent will never find a husband.

Your thoughts and attitudes alone can perpetuate non-assertive behaviour. If you believe it would be *terrible* for you to behave assertively, you aren't likely to give it a try. Exploring the thoughts and attitudes that prevent you from expressing yourself can actually help you to stimulate positive new behaviours.

For example, Doris Doormat may think to herself:

'If I tried to assert myself in this situation, I know I'd say the wrong thing and people would think I'm stupid and unfeminine. *That would be terrible*. I'd never live through it.' By imagining catastrophic consequences, Doris is effectively teaching herself not to be assertive. April would have quite a different attitude: 'If I try to assert myself in this situation, I will feel better because I'm saying or doing something. By expressing my views, I know I will benefit.'

Try to be aware of the imagined consequences you attach to asserting yourself. If you find you have some *attitudes* which discourage acting assertively, make a conscious effort to have those attitudes work *for you* instead of against you. Try repeating to yourself, 'I will say or do something in this situation because I believe it could be effective. I will benefit from asserting myself.' If you practise saying this as you begin new behaviours, it will be easier for you to progress in self-assertion.

Also, try to *visualize* yourself acting assertively and experiencing positive consequences. If you frequently see yourself failing to be assertive, imagine some situations in which you are successfully assertive. As you visualize yourself becoming more positive, your self-image will change also. The more you regard yourself as an assertive woman, the more likely you are to behave assertively.

For many women, attitudes about what is feminine prevent them from behaving assertively. Women who feel it is unfeminine or aggressive to behave assertively have two alternatives: to behave passively or to be coy and indirectly aggressive. The result of either approach is to avoid an opportunity to develop assertiveness.

Perhaps you have avoided acting independently and assertively because of the anxiety or fear involved in changing your behaviour. If you consider the anxiety and pain you have felt when you acted non-assertively, you will find that assertion is a welcome alternative.

Behaviours
Learning new behaviours involves at least these four steps:
1. Description or modelling of the behaviour;
2. Practising the new behaviour;
3. Reinforcing the desired behaviour; and
4. Receiving accurate, rapid feedback.

As you learn assertive behaviours, an awareness of their causes (antecedents) and their results (consequences) is also important. Let's examine each of these elements in turn:

1. *Description or modelling of the behaviour.*

Throughout this book we present descriptions and illustrations of appropriate behaviours that will serve as assertive models for you. Before you begin attempting to increase your assertiveness, be sure you understand the difference between assertive and aggressive behaviours. It is also worthwhile to talk with or observe someone you consider to be an assertive person. Research has shown that learning takes place as a result of observation as well as through descriptions of the appropriate behaviour.

2. *Practising the new behaviour*

Your first attempts at assertion should be those which will likely meet with positive consequences. Choose situations in which you are likely to experience control. If you try to tackle more difficult areas too fast, you risk negative consequences which could discourage you from asserting yourself in the future. For example, it would generally be wiser to assertively handle someone who is manipulating you. If you proceed gradually, from initial assertions to increasingly difficult ones, you will increase your probability of success.

3. *Reinforcing the desired behaviour.*

Arrange it initially so you are likely to be rewarded, rather than punished, for your assertive behaviour. As you continue to behave assertively, you will find that just the act of being assertive is in itself rewarding. We cannot stress enough that the goal of assertion is not 'victory,' but being able to express your needs and desires openly and honestly. Remember, the compulsion to 'win at all costs' is the burden of the aggressive person. More about reinforcement under 'Consequences' in the next section of this chapter.

4. *Receiving accurate, rapid feedback*

When you are practicing assertive behaviours, ask a friend to give you feedback on your behaviour:

● Did my assertive words match my body image?
● Did I use my voice, gestures, and posture assertively?
● Are there specific areas that need improvement?
● Which ones?

You can also give yourself accurate feedback with the help of a mirror, or an audio or video tape recorder. Practice assertive behaviours in front of a mirror before you try it in the real situation; use an audio tape recorder to receive feedback about the tone, volume, and quality of your voice. Videotape feedback is the clearest overall measure of your effectiveness. You may be surprised, when you use these feedback tools, to discover that your self-expression is not as assertive as you had thought.

Combining a knowledge of what assertive behaviour is with actually performing it and receiving reinforcement and feedback will provide you with a strong foundation you can build on. It is a good formula to follow as you develop assertive responses. Practice and preparation beforehand will make it much more likely that you will continue to behave assertively. Practise or rehearse your assertive behaviours using the exercises in this book. The more attention you give to *practising* assertive behaviours, the more comfortable you will be in asserting yourself.

In spite of your preparation and new knowledge, you may still find it difficult to behave assertively. If you find yourself being generally non-assertive, you may benefit from the extra support and guidance that a professional counsellor or therapist can provide. Changing your lifestyle is not easy. Many women have combined other resources to help them become more assertive: the help of professional therapists, reading books, attending workshops, or enrolling in classes.

Antecedents and Consequences of Behaviour

Knowing what causes or stimulates your behaviour and being aware of how your behaviour affects you and others are both important in learning new behaviours. Specifying the antecedents and the consequences of your behaviour can support you in your efforts to be assertive.

Antecedents. People and situations influence you to behave in certain patterns. Identifying the ones that have led you to behave non-assertively in the past will give you direction for behaving assertively in the future.

Sharon Bower, in her book, *Learning Assertive Behaviour With PALS,* has developed a comprehensive list of people and situations for use in identifying who or what may cause women to behave non-assertively. We have condensed it here. Use it as a starting point for developing your awareness of situations you can handle more assertively.

Place a tick beside the items that influence you to behave non-assertively. After you have finished, review the items you have. You will have a list to use in guiding your progress towards more effective assertive behaviour.

1. With *whom* do you feel passive or non-assertive?
   _____ a spouse?
   _____ children?
   _____ a relative?
   _____ friends?

_____ an employer?

_____ an employee?

_____ a teacher?

_____ a doctor?

_____ a police officer?

_____ a sales assistant?

_____ waiters or waitresses?

_____ an acquaintance?

_____ other: _____

2. *When* have you felt non-assertive, especially as you *ask* for:

_____ cooperation from spouse, children, employer, employees?

_____ a loan of money or an item?

_____ a favour?

_____ a job?

_____ love and attention?

_____ directions?

_____ other: _____

3. *What* subject has caused you to behave non-assertively:

_____ sex?

_____ politics?

_____ women's rights?

_____ your accomplishments?

_____ others' accomplishments?

_____ your mistakes?

_____ others' mistakes?

_____ expressing positive feelings?

_____ expressing negative feelings?

_____ other: _____

4. *Size* of the group might be a factor in your non-assertive behaviour; did the situation involve you and:

_____ one other familiar person?

_____ one other unfamiliar person?

_____ two or more familiar persons?

_____ two or more unfamiliar persons?
_____ a group of familiar persons?
_____ a group of unfamiliar persons?

Consequences. Your behaviour has consequences; it does affect other people. Women who have behaved passively for long periods of time usually acknowledge that the behaviour of others affects them, but they are seldom aware of the extent to which their passive behaviours affect others. Recognizing the consequences of your behaviour is an important element in learning assertive behaviours.

Assertive behaviour is likely to have positive consequences. When you assert yourself, you will feel more in control of your life and less helpless and frustrated. While you remain passive, the consequences are likely to be painful for you and for others. Other people may resent you for being so dependent on them or for allowing them to make your decisions for you. They may feel burdened by your non-assertiveness.

There may also be people who have actually encouraged you to behave passively. Your mate, for example, may have reinforced your passive behaviour by labelling your assertive attempts as aggressive, or by blaming you for difficulties in your relationship. In such a situation it is understandable that you would feel anxious about expressing yourself, because you have experienced such negative consequences in the past. Professional counselling or assertiveness training for you and the other family members might be recommended. If your family members are prepared and willing to try to make some changes themselves, you are all likely to benefit, physically and emotionally.

For the best results, remember to choose initial assertions that are likely to promote positive consequences. You will be less likely to be discouraged in the future. Don't attempt more difficult assertions until you have had sufficient practice and preparation, and feel comfortable with previous ones.

In summary, your attitudes and previous ways of behaving affect your new attempts to behave assertively. Structuring your learning of assertive behaviours will help you to experience success with few setbacks.

Consider your thoughts and attitudes about being assertive:
- Which ones encourage and support an assertive image of yourself?
- Are you avoiding assertion because you fear disastrous consequences?
- Be aware of the situations and people that have influenced you to be passive in the past, and use them as reminders to be assertive in the future.
- Practise new behaviours that result in positive consequences.
- Stay *away* from people who punish your attempts to be assertive. Seek out people who reward your assertive attempts with positive feedback.
- Look at becoming assertive as a positive experience, instead of a negative problem-solving venture. Remember, learning to be assertive can be fun!

In the next few chapters, we'll focus on attitudes, beliefs, thoughts, and feelings: The 'Inner Game of Assertiveness.' In later chapters, we'll deal with the behavioural skills you'll need to express yourself.

Chapter 5

The Inner Game of Assertiveness

. . . I am a fairly inexperienced, often naive young woman, who is not always certain of what is right and wrong, what's worth pursuing in life, or even what I myself want out of life . . . Knowledge has always come quickly and easily for me, whereas wisdom has been a difficult thing for me to put my finger on and be sure that's where it lay.

–a 24-year-old college student

When Tim Gallwey wrote *The Inner Game of Tennis* in 1974, it revolutionized the game. Tennis players faced their opponents differently and often dramatically increased their levels of peak performance. *The Inner Game of Tennis* taught players to relax instead of tense up before a game, to stop labelling themselves as 'stupid' or 'weak,' to see themselves winning. They imagined vivid scenarios in which they played superbly, using their inner intelligence to play the 'inner game.' Believing in the process, these players created an emotional experience of winning as if it were already happening, all before stepping onto the court! Instead of worrying about the opponent or themselves, they learned to 'become one' peacefully with the racket and ball. They let go of the idea of 'doing it right,' trusting inner wisdom and allowing it to flow like a natural channel of energy. For some, playing the inner game made playing the outer game as natural and automatic as breathing.

Athletes in other sports quickly surmised that the inner game could work wonders for them too. The concept was soon applied to other sports to improve concentration, confidence and performance. The inner game worked.

The Inner Game of Assertiveness

If the inner game can work so well in athletics, it is worth exploring its usefulness in other challenging areas of our lives. The concept of inner wisdom is an old one. Some of us already play an inner game as a result of religious education or metaphysical pursuits, but many people do not exercise their inner wisdom.

The inner game of assertiveness places importance on the spirit in which an assertive action is taken. To play the inner game, one trusts her own intuition or inner wisdom, evaluating herself spontaneously in relationship to her situation, then applying assertive skills accordingly. The inner game of assertiveness is a flowing, constant interaction between thoughts and behaviour, between inner wisdom and assertive action.

Let's look at an example of how the inner game can be applied in everyday life.

'Nobody Wants to Listen to Me'

Dorothy has recently completed a very exciting seminar on Time Management that has inspired her to get her life in order. She buys a daily planner book and spends the weekend reorganizing herself. While doing so, she sees some applications that would be beneficial at the office where she is a secretary. On Monday morning she goes into the office filled with enthusiasm and zeal to get everybody else organized, from the boss to her co-workers. She greets everyone with an instant wave of enthusiasm and creative ideas on how to increase productivity.

When people respond with indifference, agitation or resistance, Dorothy realizes that her assertions have fallen on deaf ears.

This is an opportunity for Dorothy to play the inner game. She can acknowledge that she may have caught people off guard, that her timing was inappropriate. At a quiet time, perhaps her morning coffee break, she allows herself to calm down and really think about what she wants to accomplish with her boss and co-workers. She realizes that she wants to encourage receptivity in them and a spirit of cooperation. As she quietly meditates on this, she understands that she antagonized people by attempting to force *her* ideas onto them. Now she recognizes that it would be better to approach them in the spirit of teamwork, at a time when they will be receptive. After considering various alternatives, she finally decides to type up a summary of the most innovative and practical ideas she learned in her seminar. She will make arrangements with her boss to distribute copies of these at the next staff meeting as a contribution to all. She can then invite comments, additional ideas and feedback. Such give and take opens the possibility for eventual implementation of the best ideas. However, she is now clear that others are not approving or rejecting her personally. With her ego out of the way, everyone is able to embrace some of the new ideas more easily. Dorothy's assertive action based on her inner wisdom produces winning results.

Finding Inner Wisdom and Using It

When life is calm and clear, it is easy to make time to be centred and let inner wisdom be your guide. The challenge is much greater in the throes of real life dramas. Yet, inner wisdom evolves out of trusting yourself in spite of what's happening around you. It is a product of confronting such internal barriers as runaway emotions or negative, self-defeating thoughts.

'How Could You Do This!'

Today is Sarah's mother's birthday – a joyous occasion, or so she thought. An intimate gathering of close family and friends is to meet at her parents' home for a special tribute dinner party. Sarah dresses up for the celebration and is anticipating a good time. Her mother hasn't been 'feeling well' lately but Sarah is sure this party will cheer her up.

When Sarah arrives she finds her father in an anxious state. Her mother is in bed 'sick.' Actually Sarah's mother is an alcoholic, who on occasion drinks herself into oblivion. Everyone has felt helpless at these times but has chosen to ignore the problem and make excuses. But, there is no excuse for this. The other guests will arrive soon. What to do? How humiliating.

In the midst of other people's disapproval, hysteria and/or fear, Sarah is barraged by her own defences as well: 'How could your own mother do this to *you* on her birthday?! What will people think now? You ought to be absolutely furious! Why don't you just leave this mess!' This is an opportune time for Sarah to activate her inner wisdom and play the inner game of assertiveness.

Because of the surrounding chaos, Sarah doesn't have the leisure to go off and ponder the situation peacefully. She is forced by circumstances to act more quickly and spontaneously. This she can do easily if she has been practising the inner game consciously and consistently already. In a matter of seconds she can take a few deep breaths, shut out the outward noise, and allow her inner wisdom to speak to her.

As she calms herself and lets go of her judgments about what an 'awful thing' her mother has done, she understands that her mother has chosen *the perfect time* to reach out for help. What a good idea! Within a short time Sarah has let go of her reactions and has begun to *take positive action*. She assertively reassures her father and enlists the assistance of the less anxious guests to make arrangement for her mother's physical and medical needs. She extends a loving attitude to her mother, who knows the difference even in her state of oblivion. After the immediate concerns are handled, Sarah uses this opportunity while all are gathered to address her mother's alcoholism openly. She enlists the support of the others to deal with this family problem together in a more direct and assertive way.

To activate inner wisdom during times of pain or pressure, you must *slow down*. Take time to be alone, take a walk, meditate, listen to calming music and breathe deeply and slowly. You may even practice deep muscle relaxation as discussed in Chapter 11. If you ease the pressure to find an immediate answer to your current challenge, an answer will come from your inner wisdom. The genius of it may even surprise you. And the fact that it is *your* answer and not someone else's opinion will delight you.

What is the price of turning your back on your inner wisdom? Fear and uncertainty. If you are not willing to trust yourself, other people and events will determine the direction of *your* life. Your assertions will hit and miss, because they will be buffeted about by others' ever-changing opinions and well-meaning advice. Perhaps others can provide appropriate answers for you from time to time.

However, there is no person or self-help book that knows your heart better than you do!

If you can answer the following questions with a 'yes' – even a nervous 'yes' – you are ready to find your inner wisdom and begin a new process of assertion. You are ready to play the inner game!

- Am I willing to listen to my heart, follow my passion, activate my inner wisdom even if it means giving up what is secure and familiar?
- Am I willing to lose the approval of others and risk rejection if it means being true to myself and self-respecting?
- Am I willing to give up my addiction to what I think I *should* feel, do, or have, in exchange for being who I am?
- Am I willing to go through any awkwardness and make mistakes as I'm learning to tune into my inner self?
- Am I willing to choose assertions out of the spirit within me, rather than choosing assertions that appear 'right' or 'perfect?'
- Am I willing and ready to trust myself? Do I believe that I'm worth it?

Keeping Track of Inner Wisdom

Today it is not so important to conform to rigid standards as it is to acknowledge and appreciate our uniqueness. We are waking up to the passion and promise of our own energy, intuition and creativity.

We need new ways to keep track of where we're going; it's no longer enough to measure ourselves by competing with someone else. Although we still enjoy matching wits in intellectual games, keeping score in athletics, and competing in business, we are also making progress in business, science, medicine and even world affairs through the integration of intuition and logic.

On a more personal level, we can accelerate our use of inner wisdom and ability to play the inner game through some special learning tools.

One of the most effective ways to keep track of your personal progress is to keep a journal, a blank book in which you record – on a daily or less frequent basis – your innermost thoughts, feelings, questions, even dreams. You can include conversations you've had with yourself or others. It is personal, private and confidential; keep it in a safe place so you'll feel secure in being open and vulnerable with what is written. Yes, it does sound a lot like what we used to call a 'diary.' The major difference is that now you'll be more systematic and purposeful about your own growth and change. Periodically read through earlier entries and look for patterns, blind spots and progress from which your inner wisdom can be strengthened.

Another possibility to consider, especially if you are not inclined to write, is to tape record your journal entries. Listening to your own voice and its many moods and changes can be a powerful learning experience. Besides developing and tracking your inner wisdom, these tools can assist you in having compassion for yourself, letting go of the old, and forgiving yourself for past mistakes.

To get you started you might enjoy the following exercises.

- *Write a letter to the 'you' of twenty years ago.* From your current wisdom and experience, tell yourself all the 'Things I wish I'd Known When I was You.'
- *Write a letter to your Feminine Intuition,* telling this part of yourself what stands in the way of your listening to, understanding, and respecting what she tells you. Let her know your commitment to paying attention to and honouring her inner voice. Describe how you plan to do this and what you'll do when you feel confused or uncertain about her messages.

Developing Assertive Attitudes

Assertiveness is only one tool that you may choose to employ to better your life. It is not the answer to every question; it is not the solution to every problem. As you explore your attitudes and deepen your awareness, you will be able to identify the ways in which assertiveness can be valuable to you personally. You can accelerate your own 'consciousness raising' with our 'consciousness razors,' provided here for your use. The concept of consciousness raising certainly has merit; it is the process of increasing awareness and heightening perceptions. Yet we especially like the pun on the word 'razor,' because it implies that each razor has a sharp edge to help you cut through some attitudes that may inhibit your assertiveness.

Using Consciousness Razors

Following is a list of razors. Try to answer each item as honestly as possible. After responding to each item, review your thoughts carefully, and write your comments in your journal.

- Have you ever felt different from other women?
- Have you felt competitive with other women?
- Were you treated differently from your brother(s) as you were growing up? How?
- Have you ever felt pressured into having sex?
- Have you ever pressured yourself into having sex?
- Have you ever lied about orgasm?
- Have you ever felt like a sex object?
- Do you ever feel invisible?
- Do you often feel insignificant?
- What was your relationship to your parents?
- What was your parents' relationship to you?
- How was your education affected by your being female?
- How was your interest in sports affected by your being female?
- How was your career choice affected by your being female?
- How do you feel about getting old?
- How do (did) you feel about your mother's ageing?
- What do you fear most about ageing?
- What goal have you wanted most to achieve in your life?
- What, if anything, has stopped you from achieving this goal?
- Do you see yourself operating in a dependent and/or in an independent way? How?
- How do you relate to authority figures? (Clergy, doctor, police, etc.)
- Have you ever felt powerful?
- How do you feel about your body?
- Have you ever punished yourself? When? How?
- Have you ever forbidden yourself a pleasure, a meal, or some other gratification?
- Have you ever pinched or slapped yourself?
- Do you often feel a sense of aloneness or loneliness?
- Do you have some attitudes that could inhibit your being more assertive?

- What are they?
- Which affect you the most?
- Which affect you the least?

As you review your comments on the consciousness razors, look for:
- Patterns or habits that seem to repeat themselves over and over in your life.
- Rationalizations about why you do or don't do something.

Explore your feelings in depth, trying to avoid an intellectual exercise in pursuit of the 'right' answer. The goal of consciousness raising is to know yourself better and to accept who you are as well as to undertake the changes that you decide to make.

Choosing Your Own Labels

Developing an assertive attitude is an important part of becoming an assertive woman. If your attitudes and feelings about being assertive are positive and supportive, you can *reward* your assertive behaviour. However, if you feel you are being 'impolite,' 'bossy,' or 'bitchy' when you assert yourself, you can inhibit your assertive behaviour and seriously weaken your assertive attitude. You can strengthen or minimize your assertive skills by the *labels* you place on them.

Do the labels *you* apply to your assertive behaviour encourage or prevent you from being assertive? Use *positive* self-labels to support and encourage your assertive behaviour. ('I'm really being assertive – I love it!'). *Negative* self-labels can only serve to inhibit and prevent your assertiveness. ('What a bitch I am!')

Other people can mislabel your assertive behaviour also. Because women have been expected to behave passively for so long, becoming an assertive woman seems to be an extreme contrast. Other people's expectations of how you behave are being thwarted if you have been consistently passive with them, and are now being assertive. They will be quick to label your behaviour as aggressive in an attempt to inhibit it, fearing they may have to change, too. This is particularly true for people close to you (family members, other relatives, close friends, employers) who have in some way benefit-ted from your passivity (see Chapter 7, 'Compassion Can Be A Trap'). On the other hand, if you have been consistently aggressive in your interactions with others, moving to a more assertive way of relating will usually be encouraged, and given positive labels by those around you.

Be aware of the negative self-labels you attach to your assertive behaviour, and work toward replacing those labels with more positive ones. If you do this, other people can follow your example and work at changing their labels also. Use the following exercise to see how *you* label your assertive behaviour by comparing your responses with the responses of our four women, Doris Doormat, Agatha Aggressive, Irish Indirect, and April Assertive. Each of these situations was handled assertively, but it is the label each woman has attached to the assertive behaviour that varies here. How would you label each assertion?

'Thanks, but no thanks . . .'

You have been telephoned by a salesman who is trying to sell you a magazine subscription. You say you aren't interested in receiving the magazine and end the conversation. Do you think to yourself:

Doris Doormat: I really didn't *want* the magazine, but wasn't I impolite and irritable to say so? The next time I'm asked to subscribe, I'll be more polite and do it.

Iris Indirect: Well, I certainly was easy on him! I should have said yes, and then refused to pay the subscription to teach them a lesson about bothering me.

Agatha Aggressive: I wish I'd given that salesman a piece of my mind! What an insolent person! The next time that happens I won't be so mild-mannered and meek.

April Assertive: I was really assertive with that salesman. I feel good about being honest and direct.

'Get Ready for Dinner'

Your children are playing outside and you want them to come in for dinner. You go outside and tell them to come in now. They protest that it's not that late and couldn't they play for a while longer? You firmly tell them again to come in, and they do. Do you think to yourself:

Doris Doormat: I'm glad they came in, but wasn't I nagging and bossy? I don't want to nag, so I think in the future I'll ask once, and if they don't come in, I'll just try to keep dinner warm.

Irish Indirect: I'm sure they would have come in sooner if I'd not been so polite. Instead of asking twice, I should have just said okay and waited until dinner was burned for them to come in. Then they'd feel bad.

Agatha Aggressive: Was I quiet and passive! What a softie! Next time I'll teach those kids who's the boss around here. I'll really give them a lecture!

April Assertive: I'm glad they came in when I asked them to. I'm really being assertive and honest with them.

'You're Late.'

You are scheduled to meet a friend for an important meeting. She is an hour late when she arrives. You tell her that you are upset because she is so late, and you would have liked more time to spend with her. She acknowledges your feelings and says she will try to be on time in the future. Do you think to yourself:

Doris Doormat: I'm really pleased that she will make an effort to be on time in the future, but wasn't I awfully aggressive and mean to say anything about it? I hate being so aggressive, so I'll stop demanding things and just hope they work out from now on.

Irish Indirect: She might be on time in the future, but I shouldn't have said anything about it today. It's so embarrassing to have to go out of my way to say something about it. I should just be late next time and see how *she* feels.

Agatha Aggressive: I sure let her off easy. What an inconsiderate woman to be late! I should have really told her off.

April Assertive: I'm really glad that our meeting will be on time in the future, and I'm pleased that I was assertive and mentioned it today. I was really honest and spontaneous, and I like it.

If Doris's responses sound all too familiar to you, you have been mislabelling assertive behaviour as aggressive, bitchy, impolite, nagging, bossy. You are also inhibiting your own assertive behaviour by attaching an inappropriate, undesirable label to it. Remember that *aggressive* behaviour such as Agatha's could be labelled 'nagging,' 'bossy,' or 'bitchy' – *not* assertive behaviour.

If your labels are more like Iris's, you are looking for revenge or trying to elicit guilt rather than rewarding your assertive behaviour. You are mislabelling your assertive behaviour as too easy, too direct, or embarrassing. If Agatha's labels resemble yours, you are mislabelling your appropriate behaviour as weak, passive or meek. The assertive woman, April, correctly identifies her assertive behaviour as direct, spontaneous, and honest. She rewards her own assertiveness accordingly.

Attach appropriate labels to your assertive behaviour, and make a conscious effort to tell yourself you've been assertive. By rewarding yourself whenever you are assertive, you'll support your own progress toward becoming an assertive woman.

Chapter 6

Obstacles on the Inner Journey

Dear Stanlee and Nancy,
I've dressed for success, had my colours done, new make-up,
hair-style – in short, a complete overhaul. I've eliminated weak
words from my vocabulary and replaced them with power
phrases. I've attended seminars, absorbed the latest books on
self-improvement, joined the right organizations and profes-
sional groups, lived through divorce and am financially inde-
pendent. I seem to have done it all and have it all. But, with
accomplishing this and more, why do I still doubt myself? What
does it take to honestly believe I'm an assertive woman in my
guts?

> – 41 years old, vice president for
> marketing of a large corporation

Looking like an assertive woman can be accomplished a lot faster than feeling like one. For years women have been inundated with instructions about how to achieve the look of today's new woman. Quick-fix techniques, images and accouterments have been easily adopted and tried, with the hope that they would immediately and permanently transform the women who used them.

Instead, there are a large number of women today who look assertive, but who don't believe they *are* assertive. They have adopted styles and behaviours recommended by experts, the media, spouses, friends, colleagues, or society in general. In many instances they have paid a high price in order to make these changes – an expenditure of time, energy and money which has left many women short of the real, deep-down transformation they expected.

Some women have resigned themselves to a perpetual self-improvement campaign as if it were a life sentence. Some, weary of pursuing a new assertive woman identity, reverted to more traditional or less demanding roles. Others ride a merry-go-round of confusion, chasing quick fixes of enlightenment, followed by periods of hopelessness and lethargy. And still others cautiously guard their assertive woman image – a precariously held package of outward appearances – like a trophy that could be snatched away at any moment.

A traditional focus on the external environment and a powrful need to conform to what others expect has been a major preoccupation for many women. It is no surprise many women feel like imposters: they know that their insides don't match their outsides. They feel cheated and tired, but they are afraid to admit it. The fear of being found out keeps their defences high.

To be an assertive woman, and not just look like one, an important shift must be made toward discovery of and respect for one's inner self. A good beginning is to let go of the drive to win others' approval.

Practitioners of the martial arts understand how to be as powerful as they need or want to be. They do not meet force with force, violence with violence, defensive reaction with defensive reaction, attack with attack. They face every situation by centring their thoughts and energies from within first, remaining alert to the movements of an opponent. They pay attention to their own thoughts and feelings, and use that inner awareness to better cope with the forces of the adversary.

Tom Crum co-founded Windstar Foundation with John Denver, and created workshops on 'Positive Conflict Resolution' that they're conducting internationally, including the U.S.S.R. Tom has a black belt in Aikido and bases his seminar teachings on the use of 'Aiki energy' – the energy of positive power within us all.

Here is a simple exercise to try with a friend to see how tapping into your power within strengthens and centres you when faced with a conflict or confrontation from another:

One of you will be partner *A* and the other partner *B*. Stand side-by-side – not facing one another – about two feet apart. Partner

A stretches one arm out horizontally to the side toward *B*, and locks it in place as rigidly as possible.

Partner *B* puts both of her hands on this rigid arm, attempting to push the arm down. Partner *A* resists as much as she can, 'trying' to be strong.

What happens? The arm of Partner *A* goes down easily. The rigid, defensive stance prevented the Aiki energy from flowing into the raised arm to give it strength.

Now stand in the same position, side-by-side, with A's arm raised rigidly again. However, before Partner *B* attempts to lower *A*'s arm, *A* should take a few moments to locate her power within. She should first focus her attention 2 inches below her belly button – a point of centring in the body. Imagining energy flowing into this spot, she takes a few deep, relaxing breaths. With her arm out-stretched, she then imagines the energy rising up through the trunk of her body and flowing briskly through her raised arm. She pictures the arm as a big, sturdy fire hose that becomes filled with the Aiki energy – just like the rapidly rushing water turned on full blast and shooting through the hose. *A* wiggles her fingers freely and loosely as if to allow the energy to spray out, like the water gushes out of the fire hose. She stays calm, relaxed, positive and focused on this movement of energy from within, continuing to wiggle her fingers.

Now Partner *B* attempts to lower *A*'s arm, using as much force as possible. What happens? The arm remains outstretched no matter how much force Partner *B* uses as long as Partner *A* allows her energy from within to continue to flow!

What does this simple exercise demonstrate? It shows us that tapping into our inner strength can assist us in becoming more effective outwardly. Perhaps our assertiveness can be more easily achieved through engaging in an inner process as we face our day to day challenges.

The Assertive Woman: Fashioned From Within

The next step toward becoming an assertive woman presents ob-stacles of a different nature. A new selection of 'how-to' books, seminar workshops, and self-help manuals describes these pitfalls. Just when we thought we might relax a little and coast along on some of our mini-triumphs, we're barraged with a whole new wave of syndromes, complexes and situations to overcome. The challenges seem endless. And, there are new lists of what to *do* and what you need to *have* to survive.

The assertive woman is challenged to be a unique individual in her relationships with herself, others and her career. Again she looks not for answers about what to *do* or what to *have* but who she wants to *be*. Her answers come from within.

Barriers to the Inner Process

Sally Ride, America's first female astronaut, was the keynote speaker at a Women in Management Conference in 1985. When asked by someone in the audience, 'Did you get your brains from your father?' she replied, 'I must have, because my mother still has hers!' Her speech was warm, humorous and powerful. From the way she spoke and the information she shared about her life as a woman and an astronaut, it was apparent to all that Sally was centred from within.

Barriers to the inner process generally fall into three categories (1) cognitive or thought barriers; (2) emotional addictions; and (3) social barriers. Any or all of these can sabotage the sincerest efforts to be assertive.

Thought barriers often come to us in the guise of self-stereotyping or negative self-labelling. A constant voice in the back of your head can be heard at any time you choose to listen. We call her 'Ms. Protecto.' Her chatter provides you with a perpetual stream of judgements, positive and negative. Ms. Protecto's negative comments can be definite barriers. She thinks she's protecting you from getting hurt or other dangers. Actually she's preventing you from meeting the assertive woman inside who needs and wants to grow, take calculated risks, and pursue the adventure and rewards of being assertive. Do you recognize any of these thought barriers from your Ms. Protecto?

'This will never work . . . I can't . . . I'll never be able to change . . . I'll wait and see, wait and see, on and on . . . It's not right to do what *I* want to do . . . Nobody cares anyway . . . I'm not thin enough (good enough, smart enough) . . . What if I fail? I'm

rejected? She/he gets angry? . . . This is too much work . . . The
world will never change anyway . . . There's no such thing as inner
wisdom, especially inside *me*! . . . If you can't beat 'em join 'em . . .
Somebody needs to help me because I can't do it alone . . . This is
ridiculous, just somebody else's idea . . . I can't think . . . What's
the use anyway? . . . It's just bad luck . . . My childhood was
miserable . . . I'm being punished . . . It's against my faith . . . I
don't know.'

Emotional addictions can be the most stubborn. Not only do we
manufacture these emotions ourselves, their fires are fuelled by the
latest fads. In 'Don't Tell Me How to Feel,' her article in the
January 1885 issue of *McCall's*, Lesley Dorman describes 'designer
emotions,' which she says have become as big an industry as
'running shoes or cereal.' Dorman points out that although feelings
have been around for centuries, it wasn't until the '60's and '70's
that we were encouraged to let our feelings really 'hang out,' as long
as they were 'OK' feelings.

During the '70's it was suddenly OK to plumb the depths of anger
and sexuality. It was not in vogue to feel or express jealousy, envy,
shyness, depression, guilt or regret. Instead, the emphasis was on
selfishness and revenge: men and society were held responsible for
the repression of female anger and sexuality. In the first edition of
The Assertive Woman in 1975, we attempted to shift women's
awareness from 'What have they done to me?' to 'what am I
continuing to do to myself?'

An assertive woman seeks to take responsibility for herself,
including her anger and her sexuality. She has choices about the
intensity of her feelings and the way in which she expresses them.

Much has been said and done to de-mystify anger and sexuality
and to diminish them as taboo topics. But, the addiction to an
emotional merry-go-round is still with us. It has taken on new forms
which are just as oppressive as the old. The message is the same:
somebody else knows more about how I'm supposed to feel and not
feel than I do!

For example, today's 'designer emotions' include stress and
burnout, 'true' romance, and guilt about not doing it all or having it
all. Absorbed as we are in trying to fix the symptoms of alcoholism,

drug addiction, eating disorders and disappointments in relationships, we don't take the time to look inward.

These obsessions and emotional addictions act as barriers to our
inner selves and to assertion. Assertiveness requires a commitment
to begin an inner search for what is personal. We may not always
know what we feel or have a designer name for it; it may not be in
vogue, especially if others label it as 'selfish' or 'irrelevant.' The
woman who is growing in assertiveness knows and trusts that her
inner process will provide her with the necessary sensitivity and
clarity to be an assertive woman from the inside out.

Social barriers to the inner process are more obvious but no less
difficult. In her book, *A Lesser Life*, Sylvia Hewlett summarizes
what she believes are the predominant social forces facing women
today:

'*By the early eightes my experience had already led me to one
important conclusion: Women of my age are at the mercy of two
powerful and antagonistic traditions. The first is the ultradomestic
fifties with its powerful cult of motherhood; the other is the strident
feminism of the seventies with its attempt to clone the male competitive model. Both these traditions can be found in other industrialized
societies, but in these other contexts they are pale reflections of the
prototype. Only in America are these ideologies pushed to extremes.
A woman trying to fulfill the demands of both traditions is obviously
in something of a dilemma. It is not easy to be simultaneously the
earth mother-goddess and the hard-bitten, hard-nosed corporate
executive or fireperson. And her attempt to manage both roles is
further undermined by the fact that our society, having produced the
strongest and most antithetical dual roles for women, has left them
with the weakest support systems with which to mediate these roles.
Successive administrations have repeatedly failed to provide the
maternity leaves and child-care facilities so taken for granted by
working parents in other advanced countries.*'

It's likely that any woman who identifies with the dilemma that
Ms. Hewlett describes is caught in a perfection trap, trying to do it
all – and do it all well. In her drive for perfection, she searches for
the approval that she hasn't received or given to herself. It may even
seem a luxury to take the time to develop inner awareness.

Women must continue to challenge society's expectations and pressures of motherhood, family, relationships, careers, and independence. However, we must pause from time to time to collect our thoughts, senses and strengths, to renew and restore our vitality, vision and clarity, to dissolve the barriers to our own personal growth and joy.

Ten Commandments For the Inner Journey
Keep in mind the pitfalls you may face in becoming an assertive woman. The following commandments are helpful in steering clear of the barriers to our inner journey. You may wish to put together your own list of reminders; we suggest 3″ × 5″ index cards to carry with you or post in clear view.

- Create quiet time.
- Risk vulnerability.
- Open to inner wisdom.
- Learn to laugh at Ms. Protecto.
- Let go of emotional addictions.
- Look for and develop self-approval.
- Live without negative self labels.
- Focus on *being* – not doing and having.
- Be responsible for creating choices.

In the following chapter, we'll take a look at another barrier to assertiveness – one so pervasive that it deserves a name and space all its own: The Compassion Trap.

Chapter 7

Compassion Can be a Trap

One particularly powerful attitude that stops women from acting assertively is 'The Compassion Trap.' In a 1971 article, Margaret Adams defined the Compassion Trap as a trap exclusive to women who feel that they exist to serve others, and who believe that they must provide tenderness and compassion to all at all times. Recognizing when and how the Compassion Trap affects *you* is an important part of developing an assertive attitude.

Years ago, it was up to Doris to 'keep the family together' through self-sacrifice and compromise. The man of the house endured hassles outside the home, at work. Overall, the totally compassionate woman benefited society by making things comfortable, so that men could tend to the 'more important concerns,' of work, business, science, or politics. Now, many women still tend to cluster in the 'helping professions' (social work, nursing, teaching, domestic services), in which they may extend their caretaking roles. However, many a Doris becomes frustrated and confused as she tries to honour her own individual preferences. She is torn between expressing herself directly – and thus reaping firsthand rewards – and supporting others, and receiving vicarious pleasure from their accomplishments.

Because the Compassion Trap dictates that a woman express herself chiefly through meeting others' needs, it frequently prevents women from being assertive. Climbing out of the Compassion Trap does not mean that, like Agatha, you must close yourself off from others' feelings. Instead, it means valuing your *own* feelings and treating them with the same care that you give to others, as April does.

Generally, there are five areas in which Doris, Agatha, or Iris may find herself trapped by compassion:

1. She may see herself as a protector, as a mother who is afraid to act on her own behalf for fear that her children will suffer.

2. A single woman may give up a career to take care of her ageing or sick relatives.

3. A woman may be reluctant to leave an unsatisfactory job for fear that her clients will suffer in the short run, even though she may benefit in the long run.

4. When no one else is concerned about a problem situation, a woman may enjoy being the one who has special understanding or compassion.

5. When a crisis arises, a woman may push aside a creative project to give her full attention to the crisis; she feels indispensable.

Some profiles will illustrate the chief variations of the Compassion Trap:

'I Felt Sorry for Him'

Situation: A seventeen year old girl and her boyfriend are alone at a very 'romantic' place. They have been getting closer and closer to sexual intercourse, but have always stopped just before that. Tonight, he has decided to 'go all the way.'

Aggressive: Agatha, caught in the Compassion Trap, feels an attack is the best way to avoid a confrontation. She accuses her boyfriend of being a sex maniac, and only having 'one thing on his mind all of the time.' She feels it unnecessary to listen to him; her philosophy is 'a good offence is the best defence.' She prevents him from expressing his feelings, and continues to overreact. For Agatha, it is embarrassing to think that she could be caught in a weak moment of compassion, so she uses her aggressiveness to mask her indecision. Agatha cannot believe that expressing her feelings in an assertive way will have any impact, and she feels that the only way she can get her point across is to act aggressively.

Passive: Doris listens intently as her boyfriend recounts the times when he felt so frustrated after being with her that he couldn't sleep all night. Doris feels guilty as he describes the 'pain' he felt by not being able to ejaculate so many times in a row, night after night. She's far too embarrassed to ask him if he ever thought of masturbating to relieve the pressure. Instead, Doris is swept up in his intense feelings, and forgets about her own desire not to have sex. She gives in because she feels she can no longer allow him to 'suffer,' and she is secretly fearful that if she refuses, she'll lose him and maybe nobody else will want her.

Indirect: Iris, like Doris, is not immune to the Compassion Trap. She feels sorry for her boyfriend, but she tries to mask her compassion and her panic by making excuses. For example, Iris lies about having her period and says intercourse would be 'very messy and not much fun.' If this excuse does not have the intended impact, she will add that she has a headache or is too tired. Iris may even pretend to want him passionately while she makes up another story about having to get home early, or say she has promised her parents or her best friend that she would not indulge in any sexual activities that night. Iris fears that her boyfriend will not accept the truth, but she is convinced he will accept excuses!

Assertive: April listens to her boyfriend's feelings and complaints. She acknowledges how miserable he is feeling. She says, however, that she does not want to have intercourse. When he accuses her of being unfair and leading him on, she again repeats that it is very important to her at this time not to have sex, that she respects his feelings, and that perhaps they need to talk about alternatives such as masturbation, avoiding heavy petting sessions, or not seeing each other. She expresses her concern for her own feelings without feeling guilty or compelled to take care of his needs. She feels confident that, if he decides not to see her anymore, she can find someone who will be willing to respect her wishes.

In this situation April may refuse to go along with what her boyfriends wants for legitimate reasons of her own. For example, April may hold a religious belief about the importance of remaining a virgin until she marries. Or perhaps she simply does not feel that the relationship is ready for sex. Or, April may be refusing her boyfriend's request because she has a health problem that may make intercourse painful for her. Whatever her reason, April chooses to offer it without feeling that she is making excuses.

From this situation alone, we hope it is clear that it does not require a special background or unique personality type to become an Assertive April. Everyone can be assertive in their own personal ways, and within the contexts of their own unique life situations.

'They Need Me – the Poor Things'

Situation: A married woman, who is also a competent, experienced nurse, works for a large city hospital. Her salary is below average and the working conditions poor. Her income is not vital to the family's welfare; she works primarily because she loves nursing. However, she is confronted with a disorganized hospital administration, understaffing, inadequate supplies, and low morale among the nursing staff. A union organizer is trying to unite the nurses to take a stand and, if necessary, to strike for better conditions.

Passive: The Compassion Trap tells Doris that she and the other nurses would only be selfish to engage in hard-nosed negotiations that may lead to strike. After all, who would see to it that Ms. Jones down the hall really swallowed her medication instead of hiding it under her tongue? Doris decides to put up with the poor conditions 'for the sake of' her patients. She's frightened of confrontations and believes that a 'good nurse' has to think of others first, keep peace and keep smiling.

Indirectly Aggressive: Iris feels helpless when she's caught in the Compassion Trap. She is sorry for her patients, herself, and the other nurses. However, her inability to directly express her frustration leads her to find fault with other nurses, neglect her patients, and develop a 'who cares?' attitude.

Aggressive: Agatha, also caught in the Compassion Trap, is unable to communicate her concern. Instead she gives the impression that she is just an 'angry bitch.' As usual, she overreacts by making hostile demands and threats. She goes to the right people at the top, but she says the wrong things. The net result is that she widens the gap of misunderstanding.

Assertive: Like Agatha, April believes in the value of action. She is concerned about her patients' welfare, but she chooses to risk a possible strike to obtain better conditions for all in the long run. She is confident that the nurses, if united, can make a substantial impact to improve the hospital. April puts her compassion to good use and doesn't allow her energies to dissipate in a flurry of worry. She expresses her concern to the other nurses and urges them to organize and to take a strong, but fair, stand.

On a practical level it is important to look at the consequences of what we do. April asks: are we *really* helping other people so much by always pampering them and taking care of things that cause them discomfort? What price do *we* pay as individuals when our giving and compassion is done at the expense of our own happiness? What price does the *receiver* of our compassion pay when we have felt obligated and resentful? Just as much or more can be accomplished if we allow others to be assertive and take responsibility for themselves, while we pursue what is best for us. When you are assertive, you make it possible to grow and change without cramping anybody else's style.

The Compassion Trap Quiz
Gauge the extent to which you are in the Compassion Trap by taking our quiz below. Answer each question *honestly*. If you have not personally experienced some situations, choose the response that most closely approximates the way you think you would respond. After you have finished, turn the page and add up your score. The corresponding key will help you to determine how 'trapped' you really are.

1. You have been seeing a man socially for several weeks, but you are beginning to feel bored and disinterested. He likes you very much and would like to see you more often. Do you:

    a. tell him you'd prefer not to see him, feeling you've been honest with yourself?

    b. feel a sudden attack of the Hong Kong flu coming on?

    c. continue to be the object of his affections, because leaving would really hurt his ego?

    d. tell him that he bores you to tears, and that even if you were both marooned on a desert island, you would camp out on the opposite shore?

2. You invited a friend who lives some distance away to spend her/his two week holiday with you at your home. It is now one month later, and your friend shows no intention of leaving, or reimbursing you for food and telephone bills. You would like your friend to leave. Do you:

a. not mention anything about your expenses or feelings, because you don't want to damage the friendship?

b. leave a note saying that you're terribly sorry, but your mother has decided to live with you and you'll need the room?

c. tell your friend that you really value your friendship, that the extended visit is putting a strain on it, and ask that your friend make plans to leave?

d. put all of your friend's belongings out on the doorstep with a note: 'Don't call me; I'll call you'?

3. You are enjoying one of your rare visits to London, and you are staying with your brother and sister-in-law. One of your favourite things to do in that city is to sample the fine restaurants. Your brother and sister-in-law are terrible cooks, but they insist on 'treating' you by cooking for you themselves. You would much prefer going out to eat. Do you:

a. decide to have dinner at your brother and sister-in-law's home because you don't want to disappoint them by refusing their offer?

b. tell them that you appreciate their thoughtfulness, and explain that one of the reasons you come to London is to enjoy the restaurants, suggesting that all of you go out to eat instead?

c. loudly tell them that you're not there for *their* food?

d. call and claim that you are unavoidably detained, and tell them not to wait dinner for you – then sneak out and eat by yourself?

4. You are working on a project that is very important to you. Some friends drop by unexpectedly. You'd really like to continue working on your project. Do you:

a. shelve your project, prepare hors d'oeuvres, and apologise for your cluttered living room?

b. loudly berate your friends for not having called first?

c. explain that you're in the middle of an important project and arrange to see them at a mutually convenient time?

d. ignore your friends and continue working on your project while they are there, hoping they'll get the message?

5. Your ten-year-old daughter customarily walks to school, but today she wants you to drive her. You have driven her on rainy days, but it is not raining today. She continues to ask you to drive, adding, 'Besides, everyone else's mothers drive them.' Do you:

a. tell your daughter she can walk to school as usual?

b. begin by telling your daughter that you won't drive her to school but after a short time you give in, feeling only guilty that you hesitated?

c. reply 'Oh, okay, I'll drive you,' thinking of all the other children whose mothers faithfully drive them, and feeling like a neglectful mother if you don't drive your daughter to school?

d. threaten to call the truant officer and report on your daughter if she doesn't leave for school immediately?

Key

1. a) An assertive choice. (3)
   b) Honesty is the best policy here. (0)
   c) Don't forget *your* feelings. (0)
   d) Don't forget *his* feelings. (0)
2. a) You'll feel resentful later. You're trapped. (0)
   b) This may get her/him out, but how do you feel about trapping yourself with *that* one? (1)
   c) Right. This will also get her/him out, and leave you with your self-respect. (3)
   d) This will get your friend out of your life, also. (0)
3. a) This Compassion Trap will result in your disappointment and indigestion. (0)
   b) The assertive thing to do. (3)
   c) Better look for a hotel room – your brother and sister-in-law won't want to have you as a guest for some time. (0)

    d) You'll soon run out of excuses. Then what?   (0)

4. a) The Compassion Trap.   (0)

    b) Only if you *never* want to see them again.   (0)

    c) Ain't it the truth?   (3)

    d) You're wasting time; it may take hours for them to get the hint!   (3)

5. a) You've got it!   (3)

    b) A good start – but you're in the Compassion Trap here.   (1)

    c) Are you really neglectful? The Compassion Trap again.   (0)

    d) You avoided the Compassion Trap, but stepped into the Aggression Trap!   (0)

Add up your total points and gauge the extent of *your* Compassion Trap:

14+: We couldn't ask for more. You can choose what to do without being trapped. Be on the lookout, though, for other situations that may trap you.

9–13: You can avoid the Compassion Trap most of the time, and you're moving in the right direction. Give some extra attention to the people and situations that continue to trap you, and attempt more assertive ways of handling them.

2–8: Consider the price you pay when you do things at the expense of your own happiness. With some practice, you *can* leave the Compassion Trap and *enjoy* what you *choose* to do. Be an assertive woman and be loved for it.

Chapter 8

Empowering Yourself to Be Assertive

I personally feel that I am an assertive woman in many ways now. But, the problems that I am dealing with recently occur from lack of confidence within myself.
– Marketing Administrator, married, in her 30's.

Ever since Eve's temptation of Adam resulted in banishment from the Garden of Eden, women have learned to be accessible to blame.

Apology and powerlessness have characterized the lives of women for generations. A woman's traditional social role has been dependent, submissive: women have been expected to react rather than act, to have decisions made for them rather than make decisions for themselves. What women deserve is the power to determine the course of their own lives without apology to make their own decisions, and to be free from the absolute authority of others.

Stereotypes start early. We hear jokes about mothers-in-law being to blame for family conflict; Jewish mothers being responsible for fostering helplessness and dependency in their children; women school teachers making 'sissies' of little boys. Women have been so involved in defending themselves against these accusations that they have rarely questioned their legitimacy. Instead, they have reacted with guilt and apology, and they have incorporated these feelings into many other situations.

Developing Your Sense of Power
This chapter is concerned with helping you to develop a sense of personal power. Personal power is so important to effective asser-

tive behaviour that it deserves our special emphasis and your alert attention.

The issue of power is beginning to assume new importance. There seem to be two major aspects of personal power for women: how to get it and keep it, and attitudes about having it and using it.

Personal power is something we all need. Yet women have been denied the opportunity to exercise power; they have been told it isn't 'natural' or 'feminine' for them to want it. They have swallowed their anxiety, buried their anger, and experienced the personal anguish and disappointment produced by powerlessness and non-assertion.

We neither insist upon nor object to women competing with men for success, money, prestige, or authority – the external barometers of power. Instead, we are concerned with power as a positive, creative force that helps you choose for yourself, gives you a feeling of worth and purpose, and fosters a strong conviction to overcome feelings of anxiety and helplessness.

The Tools of Power

Your mind is one of the most powerful forces on earth. It can be your strongest ally or your worst enemy. How often have you imagined failure and fulfilled that negative expectation? What would happen if you put as much creativity and emotional energy into picturing *success*? Here is a set of tools to enhance the part your mind plays in becoming assertive.

Imaging. Leland Cooley calls this 'imaginology.' Imaging is a process of visualization – creating images in your mind as if what you imagine is *already* happening – coupled with the emotional desire to make it happen. If your image has been chosen from your inner wisdom while you're in a relaxed frame of mind, it can become real in your life quickly and solidly. Regular practice of positive imagery will enable you to reproduce the pictures in your mind as real-life results.

To *become* an assertive woman, create a vivid picture in your mind of how you would *look, think, and feel* as an assertive woman. Create the assertive you that you want. Concentrate on this image in moments of relaxation. Fix it in your mind.

If you are uncertain that you can create your own images, ask a friend to do a guided imagery exercise with you. As you relax, perhaps with your eyes closed, that person can vividly describe to you an image – in specific detail – that you want to have of yourself. This can be done in story-like fashion or can be related to a real situation in your life. Give your friend as much information as you can about your desired result. The more detailed your goal, the better and faster it can be achieved.

Meditation and Relaxation. There are many forms of meditation and relaxation, from a simple walk on the beach or bubble bath to the more disciplined Transcendental or Zen meditation, Tai Chi Ch'uan (a moving meditation, a way of learning to centre and balance one's energies), and deep muscle relaxation (as described in Chapter 11). These approaches work to free the body and mind from stress while expanding the capacity to freely contemplate, feel joy, create. In each case, you remain awake and peaceful. The point is not to relax to the point of indifference, but to become fully open and alert to new possibilities.

Once in a meditative or relaxed state, you can give your attention to whatever subject you choose. You could, for example, empower yourself to work on a particular goal in becoming more assertive. If you don't know what you want as you are going into meditation or relaxation, be patient and ask your inner wisdom to guide you. Trust that you are the source of direction for your life as you want it to be, that you are in control and not being controlled. Just realizing that you have the power to be assertive will move you closer to positive action.

Affirming. In Chapter 6, we introduced Ms. Protecto, that defensive inner voice that constantly feeds us messages to direct our behaviour. 'Affirming' can keep Ms. Protecto from ruling your inner self and causing you to act non-assertively or aggressively.

Affirming is a way to be assertive with yourself. It is a creative, conscious process that enables you to express yourself more fully and confidently. An *affirmation* is a spoken and written declaration of something you want, phrased as if it were already happening. By your statement you are planting a powerful, positive suggestion in your mind. Repeating it many times daily reinforces it. The more intensely you imagine it and create an emotional experience of it (rather than repeating it blandly) the better it works.

It is important to phrase your affirmations in a positive, proactive way. For example, 'I am becoming more assertive with my boss' is better than 'My boss doesn't annoy me.' Don't pressure yourself for instant results. State your affirmations as concrete, achievable steps toward your goal. If things change gradually, the change is often more lasting and appropriate. Allow things to happen naturally and allow yourself to be surprised, especially when something turns out better than your wildest dreams!

Another way to express your affirmations aloud is to tape record them and listen to them while driving, at home, or during coffee breaks at work. You can also include affirmations during medianations. You can tape them on your mirror or put them anywhere you look frequently. If there is a particular song or piece of music that makes you feel strong, it is helpful to record it along with your affirmations, or even sing your affirmations to its tune.

Affirmations for an Assertive Woman

- I am becoming an assertive woman from the inside out!
- I am dissolving the barriers to my self-expression!
- I feel more powerful!
- I communicate more clearly and effectively all the time!
- I handle confrontations with greater ease!
- I express my enthusiasm and joy more freely and fully!
- I am becoming stronger and more courageous!
- I am more and more pleased with who I am!
- I am taking charge of my life!
- I can create love, success and happiness for myself!

Music. A powerful way to communicate with our inner selves, music reaches us at such a deep level that at times it almost seems possible to feel it rearranging our molecules! It is definitely felt in the body as it is perceived in the mind. Because it has the capacity to move the emotions so strongly, it is also a tool of empowerment. Films use strong musical sound tracks to amplify the action. In some instances the music precedes the action; we can sense what's coming before it has happened.

Other examples of how music magnifies our experiences include church services, weddings, concerts, movies, or majestic ceremonies. We take music for granted as an integral part of our outward lives. Why not use its power in our inner lives?

Explore your own music collection for inspiration. Observe how others use music. Experiment. If you're depressed, instead of playing Gregorian chants or moody lost-love songs, try your assertiveness selection and see what happens.

Treasure Maps. Perhaps the most playful tool is the treasure map. A visual tool that makes it easier for you to picture what you want, a treasure map is a more concrete way of telling your inner self what it needs to do to achieve your goals.

A colourful drawing or collage that represents what you want can include all the things necessary to achieve your goal – much like scale drawings and models help architects and builders get the job done.

To create an effective treasure map, use colourful pictures, photos or drawings to display what you want in detail. These can be glued or taped to poster board or any size or type of paper you desire, small enough to carry with you or large enough to cover an entire wall. You might place a recent photo of yourself in the map as a symbol of your ability and power to achieve your goal. Keep the design simple and real enough to maintain clarity. Include anyone or anything else that you feel is necessary: money (play money will do); another person's photo; a symbol of a higher source (to acknowledge your faith in God or the universe). Spend a few moments every day quietly contemplating your treasure map, preferably at the beginning and the end of your day.

Power Grabbers
The assertive woman knows that the best way to protect her rights is to use them. Yet, many women have trouble developing confidence in their own power. Becoming comfortable with power and enjoying a feeling of competence will take some practice. By using the

exercises and examples in this chapter for practice, you can develop an assertive attitude and experience a feeling of being in control.

Before attempting each situation, relax and imagine yourself successfully completing the exercise. After you are able to do that without feeling anxious, try it out alone in front of a mirror. Then you are ready to try it with a friend with whom you feel comfortable, or in a relatively low risk situation. Do not push yourself too fast, and don't try to be assertive with an intimidating person, or in an uncomfortable situation, until you have mastered relaxation and successful imaging.

Need for Approval. Working for others' approval limits your autonomy because you voluntarily concede your power to someone else. Doris Doormat, for example, is a reliable, responsible employee. She makes decisions, but once she's made them, she presents them to someone else because she wants that person to tell her she's done a good job, to give her approval. April Assertive can make decisions without the need to present them to someone else. She uses her own power and resists seeking the familiar comfort of approval. Her autonomy and personal power are more important to her. As an assertive woman, April stands up for what she believes, and makes decisions independently for herself.

'I'm Sorry, But . . .' Many women find themselves struggling against years of easy apology. The phrase 'I'm sorry, but . . .' is a common refrain. Women frequently feel compelled to apologize for saying 'no,' for exercising their authority, for expressing their anger or for requesting something. A woman's inappropriate use of apology reflects her feelings of powerlessness, indecisiveness, and ambivalence about whether or not she even has the *right* to make a request, or to disagree. When women apologize unnecessarily, they are really saying, 'I know I don't have the *right* to say this, and I don't want to bother you with it, and I'm sorry for saying it, but . . .'

There are legitimate and appropriate occasions for an apology. The legitimate apology conveys understanding and appreciation of the other person's feelings, such as 'I'm very sorry I was late; I must have kept you waiting for an hour.' The examples below illustrate inappropriate and appropriate uses of apology.

'Guess Who's Coming To Dinner?'

Situation: Doris Doormat has invited several women to her home for dinner this evening at 7 p.m. They finally arrive at 9, two hours late. The dinner Doris prepared is cold and ruined. One of her guests, Agatha, is critical.

Agatha: 'Weren't we invited for dinner, Doris? You didn't plan very well, did you?'

Doris: 'Oh, I'm so sorry, Agatha! I feel awful about this. I'm really sorry to cause such an inconvenience.'

In this situation, Doris apologizes inappropriately. It is Agatha and the other guests who caused Doris the inconvenience by arriving late. The apology should have come from them.

'Dinner is Served – Late'

Situation: April Assertive has invited two of her friends to dinner at 7 p.m. She is late coming home, and doesn't arrive until 6:45. When her friends arrive at 7, April is just preparing dinner, which won't be ready until 8.

April: 'I'm really sorry that dinner will be late. You must be absolutely starving. How about some cheese and crackers, while we're waiting?'

In this case, April apologizes legitimately to her friends for the late dinner. She acknowledges that they must be hungry and makes a positive suggestion, but she does not over-apologize.

The next time you find yourself apologizing, ask yourself what you are apologizing for:

● Was the apology legitimate and appropriate?
● Did you feel compelled to apologize?
● Did you apologize for something even though you have nothing to be sorry about?

Getting Your Questions Answered

Have you asked an important question, only to be sidetracked when the other person changes the subject to avoid answering you? If so, you probably felt frustrated and confused.

Try the following outline to help you to exercise some control and get your questions answered:

1. Start with a brief, specific question.

2. Picture yourself asking this question of a comfortable person and as you do so practice relaxation.

3. Put step (2) into action, and ask a friend your question. Instruct your friend to try to avoid answering by every means possible until she feels she has run out of excuses and evasive comments. Each time she gives another rationalization, continue to ask the question as if it were the first time it was asked, without varying your voice tone.

4. If you don't receive an appropriate answer, precede your questions with 'I will repeat the question,' or a similar neutral statement, followed by a repetition of the question.

5. If your friend responds with a *feeling* instead of an answer to your question, *acknowledge* the feeling, but continue to repeat your question.

6. When a direct answer is given, acknowledge the answer in a neutral, non-judgemental way, 'Thank you for telling me.'

7. If your friend makes insulting or other negative remarks, you may follow your acknowledgement by telling your friend how you feel about these remarks. You can do this assertively, without punishing your friend for not answering you honestly. What you are concerned with is your right to exercise your power to have your questions answered. So, remember the assertive woman remains non-judgemental and non-abusive, and keeps her voice evenly modulated – not loud or angry.

'Are You Having an Affair?'

A situation which has come up frequently in seminars involves confronting a lover whom one suspects of having an affair. The woman has usually experienced a great deal of emotional pain, and has attempted to deal with it by ignoring it, playing the martyr, or by fighting fire with fire. At this point, she is ready to try the alternative of being assertive. The following dialogue illustrates a classic assertive response to this emotionally-charged situation. Each woman must tailor her response to her own needs and style; this may mean that her assertiveness is interrupted by angry outbursts or tears. Remember that to be assertive does not mean to be perfect.

April: I have been concerned lately about the amount of time you are away from home. You have been telling me that you are busy and have to work late, but I have the feeling you are holding back on me. Are you having an affair?

Lover: Don't be ridiculous. I've got important work to do. It takes too much time to explain it to you. You don't understand.

April: I feel you're being evasive with me, and I'm very concerned about what's happening. I will repeat my question. Are you having an affair?

Lover: How many times have I told you not to nag me with your stupid questions? I'm really angry! Why don't you trust me?

April: I know that you're angry about my asking you the same question over again. I really do want to trust you, and I can when you are open with me. I'd feel more comfortable knowing the truth and being given the choice to deal with it, rather than being in the dark and feeling anxious and insecure. I would like to know if you are having an affair.

Lover: You really know how to back somebody up against the wall, don't you? You must really get a kick out of playing Sherlock Holmes. I've had enough of your nagging. How do you think it makes me feel to be interrogated like this and subjected to your high pressure tactics? I suppose your friends put you up to this.

April: I want you to feel comfortable about discussing this with me. The last thing I want to do is threaten you. It is really important to me to clear up this distance between us. I would like to know where I stand, so it is very important for me to know if you're having an affair. Are you?

Lover: Well, just remember that you asked for it! Yes, I am having an affair. I hope you're happy now that you squeezed it out of me.

April: I appreciate your telling me, even though it doesn't make me happy to know that you're having an affair. I feel at least now we can begin an honest discussion of our relationship.

Remember that the content in this exercise is extremely meaningful. It is important to choose words that are not accusatory, for example by saying, 'I feel' instead of 'you make me feel.' Even though the other person may insult you, it is important to be concerned with your feelings rather than letting yourself get side-tracked by name-calling or other manipulative devices.

You have a right to ask questions and to expect direct answers, and you should give such answers yourself. However, there are times when you will want to be forced to answer questions. Assertiveness will give you the power to decide.

Choosing Not to Answer Questions
Now that you have practiced getting your questions answered, consider what you do when you are in the opposite position. How do you respond when someone is asking *you* a question you don't want to answer? Perhaps the question is irrelevant, embarrassing, or intimidating. How do you handle this situation? Try a method that has worked for us.

First, be sure you understand the question. If you do not, then clarify it by repeating it back to your questioner. Once it is clarified and you are aware that you still do not feel comfortable answering, make a simple, direct statement saying that you do not want to answer it. If the other person persists, you might express how you feel about the question or the persistence of the questioner. Then repeat again that you do not want to answer the question.

'Where Have You Been . . .?'
Situation: A single woman just took a few days off from work to have an abortion. There are a couple of curious co-workers who seem intent on discovering the reason for her absence.

Nosey: Oh, April, you look a little pale. You must have been pretty sick to have stayed out for three days. Would you like to talk about it?

April: I'm not sure what you mean by 'it.' Could you be a little more specific?

Nosey: Well, some of us noticed that you were nauseated a few mornings here at work. And your clothes didn't seem to be fitting quite the same, if you know what I mean. Well, what I'm trying to say is – April, did you have an abortion?

April: I really feel uncomfortable with your asking me what I feel is a very personal question, and I don't want to answer it.

Nosey: Of course, I know it is rather personal, but we're asking only because we care about you. Is there anything we can do?

April: It really makes me angry for you to persist in prying into my personal life. I do not feel it is necessary to answer your question.

Nosey: I don't see why not. Everybody knows anyway.

April: I do not want to discuss your question any further. I am going to resume working, which is what we ought to be doing, anyway.

Write down three questions that you anticipate people may ask you that you do not want to answer. Then role-play the situation and practice *not* answering the question by using the process described in the previous exercise.

'Sure, No Problem'

Situation: This topic comes up quite frequently in our women's classes, especially with secretaries.

The boss (usually male) has just asked his secretary if she wouldn't mind during her lunch break exchanging some merchandise his wife bought. He then adds that he'd like her to try to get back from lunch *early* because he has some extra typing for her that must be done right away. She wants to tell him that she is not going to do it.

Doris: Oh, *I'm sorry, but* I was going to have lunch with a friend I haven't seen in years who's in town for the day. But, I guess I could call her and cancel our plans. Yes, I guess I'll do that. Sure, it's no problem. Where do you want me to go?

April: I've made plans with a good friend that I haven't seen in years. She will only be in town today, and it is very important that I see her. I know that you are rushed. I can do the typing as soon as I return; we'll get it out in time. Returning the gift is different. I am uncomfortable running your personal errands and I must refuse. You can count on me to help with office business, of course.

'Do You Have the Nerve?'

Here is another action exercise we have developed to help you to gain confidence in taking the initiative – by acting instead of waiting to react. Choose at least three out of the five following situations and rank them according to how uncomfortable the thought of doing them makes you feel. *A* being the *least* uncomfortable and *F* being the *most* uncomfortable. Then, starting with A, decide how you are going to go about doing something active about it instead of waiting to see what the other person does. You can write a script before you try it or role-play what you are going to say first. Try to visualize what your 'ideal' assertive woman would do:

- Make an appointment with your employer, teacher, or family to let them know that you feel you are doing a fine job, instead of waiting for someone to notice.
- Your children are annoying you. You take responsibility for telling them how you are feeling and that you want them to stop bothering you right now. Do *not* threaten them with 'Wait until your father hears about this,' do not wait until somebody else takes the responsibility, do not react with pent-up frustration and complaints.
- Phone a woman or a man whom you have never phoned about something you want to tell her/him instead of waiting for her/him to call you.
- Somebody makes a request of you, perhaps to borrow something or to ask a favour. If you do not feel like loaning it or doing it, say so right away instead of letting your anxiety build.
- You want to talk to your lover/mate about an important feeling you have, perhaps about sex. Set up the right time and place and initiate the conversation. Do not passively wait for the right time and place to happen, or for the other to talk about it first.
- Return a defective item to a shop, even though you don't have the receipt or you have procrastinated for weeks about returning it.

Power is as much a feeling of confidence from within as it is an outward display of your effectiveness in getting what you want. In fact, you can feel powerful even during the times when you don't get what you want.

Empowering yourself to be assertive is a long term investment that yields higher dividends than trying to be the winner in any given situation. When you make a commitment to being assertive from the inside out, the depth and strength of your commitment will earn you the reputation of a winner. You can learn from your losses, let go gracefully, and move with confidence to whatever challenge awaits you.

Chapter 9

The Expression of Assertion

I had a real test of my own assertiveness. I had got a quote from the printer on the cost of new brochures. When it came time to order, however, the price was double the original quotation.

I believe the first thing I did was break out in a sweat! After I had given him my side of it, he insisted that the second price had to stand. I suddenly had a flash which said – silence will solve this.

So I sat tight, he squirmed, I got the original price.

What more can be said about how assertiveness is expressed? Over the past decade – and from all indications well into the next – thousands of articles, quizzes, books, how-to guides, seminars, workshops, classes, and lectures have been designed to help people become more assertive, less aggressive; more confident, less afraid; more effective, less wishy-washy. To be able to express oneself assertively – to stand up to bullies, defend one's position, congratulate a colleague on a job well done, ask a new person out – become the goal of the non-assertive over the years. To speak up when it mattered most – that was the idea.

Along the way, we discovered there's a difference between using assertiveness as a *method* to accomplish a goal, and the longer term prospect of developing an assertive *identity*. As a method, assertiveness is available to anyone – you don't have to think of yourself as assertive to be able to use it successfully for a specific reason. Someone who has trouble expressing a conflicting point of view among friends, say, may nonetheless be quite good at dispatching the vacuum cleaner salesperson at the door. The assertive identity part – assertiveness is your middle name, finding that assertive responses outnumber the others – well, that's something else again.

Assertiveness was, in the beginning, a way of confronting the unpleasant or difficult without getting squashed (or squashing others) in the process. Newly learned assertive skills were plied on waiters ('I ordered this steak well-done. It's quite rare. Please take it back and bring me a well-done steak'), on spouses ('When you interrupt me, I get frustrated and angry'), on cold-calling sales-people ('No, I do not want to buy a set of porcelain corncob skewers'), and on bosses ('I am willing to work overtime as long as I am paid to do so'). The keynote, usually, was standing one's ground, and firmly. An early objective was to find out how good we were at asking – and then standing up – for what we wanted. We practised saying and doing the things that gave us sweaty palms and cold feet until we could perform them with a certain amount of comfort. It got easier as we went along.

After a while, we realized that using assertiveness the way you might use any handy tool left something to be desired. In some university extension classrooms, 'Assertive Skills Workshops' pro-duced identical responses to the top ten situations in which assertive-ness was the antidote. The techniques learned there were neither universally accepted nor admired, as we quickly saw when we tried them out in the real world. At the same time, even partly successful assertive encounters produced a rush of pride. It could be done! We lived to tell about it! Honouring our own wishes didn't mean turning our backs on friends!

One Size Does Not Fit All
It was especially gratifying to learn that there was no such thing as an 'ideal' or 'perfect' way to be assertive – no pressure to live up to that perfect assertive woman image – but instead there were many legitimate variations of assertive expression. Those who considered themselves shy by nature were relieved to discover they could express themselves assertively without feeling phoney, acting a part. Their style was simply a little softer, a little toned down – but without hesitation, insecurity, and without apology. The more extroverted discovered that they, too, could weave assertiveness

into their own unique expansiveness with good results. They didn't
have to give up any of their exhuberance for the sake of assertive
communication. Women who had always thought of themselves as
spontaneous and daring were happy to see that assertiveness didn't
require putting a damper on their intensity, or make them less
interesting. Assertiveness could actually enhance the things we
liked best about ourselves. We could get what we wanted and we
could be nice about it. Little by little, we imagined assertiveness not
as a checklist of behaviours which we had to perform competently,
but as a natural extension of our own personalities, with all our
differences, preferences, and eccentricities.

Wait a minute, you might be thinking. Are you saying that Joan
Rivers is assertive? How about the so-called 'Mayflower Madam,'
Sydney Biddle Barrows? And while we're on the subject, how
about Princess Diana, formerly 'Shy Di?' Can you really call these
women assertive given their remarkable differences?

Let's start with Rivers. Her on-screen personality is undoubtedly
more intense than her private one. But on-screen, she's made a
career of entertaining audiences with aggressive, outrageous one-
liners. There is no question the woman is expressive – during her
monologues, she's downright astonishing. When she talks with
guests, however, her ability to listen and to make them feel comfortable is more apparent. She has a range of skills open to her, and as
long as she doesn't misread when her verbal zingers are too far over
the line, she's effective in the role.

Another controversial figure is Sydney Biddle Barrows, who for
several years presided over her own high-priced New York call girl
service. When she appeared widely on television and radio to
promote her book, *The Mayflower Madam*, many people were
outraged that she should receive so much air time to push a book
written about a questionable way of life. What was interesting about
Barrows was the way she handled herself during the interviews and
particularly how she responded to the many stinging criticisms from
callers and people in television studio audiences. She remained the
model of assertive expression through it all: you would have to say
she handled the whole thing with dignity. She was calm, direct,
never made excuses for her behaviour, and never hedged a single

question. While we may certainly argue about her ethics, she was a model of strength under considerable pressure.

'Shy Di' has since been dubbed 'The Mouse That Roared,' by nothing less than *People* magazine! Princess Diana's trademark downcast eyes and reserved demeanour made her famous. As she warmed to her new role and responsibilities, however, she felt more comfortable in speaking up. Because it was such a contrast to the quiet little nursery school teacher who married a prince, her self-expression was probably mislabelled 'aggression,' at least as far as the rest of the world is concerned. By all accounts, she, more than anyone or anything in recent times, has rekindled an interest in British royalty. She and her sister-in-law, Sarah Ferguson, now appear on most-admired women lists the world over.

The point is not to debate whether certain well-known public figures are or are not assertive. Authentic assertiveness can look, on the surface, very different from one person to the next. The goal is not to be less like Joan Rivers and more like Princess Diana; the idea is to learn to blend assertiveness with your own way of doing things. Personal style can, and should, play a big part in developing assertive behaviours that will last.

Slowly, we started to think of assertiveness as a natural, highly individual process, not a competitive event. It didn't matter if we weren't perfectly assertive, identically assertive, or if we decided not to be assertive in some situations. We didn't have to be 'assertive robots' constantly looking out for number one. We didn't even need charismatic or magnetic personalities. Assertiveness could be part of us, the way we were. It could make the good better and impart a sheen to the lacklustre. It made us feel courageous.

The more we thought about it, the more we saw that assertiveness, as a process, gets better with age: the newly-assertive woman is less sure of herself because she's still experimenting, learning how the process works. After some time, not to mention feedback from other people, the assertive woman begins to see that she's the one in the driver's seat. It's up to her to decide when and how to be assertive: She doesn't *have* to be just because she *can* be.

Side Trips

We've learned that moving from the early learning stages to being able to claim assertiveness as one of one's personal characteristics is a process with certain predictable features. As you build confidence in your own ability to be assertive, you become acquainted with some specific side trips or traps on the way. Part of the process is to be able to recognize them and move on.

We think psychotherapist Andrew Salter was the first to point out that what often passed as assertive expression actually was not. As much as twenty years before assertiveness gained acceptance in circles outside therapy groups, Salter described variations of what he called 'fraudulent assertion,' including 'fake assertion,' 'actor's assertion,' and 'manipulative assertion.' Salter correctly observes that fraudulent assertion involves '. . . no search for accommodation. It's just a disguised steamroller.' He characterizes actor's assertion as a sort of stream of hail-fellow-well-met greetings – 'Hello, how are you, good to see you,' all delivered in a 'slightly breathless' manner. Manipulative assertion Salter describes as 'dishonest, not real assertion in the first place.' Last, Salter includes a brief mention of 'Pollyanna assertion,' where everything is 'just great, just dandy.' We have borrowed from Salter's descriptions to take a closer look at four popular side-trips on the way to becoming an assertive woman: Reckless Assertion, Pollyanna Assertion, Fraudulent Assertion, and the Superwoman Syndrome.

Reckless Assertion

You made it through a prickly encounter with a hostile person. You initiated a difficult conversation. You pushed for a point of view you believed in. You didn't cave in when criticized by someone whose opinions you care about. That first flush of victory is heady stuff. You want to do it again. Another chance to assert yourself is just around the corner, each success more encouraging than the last. As long as you and others agree that you are doing something worthwhile, a little overkill is okay by your pals; the recklessly assertive carry it a bit too far.

As they watch your self-assurance give way to recklessness, even the most tolerant of your friends will have misgivings about your tactics. To be 'recklessly assertive,' as we call it, is rashly to plunge ahead ever more assertively, with little or no attention paid to the consequences or dangers involved.

Most authorities would argue that if you are not in tune with the consequences of your assertive actions, you really aren't being assertive. In practice, however, we find that the process of learning to be assertive usually involves at least one detour into recklessness. It's not that you are so fired up with newfound power that you want to steamroll everyone you see. It's that you are still new at this assertiveness business, and your judgement about what is appropriately assertive behaviour isn't as good as it will be: for now, you may not notice or take seriously the fact that your constant assertiveness wears thin with some.

That's the problem faced by many working women who want to project a professional image in the office, especially if they have just started a new job. They feel real pressure to perform better than expected and to make few mistakes, which they suspect would not be easily forgiven or forgotten. If they express too many traditional feminine behaviours, they jeapardize their hard-won status by 'acting like wimps.' They believe they must never let anyone catch them behaving as anything less than strong, assertive professionals. Questions or suggestions from more senior people about how the job might be done better are seen as attacks, which provoke the need in the newcomers to prove that they are better than their colleagues think.

So how can recklessness be overcome and self-assurance rediscovered? The first step is to slow down enough to see that the independence and capability that has served you well in your job so far need not be relentlessly proved. The advice and counsel of a more experienced co-worker might help you understand how you can be more effective in your role. Such a person can provide a more realistic, practical perspective, especially if she has been through it before herself. You'll also learn an important lesson in assertiveness: you have to be sensitive to, but not enslaved by, others' perceptions of your behaviour. You are free to reject their assessment, of course. But consider that they may know something about the company that you don't. You may be assertively – but blindly –

trespassing on a sacred organizational cow. Or, you may simply be trying to take on too much responsibility too early. Tactical errors like these are very difficult to spot and correct without the help of an interested outsider.

The dangers of reckless assertion can be diluted if you can be receptive to feedback from others. You can tackle some of the job yourself by taking the time to reflect on the situations that seem to bring out your 'fighting instinct.' What circumstances seem to fuel reckless assertion? How might the situation have been resolved if you had behaved differently? When do you feel most defensive? Has reckless assertion damaged your credibility in your organization or elsewhere? Your answers can help to short-circuit what might become a persistent pattern.

Reckless Assertion: Does She or Doesn't She?
Here's a list of significant behaviours and ways of getting things done that might indicate recklessness. The more you believe the statements apply to your approach, the more likely it is that you've detoured into reckless assertion.

- It seems that you nearly always take the lead in your relationships with others.
- Friends are telling you that you're defensive or argumentative.
- It's more important that you get what *you* want in the end than it is to go along with what others want.
- To describe you as a 'fist in a velvet glove' would be accurate.
- You crave being the centre of attention.
- After so many years as a pushover, it is exhilarating to finally be able to turn the tables.
- Though you can be direct and assertive with different people, they don't seem to want to see as much of you as before.
- There are certain specific instances which ignite your anger to the point you cannot control your outbursts.
- Compared to other people you know, you are much more likely to persevere to get what you want.
- People tell you that you never give up, or that you are almost incredibly singleminded.

- You find it extremely difficult to apologize even when an apology is called for.
- Winning isn't everything: it's the only thing.
- You resent others' good fortune.
- You find that you cannot predict how other people will react to your assertiveness.
- You feel that you do not get the recognition you deserve in life.
- You aren't comfortable playing a purely supportive role at times with your spouse or friends.
- You believe that if you don't look after your own interests, nobody else will.
- People tell you that you have a forceful personality.
- You are not as flexible as some other people you know.
- You cannot tell when your assertiveness wears thin with some people.
- In general, people tend to let you down.

Pollyanna Assertion

Like the storybook character, everything is just perfect with Pollyanna – on the outside, at least. On the inside we have a different story indeed.

Pollyanna assertion tends to come from the mouths of those who think of themselves as passive, non-assertive people. It's the Pollyanna in you who is overfocused on 'acceptable assertions,' the ones that may be enthusiastically received because they pose no challenge or threat to anyone else. Pollyanna assertion has to do with wanting to be accepted, with wanting to fit in. The main focus of your attention is still what's going on around you, with less, if any, allegiance to how you feel about it and how you might change or contribute to it. Like the Compassion Trap, Pollyanna assertion attaches more importance to making room for others' opinions and preferences than it does to honouring your own.

We don't suggest that this class of assertive responses – expressing agreement, support, love, appreciation, praise, or enthusiasm – has less value than some of the others, including giving critical feedback, expressing a discordant point of view, expressing anger. Both sets are available to the assertive woman, but Pollyanna is uncomfortable with all but the 'nice' ones. She likes to be assertive, but mostly within 'safe' limits (usually determined by others). She may be willing to take the initiative, but only when she knows she's expressing the majority view. At the first sign of disagreement, she is likely to back down and revert to passive behaviours.

A friend discovers that Pollyannaism damaged her effectiveness in her first supervisory job. She was promoted for her proven ability to get along with her peers. She could always be counted on to pitch in and to set a new, more productive standard for her group. When she hit management, however, she encountered problems. She would go into salary reviews armed with responsible proposals for increases for her people, but her recommendations were seldom reflected in the increases that were approved by top management. She watched as other supervisors received approvals for their recommended increases, and she couldn't understand why her proposals had been 'singled out,' as she put it. Worse, her people began to question her ability to represent their interests to higher-ups.

It took some time and soul-searching, but she began to see that while she genuinely wanted to 'take care' of her team, she had trouble standing up for them when she felt the most pressure to perform: in front of senior executives. She had no difficulty providing assertive support for her team or in handling touchy situations, like scheduling vacation schedules when several key people wanted the same weeks off. But when she faced those executives, she was too quick to accept their counterproposals. She didn't realize that as a supervisor, she was expected to defend her recommendations further. Instead, she interpreted the executive's responses as the last word on the subject. She judged it best to cut her losses and try to find some way to explain the disappointing result to her team, which was, to put it mildly, profoundly unsatisfactory.

Our friend behaved assertively, to a point. She could be assertive in situations where she didn't have to ask for too much, but would seek familiar, passive ground when the going got tough. Although she did not agree with the executives' decision, she tried her best to put a smile on her face and accept it as she thought a 'real team player' should. She would simply have to settle down and try harder next time to come up with a better, more carefully thought-out proposal. In the meantime, her Pollyanna assertion was earning her an unwanted reputation for being politically naive and ineffective in management.

Pollyanna assertion is incomplete. It goes only as far as custom will allow. It can be a legitimate option, but never works as a consistent strategy. What could our friend have done to get out of the Pollyanna trap? She could have listened to what the executives had to say, and calmly reiterated the reasons why her recommendations should stand. It goes without saying that she was fully prepared for this meeting, and could have produced reams of data to support her position. Armed with the information she needed and the willingness to confront her fears of rejection directly, she would likely have won the raises she asked for.

Which is exactly what she did the next time around.

Pollyanna Assertion: Does She or Doesn't She?
How about you? If, in the descriptions that follow, you see yourself – you also see Pollyanna. Review the chapters which seem to present the toughest challenges to your assertiveness: 'Saying No,' 'Compliments, Criticism, and Rejection.' Gradually work toward a real balance of expression, when you can be comfortable giving 'bad news' as well as good.

- Your assertiveness has been enthusiastically received by your friends and family.
- You don't express anger directly when you feel it.
- You don't think your 'negative' feelings are justified or important enough to share.
- You crave acceptance and approval.
- Authority figures continue to intimidate you.
- You are afraid of disturbing the status quo; your motto could be 'leave well enough alone.'
- When you and friends decide to go to the cinema, you are much more likely to go along with what your friends want to see than you are to suggest a particular film.
- Stating your opinion makes you feel trapped and uncomfortable.
- It is second nature to you to be warm and encouraging of others.

- You are afraid of expressing powerful emotions.
- You consider yourself shy.
- Admitting that you are angry seems like a major imposition.
- Even when you feel depressed or anxious, you would never dream of admitting it to anyone.
- Having good manners is very important to you; you know all about etiquette.
- You are super-conscious of 'overstepping your bounds.'
- You want others to appreciate you.

Fraudulent Assertion

Like Pollyanna assertion, the fraudulent variety also masks an underlying fear or anxiety, but with very different tactics and results. As the name suggests, fraudulent assertion isn't assertion which takes direction from a sincerely held feeling or opinion – it's a fake. Often it's nothing more than thinly disguised manipulation, dressed up to look like assertiveness. At other times, it can be 'textbook assertion,' the kind that looks and sounds authentic, but actually covers up a hidden agenda. The assertive 'fraud' wants to be thought assertive, but she can't really claim the part.

Fraudulent assertions are well remembered and energetically resented. Like other indirect manoeuvres, they have the capacity to provoke a desire for revenge. While the 'fraud' herself may be honestly unaware of any discord, those on the receiving end have a very different perspective.

But fraudulent assertiveness is not something that can be attributed to mean, vindictive, or sick people. It's not the province of a particular class of rotten individuals with deceit in their hearts. It's opportunistic. It's the desire to be assertive without the corresponding faith in oneself to live up to the responsibility assertiveness entails.

We all probably know an assertive fraud. She's the one who accepts a leadership position in her child's fourth form parent's night committee, but telephones you the night before the big event to say that she's run into a problem and could you bake three dozen cakes by 8 a.m. tomorrow? She's the boss who urges you to spearhead a controversial task force, but when you receive heated criticism for your part in it, recedes into the background and may even publicly denounce your participation. She's the friend whose brutal, insensitive criticisms are excused with a murmured 'Well, I was just being direct!' Transgressions like these might be forgiven the first time, but if it's fraudulent assertion, they are part of a pattern which tries the patience and the understanding of those left to pick up the pieces.

To the fraudulently assertive woman, assertiveness is merely a thin, if useful, veneer. Unfortunately, it's not the kind of assertiveness that inspires trust. It's the fraud who commits and the friends who have the responsibility for making good on the promises. Assertiveness isn't assertiveness without the willingness to accept responsibility for one's actions.

Fraudulent Assertion: Does She or Doesn't She?
Do you know an assertive fraud? As you review the list below, notice whether a particular person or event comes to mind. Are there special people or times that spark fraudulent assertion in you?

- Maintaining a strong, independent, assertive image to others is the most important thing to you.
- You have the tendency to cry off previous commitments at the last possible moment.
- Assertiveness seems like a useful tool which would enhance your 'marketability' or attractiveness.
- You use assertiveness as permission to say anything you want to anyone at any time.
- You are more tenacious than anyone you know.
- You dismiss others' criticisms by explaining that you were 'just being direct and honest.'
- You know how to use assertiveness to get what you want, but if it fails, you attack.
- People seem to carry grudges against you.
- You have been known to throw 'temper tantrums' or make a scene.
- At work, people make excuses to avoid being on committees with you or working in the same area as you do.

- You feel that you have been treated unfairly in the past and have resolved never to let it happen again.
- You feel compelled to contribute your 'tuppenceworth' to any discussion; if you don't, you feel cheated and frustrated.

The Superwoman Syndrome

The most pervasive trap for the assertive woman is that of the Superwoman – wanting to do and be everything to everyone. A friend, Carol Orsborn, founded 'Superwoman's Anonymous,' an organization dedicated to the proposition that 'Enough is Enough,' the group's official motto. Carol learned about being a Super-woman firsthand when she woke up one morning and realized that life on a treadmill was no life at all. There was always one more responsibility than she could handle, like the juggler who tries to keep one more ball in the air. The assertive woman opens new doors, to be sure, but there comes a time when all those options become one too many.

It's a special trap that assertiveness can bring, the woman who does it all – and well, too. We cover it in more detail in the 'Assertiveness on the Job' chapter. Suffice it to say here that the desire to be a Superwoman sneaks up on you before you know it. It's the wish to be the best you can be gone awry. Assertiveness becomes your obligation, not your choice. Every opportunity carries the expectation that you will surmount any difficulties and succeed in spite of it all. That, in itself, isn't so bad. It's when the obligations overwhelm you, leaving you limp and weary, that life as a Superwoman shows its true colours.

The fulfilling part of becoming assertive is the new options and choices and sense of accomplishment that come with it. You can do things you couldn't imagine yourself doing before, and do them with style. The successes you are enjoying may make it hard to see the hazards that line the path along the way. For the Superwoman, the chief hazard is simply the variety of new and enticing choices! An assertive woman chooses her commitments carefully. She relies on her own judgment about what constitutes success for her. The answer you reach will be different from that of your friends, possibly even different from your own answer last year – but the important issue is that you understand not only that 'enough is enough,' but *you* are enough.

The Superwoman Syndrome: Does She or Doesn't She?
The following descriptions fit a woman who is doing a dozen things at once, but she may not realize it. If most of these descriptions apply to you, ask yourself whether you're attempting too much of a good thing.
● You feel overwhelmed by obligations and responsibilities.
● You sometimes wonder if you are going crazy.
● Lately you've been daydreaming about going off to a tropical island by yourself.
● When you don't accomplish something as well or as quickly as you expected, you punish yourself.
● You feel like a failure.
● You still cannot say no without a lot of guilt.
● You feel very different from other people you know.
● You're more susceptible to illness than your friends.
● You are eating too much and/or drinking too much.
● Or, conversely, you aren't eating.
● Nervous habits have a permanent home with you.
● It is impossible for you to relax.
● You grind your teeth in your sleep.
● As a girl or when you were younger, you suffered from eating disorders, such as anorexia or bulimia.
● At work, you feel so much stress you think you will scream.
● You overreact and become harshly self-critical when you haven't returned a telephone call within a day.
● You're secretly proud of the fact that you haven't taken a holiday in years.
● You want to prove that you can cut it in this world.

The Eye of the Beholder
Each trap – Reckless Assertion, Pollyanna Assertion, Fraudulent Assertion, and the Superwoman Syndrome – can be avoided with the help of friends and colleagues; their honest, supportive feedback can teach you something about how well your idea of

assertiveness squares with the way your behaviour is perceived. Your own assessment is equally important and valuable. Fortunately, there are lots of ways to express yourself assertively – from the intelligent, deliberate use of silence as illustrated in the epigraph which opened this chapter, to the steady persistence needed to move a mountain. The options, and a thousand variations in between, are all part of the expression of assertion.

Chapter 10

You're Worth It!

Nobody can make you feel inferior without your consent.
— Eleanor Roosevelt

In a 1973 article for the *Transactional Analysis Journal* called, 'The Down-Scripting of Women for 115 Generations,' Muriel James, Ed. D., traced historical patterns that influenced women's views of themselves. She noted the importance, in every generation, of the culture's views of women: the inferior sex; defective physically; lacking intellectually.

Although these perceptions seem old and tired, even modern women remain disenfranchised. It is equally difficult for individual women to reject these outdated perceptions and expectations. The paradox is that women are achieving more – outperforming previous generations of women *and* men – while they tenaciously continue to devalue themselves.

Self-Esteem and Confidence

Most women today, including those who can be assertive women at times, need to build self-esteem and confidence. Self-respect is not a matter of acquiring the approval of others: every woman knows in her heart that friends and foes alike can be fooled by pretences of confidence, if the performance is well rehearsed. Genuine confidence, of course, is born and validated from within.

Imagine for a moment that you are at a gathering of family, friends or work associates. You have been asked to give a brief talk on 'Calculating My Confidence: Knowing I'm Worth It.' You accept the invitation. Here is what you say:

I Know I'm Worth It When . . .

- I am excited about new situations.
- I believe what others say about me is their opinion – not my worth.
- I approve of myself.
- I think and choose for myself.
- My needs and desires are important enough to make them happen.
- I share my talents and triumphs openly without embarrassment.
- I am free to express my feelings and thoughts.
- I don't measure my worth by comparisons with others.
- I accept my mistakes as useful lessons.
- I give myself credit for my efforts aimed at success, whether they succeed or not.
- I can look in the mirror with a genuine smile and say, 'Hey, I *really* like you. You're O.K. in my book.'

Did this exercise in imagination catch you off guard? How comfortable did you feel imagining yourself in this scenario? Were you able to imagine it at all? Or, did you reject it or resist it? Why? How do you feel *right now* about your confidence level? Are you willing to do whatever it takes to know and feel that *you're worth it?*

Satisfaction vs. Survival
Knowing that you're worth it is the result of adopting a *satisfaction mentality* instead of a *survival mentality*. When you have a satisfaction mentality, you believe that there is more to life than merely coping with problems in order to survive. You believe that you are worthy of satisfaction from early in the morning until you close your eyes at night, including the expectation of rest and renewal in order to begin the next day afresh.

Choosing a satisfaction mentality means beginning each day with an appreciation for what the day has to offer, expecting to feel good, strong and enthusiastic. Ready yourself for interactions with people personally and professionally by imagining that you will achieve satisfaction in what you do. Expect abundance, comfort, success, enjoyment and love.

The end of the day is a time to appreciate yourself and how you've handled the day. It is a time to feel your confidence boosted and an awareness of your worth to yourself and others. You can be at peace, letting go of the day's events – finished and unfinished business – in order to treat yourself to some relaxation and anticipation of the following day.

The Need for Nurturance

In 1971, Mildred Newman and Bernard Berkowitz, two noted New York psychoanalysts, wrote the hugely successful *How to Be Your Own Best Friend*. The book was a dialogue between patient and therapist about how to start helping or nurturing oneself, rather than hurting oneself. Newman and Berkowitz assert that many people are their own worst enemies because they do not pursue the things in life that give them pride and pleasure. The book strongly recommends that you give yourself recognition, praise and compliments, instead of waiting for others to do so.

One of the most challenging obstacles to being your own best friend is letting go of the belief that you are simply self-indulgent. Yet nurturing yourself is the *opposite* of self-indulgence. Instead of pleasing an isolated part of you, it is satisfying yourself as a whole person, *including your rights and responsibilities to others*. Self-indulgent people go for immediate, short-term gratification of their own egos. Nurturing oneself is fostering long-term loving of oneself and of others, not self-denial, worthlessness, or guilt. It is a very high form of assertiveness.

In the 1970's women learned we could no longer afford to be helpless. In the 1980's we have learned that we can no longer afford to deny our tenderness – to ourselves first. With a sincere commitment to nurturing ourselves, we can continue in the 1990's and beyond to grow and change as assertive women. To accept ourselves as worthwhile human beings, to understand and appreciate our own needs, to validate our own feelings and self-esteem, to approve of ourselves as beautiful from the inside out, to continue to seek the education, skills and support to grow – these are all facets of self-nurturance which reflect an assertive commitment to yourself.

Rebounding from Failures

Failure is inevitable. It can be debilitating, but it need not be. Failures are really stepping-stones to success. Most of the success stories we've heard or read about are filled with the anguish of many failures. What seems to distinguish the most successful people from also-rans is not a lucky break. What seems to make the difference is attitude and the capability to rebound from what is labelled a 'failure'.

The person who openly accepts mistakes and sees failure as a measure of progress has a better chance of winning. Such people often even look forward to the tests of confidence that failure brings, knowing that these obstacles are opportunities to improve and to grow even stronger.

Of course, every test of failure can be a jolt to the spirit and emotions. The strongest and most assertive among us can at times feel themselves 'bouncing off the four walls.' We are human and vulnerable. Therefore, we need to know how to *rebound* from these failures; when knocked down to be able to get up, brush ourselves off, and continue going forward – with or without a smile, but forward nonetheless.

Though we don't know who wrote the following poem, the words come from an assertive person who knows this process well. (If you know who wrote these wise lines, please let us know; we'd love to give credit in a future printing of this book!)

After a while you learn
The subtle difference
Between holding a hand
And chaining a soul.
And you learn
That love doesn't mean leaning,
And company doesn't mean security.
And you begin to learn
That kisses aren't contracts
And presents aren't promises.
And you begin to accept your defeats
With your head up and your eyes ahead
With the grace of a woman or man

Not the grief of a child.
And you learn to build all your roads on today
Because tomorrow's ground is
Too uncertain for plans
And futures have a way of falling down
In mid-flight.
After a while you learn
That even sunshine burns if you ask too much.
So you plant your own garden
And decorate your own soul
Instead of waiting for someone to bring you
Flowers.
And you learn
That you really can endure
That you really are strong
And you really do have worth.
And you learn . . .
And you learn . . .
With every failure
You learn.

A Love Letter
As an exercise in self-nurturance, sit quietly alone, perhaps play some gentle music in the background, and imagine writing to someone you love: *YOU!* Think about what you would say to yourself if you were someone else who could express love for you. When you feel the feelings and words flowing, begin to write a love letter to yourself. Feel free to say everything you want to say about your past, present and future. You may include observations of what you love in yourself, how great you make yourself feel, what promises you want to make to improve your life, forgiveness for past mistakes and failures, and even a loving pep talk directed toward challenges to come. Sign it with as much love and appreciation as you can feel for yourself. Keep it and read it occasionally. You can repeat this process on your birthday, at Christmas, or anytime. If you feel hesitant or foolish, it is O.K. Remember you are *worth* this effort and it *will* feel good.

The Freedom to Take a Stand

There are many ways to take a stand for yourself, for what you believe to be just, or toward threats to your freedom. Connie Yambert, who teaches people 'How to Speak with Authority' in her public speaking classes in Los Angeles, described an assertive stand she once took:

Accosted by two men with a gun who demanded her handbag, Connie said, 'You don't want my handbag. You want my money. I've got £ –.' She handed them the money while looking them over, studying their car and licence number. When they left, she notified the police. The thieves were apprehended within two hours. Later, as she faced the two in court, the judge commented to her, 'Most women won't come to court to testify.' Ms. Yambert, obviously, is not 'most women.' She believed she was worth the effort it took to make her assailants accountable for their action.

Recently we received a letter from a woman who read *The Assertive Woman* in 1975 when it was first published. Owner of two music stores, employer of 15, she has published two books, worked on numerous committees to help young women, and served as an expert resource for piano teachers. In her letter she shared what it means to her today to be free, to be assertive, to take a stand:

> *'Sometimes I meet a 'newly' awakened woman just stepping into her assertiveness and I recognize the fury, frustration and rage that are now history for me.*
>
> *'There is a mellowing for me. A softness that is purposely being explored by myself in relationships. Now when a man says that he really believes that men are better than women I don't argue. I usually just laugh. Because the remark doesn't wound me as it used to.*
>
> *'When a vendor marvels at my business sense and the multiple-store operation and then asks, "You run this all by yourself? Such a little girl" [I'm short]. I just pat the European gentleman [non-patronizingly] on the hand and smile.*
>
> *'I guess that I'm trying to say that I choose not to let "outsiders" hurt me as I used to. Sure, I still correct my live-in*

*lover when he refers to the "girls" in the office. But it is with
firmness, not anger.'*

In early 1986, Nancy Austin filed a claim against the A. H.
Robins Company, manufacturers of the Dalkon Shield intrauterine
contraceptive device:

'Like thousands of other women in the early 'seventies, I was
warned against "the Pill." The IUD, to the women who used it and
the physicians who prescribed it, seemed a sensible, predictable,
safe alternative. I wore the Dalkon Shield IUD for two years. When
my doctor called to say he wanted to remove it because he didn't
like the way some patients were responding to it, I was surprised,
but I agreed.

'Much later I discovered that the severe, chronic infections I
experienced may have been linked to the presence of that IUD. The
infections led to pelvic inflammatory disease, which grew more
serious and complicated each year. One by one, I developed
immunity to the antibiotics used to treat the infection. Finally, after
several years of worsening illness and only temporarily successful
treatments, I underwent surgery to remove my uterus and ovaries –
a total hysterectomy. I was 28.

'Then, in 1984, six years after my surgery and a decade after the
company stopped manufacturing the Dalkon Shield, Federal Dis-
trict Court Judge Miles W. Lord delivered a remarkable speech.
The judge, in his Minneapolis courtroom, made his remarks as he
approved a $4.6 million product liability suit against the A. H.
Robins Company. (That settlement covered only *seven* of the then
9,000 Dalkon Shield claims that had been brought against the
company.)

'According to press reports, Judge Lord spoke directly to E.
Claiborne Robins, Jr., president; Carl D. Lunsford, senior vice
president for research and development; and William A. Forrest
Jr., vice president and legal counsel, and titled his address 'A Plea
for Corporate Conscience.' A small part of his remarks are excerp-
ted:

*". . . I dread to think what would have been the consequences if
your victims had been men rather than women – women, who
seem, through some quirk of our society's mores, to be expected to suffer pain, shame, and humiliation.*

*"If one poor young man were, without authority or consent, to
inflict such damage upon one woman, he would be jailed for a
good portion of the rest of his life. Yet your company, without
warning to women, invaded their bodies by the millions and
caused them injuries by the thousands. And when the time came
for these women to make their claims against your company,
you attacked their characters. You inquired into their sexual
practices and into the identity of their sex partners. You ruined
families and reputations and careers in order to intimidate those
who would raise their voices against you. You introduced issues
that had no relationship to the fact that you had planted in the
bodies of these women instruments of death, of mutilation, of
disease.*

*". . . Your company, in the face of overwhelming evidence,
denies its guilt and continues its monstrous mischief."*

'I decided I would file after I read the Judge's stunning comments. Up to that time, I reasoned that there were others who may
have been injured more severely than I; no one could give me back
what I had lost, what would be the point?

'It took some time, but gradually I saw that I had to do this for
myself. I could not, even tacitly, act as though nothing had happened. I couldn't let myself be intimidated – even at a distance – by a
Fortune 500 company whose net income in 1986 was an incredible
$81.8 million, up almost 8% from the previous year.'

'It was a matter of self-respect. The more I kept my experience to
myself, the more I tried to put it behind me, the harder it became.
To stand back passively seemed irresponsible, a kind of surrender, a
positive disgrace when I had the capacity to act in my own behalf.
Taking a stand demands time and record-gathering and file-sifting.
It means recalling events that are painful. But from it I might see
that I am the kind of person who can face the unpleasant, who does
not run away.

'The price of silence is the private knowledge that you can't, really, be trusted to count on yourself. Living without self-respect is like stealing from yourself, a little at a time, with the promise to make good tomorrow: All you can do is worry about the new demands to pay up, and hope for rescue. The shame of it is the willingness with which you turn yourself over to the wolves at the door.

'It will likely be years before the legalities are resolved. But the wait pales next to the thought that, had I done nothing, I might have come to believe it was noble – but every morning, I'd have a tough time convincing that face in the mirror.'

Part of knowing that 'you are worth it,' is being willing and able to take a stand on your own behalf. Powerlessness, lack of self-esteem, and decaying self-confidence are products of the passive inferiority women have accepted. We urge you to reject it.

Give up self-doubt and trust your perceptions. Stop blaming yourself unnecessarily when something goes wrong; stop fantasizing about the Knight in Shining Armour who'll come and rescue you from the perils of the world.

Trust that you can rescue yourself, take a stand, see it through to completion, and feel great about acting in your own behalf. All of this can be done with the support of others, but don't wait for that support. Be the initiator, the primary power to create positive change for yourself, the assertive woman.

Chapter 11

Developing an Assertive Body Image

Your body communicates as clearly as your words. Your style of emotional expression, posture, facial expressions, and voice quality are all tremendously important to you in becoming an assertive woman. This chapter will help you to develop an assertive body image to make your body, as well as your words, communicate assertively.

An Inventory of Body Image Components
Check yourself from head to toe, as you probably do frequently during the day, but this time measure yourself on a scale of assertiveness.

For example, women often have a problem making *eye contact* because many of us have been taught that it is more feminine to look away or look down. At times it is considered coy to give little side glances and not to look directly at someone for any length of time. In some cultures, it is considered disrespectful for women to make direct eye contact with men or authority figures. However, in our society, direct eye contact and holding your head erect is essential when you want to appear assertive and interested. This is not staring at someone; look into the eyes, then perhaps look away for a few seconds or drop your gaze slightly so that you focus on the mouth of the person speaking to you. Practice making good eye contact with someone as you are talking and be aware of any differences in the quality of your communication. Are you listening better? Are you conveying more interest and receiving more interest in what you are saying?

What do your *facial expressions* say about you? Many women find it easy to smile and to demonstrate warmth, but when it comes to expressing anger or disapproval, they may do so with a smile. Look in a mirror and see how you look when you are expressing anger, joy, sadness, fear, and other emotions. Get feedback from your friends, too. Practice making your face and head look assertive: make direct eye contact, feel the control over your facial muscles, and hold your head high.

While you are looking in the mirror, check out your *posture*. Changing your posture can change the way you feel about yourself. Try assuming a passive stance. Then change to an assertive stance – lean slightly forward with feet solidly grounded. Enjoy feeling centered with your body. Learn how close you like to stand or sit next to another person. This is your 'optimal distance.' To find your optimal distance, stand across the room from a friend, face each other, and walk slowly toward your friend as she remains stationary. Make eye contact with her the whole way and then stop walking as soon as you feel that you are at a comfortable distance from her. Measure this distance, and then have your friend repeat the process. You will discover that each person has her own optimal distance that aids assertion. If you can be aware of this fact with other people, it will help you to maintain an assertive posture. Assertiveness allows you to move toward a person, while passiveness involves hesitation, or moving away.

Next on your checklist for an assertive body image, notice your *gestures*. Do people say that you could not talk if someone tied your hands behind your back? If so, your gestures may be so distracting that they prevent you from delivering an assertive message. On the other hand, if you hold your arms rigidly against your body or fold them across your chest, you create a passive or indirectly aggressive image. Being able to move your hands and arms about in an expansive way demonstrates a sense of confidence and freedom. There are two kinds of gestures to practice. *Descriptive gestures* are those in which you practically 'paint a picture in the sky' by sketching a scene or object in the air. Try this while describing your house to someone. Other gestures are *emphatic*. These underscore the significance of what you are saying, e.g. shaking your fist to show anger or pounding on a table to get someone's attention or putting your hand on someone's shoulder to connote caring and concern. Practice using emphatic gestures to show positive as well as negative feelings.

How are you dressed today? What sort of image do your convey by your *style of dress?* It is common knowledge that dressing appropriately for a job interview increases your chances of getting the job. But do you realize that you can dress assertively too? Dressing in a favourite outfit can give you that extra touch of confidence to help you be assertive. Whenever you are feeling down, you can be assertive with yourself by wearing an outfit that doesn't let you 'fade into the woodwork,' but attracts attention and helps you to project an outgoing appearance without being 'loud' or 'coarse.' Of course, these styles vary with each individual. So, check out your own particular wardrobe and decide what your most assertive outfits are and use them as allies to help you.

There may be some special concerns you have about developing an assertive body image. For example, some overweight women have admitted to us that they have used their weight as a way to remain passive sexually or to avoid sex altogether. Similarly, women who are self-conscious about skin problems such as acne may be withdrawn and passive. Long after blemishes clear up, many women continue to see themselves as 'overweight' or 'acne-prone.' At this point, an assertive attitude can be more helpful than losing weight or visiting a dermatologist.

Probably one of the most vital tools you can develop in becoming assertive is your *voice.* If you have a tape recorder or a friend to listen and give feedback, evaluate your voice in several different ways. Women, for the most part, seem to have higher-pitched but softer voices than men. However, for some, this is a conditioned tone rather than natural voice. In many instances Doris has tried to sound like a 'baby doll' by raising the pitch of her voice, or Iris has considered it feminine and sexy to 'purr like a kitten.' Unfortunately, these tones do not sound sincere, straightforward, or assertive, but are obvious distortions of what is natural. A lower-pitched voice is more often associated with assertion. Try to recite a poem in which you alternate raising and lowering your pitch to get a feeling for how you can vary and control your voice.

When analyzing your voice, gauge its *volume*. Are you afraid to speak up for fear you will sound masculine? A woman can be loud and clear and still sound like a woman. It is better to be heard than to be disregarded. And yet, like Agatha, if you speak very loudly most of the time, you will risk turning people off.

Many times women give away the fact that they are nervous or anxious by speaking too rapidly. Your *rate of speech* needs to be evenly paced, not too fast or slow. Sometimes a slower rate is good in order to emphasize an important idea. Again, when angry, a woman may tend to talk very fast, trying to get it all said before she 'runs out of steam.' You can command someone's attention for a long time if you remember to use good eye contact and the other body elements we have mentioned. Also, *stressing* important words (usually nouns and verbs) can help you to sound assertive. Try emphasizing important words in a sentence, sometimes pausing before or after the word, by speaking key words louder, or by enunciating slowly and precisely.

Finally, you should be aware of the *quality* of your voice. Do you tend to whine when feeling helpless, powerless, or manipulative? Or, when nervous, does your voice become raspy and harsh? Practice asking for favours without whining. Try saying things that you are normally uncomfortable in saying, without a harsh, rasping tone. Most people will listen and respect a full-bodied voice rather than a squeaky, strident one.

You do not need a college education or a big vocabulary to be assertive and make yourself heard. If you practice the behaviours we have described and keep your messages simple, direct, and spontaneous, you will be on the way to becoming an assertive woman. In later chapters, we will offer specific suggestions to deal with particular situations where the content of what you say makes a big difference.

Reducing Anxiety and Promoting Relaxation

The assertive woman not only knows how to develop her body image, she knows how to promote her own physical well-being. There are many sources of information on healthful food habits and exercise. We assume these are available to you. Our concern is with more subtle body influences, especially nervousness and anxiety, which afflict many women.

Anxiety will detract from your assertive body image because it shows itself in your behaviour. For most people, acting assertively in new situations evokes some initial anxiety and nervousness, which can be alleviated by learning to relax.

What happens to your body when you feel anxious? Headaches, a 'nervous stomach,' asthma, and 'dizzy spells' are common bodily indicators of anxiety. In more extreme forms, anxiety can be severe enough to be a contributing factor to ulcers, migraine headaches and heart attacks. In addition to the physical discomfort anxiety can produce, it can also cause emotional discomfort. Some people get 'cold feet' and so avoid approaching employers for a raise in salary. 'Stage fright' prevents many people from speaking in front of a group, even though the speech may have been interesting and valuable to the group; others 'clam up' when they are treated unfairly and sacrifice their self respect in the process.

When facing threatening and anxiety provoking situations. Doris Doormat feels she has *no control* over her anxiety. Her anxiety immobilizes and controls her. Her anxiety is often at such a high level that she suffers severe headaches or fainting spells. She avoids anxiety-provoking situations because she feels powerless to do anything about them. The more she tries to avoid those anxiety-provoking situations, the stronger her anxiety becomes about facing them.

The assertive woman, in contrast, is not a helpless victim of anxiety; she alleviates it by taking action. By acting and therefore having control over what you do, you make it impossible for anxiety to control you. If you have felt that you couldn't tolerate a threatening situation – that your anxiety is so great that you really couldn't 'live through it' – you have probably felt helpless to say or do anything. When you know that you can choose to assert yourself, you can live through threatening encounters and alleviate your anxiety because you can *benefit*, physically and/or emotionally, by saying or doing something – it doesn't have to be the 'perfect' thing.

Learning to relax can combat anxiety and be a good complement to assertion. You probably already practice forms of relaxation such as meditation, yoga, or a walk on the beach. While relaxation is not *necessary* for effective assertions, it can help you to feel more in control of your body.

You have probably noticed that you feel calmer and more relaxed after you have rested quietly even for a short time. By learning deep muscle relaxation, or another form of complete relaxation, you will be able to relax beyond this usual point. We recommend deep muscle relaxation as the easiest form to learn, but we also encourage you to explore other forms of relaxation. With practice you will be able to relax at will and counteract the tensions of anxiety arising from threatening situations.

We suggest that you practice deep muscle relaxation twice a day for one week. Be aware of particular muscle groups that are more difficult to relax than others, and give them special attention. For many people, the stomach, shoulders, and back are almost constantly tensed. When you have learned how to relax, you can practice relaxation together with acting assertively. Remember that you will alleviate your anxiety most effectively when you *act*.

To train yourself in deep muscle relaxation, choose a quiet, comfortable place where you won't be disturbed for half an hour. Go through a relaxation exercise while lying on the floor, a bed, or a reclining chair.

Constructing Your Assertive Behaviour Hierarchy

Dealing with tension and anxiety by relaxation is only a first step, although it is one that should be repeated as often as necessary. Your next step is to gain a better understanding of your sources of anxiety. What particular situations or encounters make you feel anxious? What causes you to be passive and non-assertive, causing you emotional and/or physical harm? What triggers your anger or aggression? It will be helpful for you to identify specific instances in which you would like to be more assertive. You can use an 'Assertive Behaviour Hierarchy' to specify situations in which you find it difficult to assert yourself.

The hierarchies can be used individually or in a group to help identify each person's specific assertive deficits. Group time can be spent rehearsing the hierarchy items to minimize anxiety and learn assertive responses. Items are ordered according to the degree of anxiety produced by each situation, beginning with the least anxiety-provoking. Experiencing success with the first hierarchy items will encourage you to continue to practice assertive behaviours and responses as you face more demanding situations as an assertive woman.

Constructing and using your hierarchy will help you to become more aware of the specific times you behave non-assertively. It will also provide you with a starting point for the application of suggestions from this book to your own life.

It is important that you proceed through your hierarchy in order; resist the temptation to jump to the last items before you feel comfortable with the first ones. When you are comfortable asserting yourself with minor anxiety-provoking items, you'll find it much easier to proceed to the more difficult ones, and so increase the likelihood that you'll become an assertive woman.

Before completing your own hierarchy, review these examples:

Doris Doormat Hierarchy
1. Returning that faulty toaster to the department store.
2. Initiating a conversation with my brother's new partner, Bill.
3. Asking not to be interrupted when Agatha starts talking in the middle of my conversation with April.
4. Cutting telephone calls short when I am busy, especially with Iris and Agatha.
5. Asking questions of my car dealer without fear of sounding weak and stupid.
6. Giving a sincere compliment to my spouse or close friend.
7. Telling April when I have done something important or worthwhile.
8. Refusing unreasonable requests from my family, employer, and friends, especially Iris Indirect and Agatha Aggressive.
9. Telling my spouse or close friend or relative that I disagree with an opinion he/she has expressed.
10. Expressing my anger to a very close relative or to my spouse in a non-apologetic way.

Agatha Aggressive Hierarchy

1. Complaining about poor restaurant service assertively, without name-calling.
2. Not interrupting Doris or April in the middle of a conversation.
3. In my classes, letting Doris and Iris speak up without answering for them.
4. Listening to April criticize me for coming on too strong, without attacking her or being too defensive.
5. Not being overly critical of Doris because I know she won't fight back.
6. Expressing my positive feelings to April, Iris, and Doris, by telling them when I appreciate something they have done.
7. Not bullying or shaming Doris into doing me a favour, knowing she'll be too guilty to say 'no'.
8. Being aware of another person's faults or vulnerabilities without teasing and making fun of her/him.
9. Talking about differences of opinion with my mate or close friend, not just saying 'you're wrong.'
10. Expressing anger without hitting, or throwing things, or being accusing or blaming.

Irish Indirect Hierarchy

1. Asking Doris to drive me to work when my car is being repaired, without making her feel guilty if she can't drive me.
2. Give a compliment and approval openly and honestly, and not by using false flattery.
3. Being more direct when refusing door-to-door salespeople; not saying 'my husband won't let me buy it.'
4. Not making sarcastic or caustic comments about others behind their back.
5. Asking for something specific from my spouse without being dishonest and manipulative about why I want it.
6. When Agatha asks something unreasonable of me, saying 'no' directly without becoming sullen and hostile.
7. Initiating the expression of love or affection with my mate without manipulating or being coy.

8. Expressing valid criticisms to my spouse honestly without resorting to indirect put-downs.

9. Asking for love and attention to be given to me without using guilt of manipulation to get it.

10. Expressing my anger openly to Doris, Agatha, or April by honestly stating that I am angry, instead of giving them the 'silent treatment.'

Your Own Assertive Behaviour Hierarchy

Instructions: To construct your own hierarchy select as the first item or situation something you feel you could handle assertively with only minimal anxiety. Continue to order your items from least anxiety-provoking to most anxiety-provoking. The last items should be the behaviours or situations that cause you the greatest anxiety and discomfort.

Chapter 12

Compliments, Criticism, and Rejection

Compliments

How do you feel about compliments?

A genuine compliment is a specific expression of appreciation, given and received in a spirit of sincerity. But we don't have to look far to find imitations. Compliments – not always sincere – run rampant in the Compassion Trap, when we 'compulsively' praise others in an attempt to make them feel good – even at our own expense. Because the Compassion Trap is a prominent part of so many women's lives, it is easy to find women who overuse compliments as a way to compensate for unacceptable negative feelings about a friend, spouse, or employer. They search for an elusive silver lining in a sky full of dark clouds, and thus avoid having to acknowledge the clouds at all. It's positive thinking gone bad.

Then there is false flattery. Women are often expected to be easy prey to flattery because, supposedly, they require constant reassurance and will respond to tiny, frivolous attentions. Just a little buttering up, and she'll go along without complaint. Bring the underpaid secretary a bouquet of flowers and she'll be dissuaded from pressing for that raise. Avoid helping her paint the living room by remarking how extremely talented she is at these things. Instead of giving her the sweater she really wants for her birthday, buy her a new blender, and tell her how glad you are she isn't selfish and self-centred like most women.

Fortunately, neither women nor men are born to be flattered! Learning to give and acknowledge genuine compliments, and along the way discovering when a different approach would be better, is all part of the process.

- A woman who works closely with you is going through a messy divorce. She looks haggard and depressed. Instead of chirping 'Oh, Tracy, don't you look wonderful?' in a well-intentioned effort to cheer her up, you might instead say: 'Tracy, are you free for lunch? I know you're having a rough time, and I'd like to help if I can.'
- You are redecorating your home, and have been working with an interior designer who comes highly recommended. After several weeks of work, the designer excitedly submits her plans. One look is enough to tell you that it's all wrong and not at all to your taste. Rather than search for the one tiny element that you do like ('This pillow fabric is nice!'), take the plunge: 'Carol, I can see you have knocked yourself out on this project, and I appreciate it very much. The only trouble is that this approach isn't what I had in mind. Let's go over it and see how it could be changed. First, I prefer stripes to polka dots for the chairs . . .'

What Gets in the Way: Embarrassment and Fear

But lots of compliments do fit the genuine/sincere criterion. Still, they make many women (and men) uncomfortable. A sizeable portion of us believe that it is embarrassing, unladylike, impolite, or just plain bad manners to acknowledge a compliment: Instead, we argue or reject what is said ('Oh, come on! Are you kidding? Give me a break!'). The response usually succeeds: the complimenter, having said the wrong thing, won't risk repeating the error.

If you feel uncomfortable when you give or receive a compliment, review the list below. Which match your own reactions?

- I tend to blush when complimented and it embarrasses me.
- A compliment paves the way for the real point – something unpleasant or critical.
- Other people may think I deserve a compliment, but I know better.
- You can't kid a kidder.
- I don't like being the centre of attention.
- I never know how to react.
- Giving a compliment is simply a request to receive one in return.

- Compliments are thinly disguised attempts to conceal the true motives of the complimenter; I don't trust them.
- Saying 'thank you' without argument sounds conceited.
- I don't need compliments; I know my own worth.
- Compliments make me very nervous.
- I can't live up to a compliment.
- I'm too shy.
- If I worked up the courage to give someone a compliment and then she or he laughed at me, I'd die.
- Giving compliments is unnecessary; the people I would want to compliment know what they're good at already.

If any of these reasons sound familiar to you, is it because you feel obligated to give a compliment in return for one you have received? You certainly don't have to reciprocate with a compliment, but do acknowledge what was said. It can be done verbally or nonverbally, with a smile or a nod of the head. If you want to say something, 'thank you' is simple, elegant, and enough. You may also add a word or two about how you feel about what was said to you: 'April, I really admire the way you said "no" to that car salesman. You didn't beat around the bush.' The assertive reply: 'Thanks, Linda. It has taken me a while to learn how to say "no" assertively, and I am really beginning to feel confident. I'm glad you noticed!'

Developing Confidence in Compliments
Use this checklist to develop your ability to give and receive compliments. As you master each item, check it off the list.
- Don't fall into the Compassion Trap by giving inappropriate compliments or false flattery in an attempt to make someone feel good.
- Do give sincere compliments as expressions of your appreciation.
- Do make your compliment specific.
- Do acknowledge a compliment you receive, either verbally or non-verbally.
- Don't get embarrassed or put down by a genuine compliment.
- Don't feel obliged to give a compliment in return for one.
- Don't use good news as a way to ease into the bad news.

Criticism

Any inhibition we experience giving and receiving compliments is heightened in giving criticism. Probably the prime fear that keeps many women from giving or accepting criticism is the fear of rejection. When your self-esteem is low, or the situation is especially sensitive, it does not take too much to paralyze you with anxiety and fear at the moment of making or receiving critical remarks. As your confidence grows, your ability to evaluate criticism objectively will also.

When you are as non-assertive as Doris, you tend to evaluate what people say to you, or what you say, in terms of your own feelings of worthlessness. However, when you are assertive like April, your self-image remains strong and intact; you can acknowledge your own faults without feeling rejected by others. In fact, being assertive in giving and receiving criticism will earn you respect, and people will turn toward you rather than away.

One reason criticism can be hard to hear is the element of surprise. Usually the criticism that is least expected is the one that hurts the most. To overcome the fear of criticism, then, set up a step-by-step process that will gradually desensitize you to critical remarks, whether anticipated or not.

Prepare in advance for three possible types of criticism: unrealistic criticism, put-downs, and valid criticism. Be careful not to over-prepare or to feel that you must be constantly on guard. *Unrealistic criticism* is the sort that is utterly ridiculous, e.g. Agatha calling a slim person a 'big, fat slob.' *Put-downs* may have an element of truth, but are said in a patronizing and/or insulting way, such as Iris saying to someone who is overweight, 'Why don't you have a banana split? You'll never notice a few more pounds!' *Valid criticism* is both realistic and stated in a straightforward, assertive manner, such as April saying to an overweight friend, 'I have noticed that you have gained some extra weight. I think you really looked better and healthier before.'

Check your C.Q. [*Criticism Quotient*]

Use our checklist to determine how sensitive you are to criticism. Put a 'plus' (+) by those that you handle assertively, a 'minus' (−)

by those that you avoid handling at all, and a tick ($\vee$) by those that you face but handle awkwardly. Your ratings here will help with the exercise on criticism later in the chapter.

_____ Someone criticizes you about a fault that you cannot deny is yours.

_____ You give a friend an honest criticism of what you see as a legitimate problem.

_____ Someone criticizes you for an act that you know without a doubt doesn't apply to you and is ridiculous.

_____ Someone has put you down in an indirect way; there may be some truth to the put-down, but it's basically unfair.

_____ Things have not been going your way lately and you are lacking confidence. You're criticized for 'being down.'

_____ You have just gained the courage to give a friend a valid criticism. Your friend cannot handle this and retaliates by criticizing you with a mixture of valid and invalid complaints.

_____ You are feeling very happy and high spirited. Someone not so happy is jealous and tries to bring you down by reminding you of things she knows can hurt your feelings.

Rejection

Everyone wants to avoid being rejected as a person, but it is natural and unavoidable to have one's ideas or acts rejected. The most common form of rejection occurs when someone says 'no' in response to your idea, request, or action. Becoming assertive means learning to accept a 'no' as meaning 'no' to the specific situation, instead of interpreting it as total rejection. Nevertheless, it is possible that the other person may wish to convey that you are 'worthless.' But, if you are feeling good about yourself, you will not accept this interpretation. You'll be able to accept some 'no's,' because your reward is primarily in asserting yourself, not just in getting what you want.

A Rejection Checklist

Use the following checklist to determine in what ways you may fear rejection. Put a tick ($\vee$) in front of each item that causes you to feel rejected regardless of its truth. Put a cross (+) before each item that you can handle assertively.

—— Your parents, spouse, or boss tells you that you are stupid and can't do anything right.

—— Your lover criticizes your appearance.

—— A friend says she or he is busy and cannot go with you someplace you wanted to go.

—— Your child or another's child tells you that you're mean and that she/he hates you.

—— Someone whose intelligence you respect tells you that your latest brainstorm isn't a good idea.

—— You're playing a game where sides are chosen by leaders – you're last to be picked.

—— In a group, you make an important statement which is ignored.

—— You have completed a job as well as you can, but you are told to do it again.

—— You look for physical affection from someone you love who is too busy to give it to you at the moment.

—— You have asked someone to do a special favour for you, and she refuses.

—— A significant person in your life forgets your birthday or anniversary.

—— You apply for a job or admission to a certain school or organisation, and are turned down.

Review the items that cause you to feel anxious and fearful about rejection. If you feel discouraged about the way you answered, the first exercise below will be a good antidote.

Action Exercises

Like Yourself First

Write in your journal ten positive statements about yourself – things you like about *you* as a person, e.g. 'I like the fact that I'm trying to become a more assertive person.' Stand in front of a mirror and read each item on your list aloud. While practising good eye contact and smiling appropriately, acknowledge each compliment that you give yourself either verbally or non-verbally. Practice adding some free information to some of your 'thank-you's.'

Use this list to gain confidence. Refer to it often and add to it by telling someone, in regular conversation, something positive about yourself.

Giving and Receiving Compliments

Try giving and receiving spontaneous compliments with a friend. If you try this in a group, have each woman turn to the woman on her right to give her a compliment. After the woman acknowledges the compliment, continue around the circle until you are all feeling quite comfortable with both giving and receiving. Be sure to give each other feedback: first, on positives about the way in which compliments are delivered or received; then, give each other specific suggestions for improvement that might be necessary.

Giving and Receiving Criticism

Take at least 15 minutes and write two separate lists with 5 to 10 items on each list. Title the first list 'Unrealistic Criticisms' and write down what you feel would be ridiculous criticisms of yourself. On the second list, 'Realistic Criticisms,' write down things that you feel are quite valid criticisms of yourself. Then exchange both lists with another person and take turns reading to one another from your lists, alternating preposterous and realistic items while being as believable and dramatic as possible.

Whenever you are confronted with an unrealistic criticism, contradict it openly, as in the following example:

'Why Don't You Try Social Work?'

Careers teacher: 'April, I think your decision to become a psychiatrist is impractical. You aren't good at science and maths, you know. Why don't you try social work?'

April: 'That is not true. My abilities in maths and science are very strong, and I think becoming a psychiatrist is a practical goal for me.'

On the other hand, when responding to a *realistic criticism*, the assertive woman will acknowledge the criticism as being valid and then may add a statement about how she is working on that problem and is trying to change. Or, she may say that she is aware that a trait bothers others, but that it doesn't bother her and she's really not motivated to do anything about it now. For example, April's reply to her careers teacher might sound like this:

April: 'You're right about science and maths not being my strongest subjects. However, I've arranged for individual tutoring and plan to master those subjects. I will do whatever I can to make sure I can reach my goal of becoming a psychiatrist.'

Handling Put-Downs

Few topics in this book have generated as much animated discussion as this one! There are several ways to handle a put-down: ignore it; respond with a direct assertive statement; respond in kind with a rapid-fire, witty retort.

Ignore it. This is often the most effective choice. We don't suggest that you walk off in a huff, working up a head of steam all the while. If you choose this option, it means you literally let the remark pass. A salesman representing an audio-visual equipment company was demonstrating a new slide projector to the support staff in her office. At one point in the demonstration, the salesman said to Cynthia, a very attractive blonde, 'This projector is so easy to disassemble that even you could do it.' Cynthia's reaction? She started laughing! Without saying a word, she responded from strength and confidence, making the put-down small and petty, not herself. (The salesman didn't get that order, either.)

Respond with a direct assertive statement. Some put-downs are part of a pattern which must be addressed. Kathleen's boss, for example, consistently patronised her by following every request with 'There's a good girl,' a remark that made Kathleen's blood boil. Ignoring it was impossible. The next time her boss uttered those four words, Kathleen said: 'Please don't call me a "good girl." It's irritating.' She made her point assertively and although she found she had to repeat it several times, she reports that it was an effective way to handle the problem.

Respond in kind with a witty retort. In the first edition of *The Assertive Woman*, this topic was chock full of quick razor-sharp retorts to some popular put-downs. In this edition, we give less attention to this approach because it was not particularly successful for many women who tried it. Although it was always a favourite exercise in seminars – and we still recommend it as a way to discover that there are alternatives to freezing up – in real life, women found it a sometimes reckless response. In the hands of Joan Rivers, a witty retort works beautifully; but for most of us, it's better to find a response that we can live with. (One we still like: 'You did a great job, considering you're a woman.' Response: 'For a man, you didn't do too badly, either.') There is nothing wrong with practising a quick retort to give you a feeling of control. Our advice, however, is: *handle with care*! The objective is to hold on to your sense of worth, not to attack.

If witty retorts aren't your style, you can always respond to a put-down directly and assertively. Saying 'I'm offended by that remark,' or a similar statement of feeling can be just as potent as any witty retort. If a sense of humour is one of your characteristics, you might discover a new application for it here (we take a closer look at it in Chapter 17, 'Humour'). In the meantime, record the put-downs you've received or heard, and see if you can come up with some effective retorts – either funny or direct. This exercise is, as you might imagine, a lot of fun to work on in a group!

Making Friends With Ms. Protecto

Here is a group exercise which will help you to reduce anxiety about giving compliments and criticisms, and aid you in being more spontaneous and open. It involves getting rid of the censor inside your head, which tells you to be overly cautious and not risk saying the wrong thing.

Have one person stand before each person in the group one-by-one and quickly blurt out a few adjectives and nouns – positive and negative – that describe what she notices about each person. Stay away from phrases and sentences and just use one-worders. Move quickly from person to person and have each person take a turn. For example, you may look at a person and say, 'short, warm smile, fuzzy, serious, unpredictable, bald, plump, caring, social, bright colours, fifty-ish.' The person being spoken to remains neutral and does not comment on anything said about her. Have each person try this until she feels she can be spontaneous with her remarks.

Then think about how comfortable or uncomfortable this exercise was for you. It's even better if you can talk about it with someone. Be specific about what types of words cause you the most trouble – negative or positive or both. Try this exercise again until you feel that you have reached a level of spontaneity that is right for you.

Accepting 'no' for an answer

Make a list with three columns: *who, what* and *when*. Under 'who' write down the names of people who you are sensitive about rejecting you. Under 'what' list specific situations in which you feel most vulnerable to a 'no' response. And finally under 'when' write down the times in which you feel most threatened by hearing a 'no.' Then order these, putting the ones that cause you the least anxiety on top of the list as 1, and continue numbering until you end with the most threatening who, what, and when at the bottom.

Sample:

WHO	WHAT	WHEN
children	asking for help around the house	at home at dinnertime
employer	asking for time off	at work during a hectic day
friend	expecting company	chores have piled up around the house
husband	making love	when feeling down
other(s)	other(s)	other(s)

Now that you have the above samples, make up your own lists, ordering them from the least anxiety provoking to the most threatening:

After you have completed and ordered your list, role-play these situations with a friend or in a group starting with 1 in each column. Keep practising until you feel comfortable with hearing a 'no' from your partner. Then move on to 2. Each time you hear a 'no' think to yourself, 'I am O.K. for making this request. I am not being rejected as a person; only my *request* is being rejected. I can make this request at another time, and it may be accepted. I feel good about asserting myself and expressing my needs clearly.'

Summary

The assertive woman can give, as well as receive, a compliment sincerely and specifically; she avoids giving inappropriate compliments. Not only can she accept a compliment without embarrassment, but she rarely feels obligated to give a compliment in return for one.

Doris Doormat feels powerless when criticized and accepts most criticism as further proof of her worthlessness; April Assertive is able to choose how she will react to criticism. April openly contradicts the unrealistic, acknowledging the valid, and uses humour or an 'I message' to counteract a put-down. The assertive woman can initiate valid criticisms when she feels it's appropriate.

Iris learns to speak openly and directly and spontaneously. Agatha recognises her habit of using put-downs and learns that they harm her more than they affect her supposed victims. She develops the ability to make her compliments direct and appropriate. She is comfortable in accepting some 'no's,' and finds her reward primarily in asserting herself, instead of feeling good only if she gets what she wants.

As you have seen in this chapter, being assertive sometimes involves defending yourself against attack. At other times, assertion requires that you reach out to others in a positive way. Becoming an assertive woman, therefore, means understanding and learning not only defensive behaviours, but positive approach behaviours as well.

Chapter 13

Saying 'No'

*The Queen turned crimson with fury, and after glaring
at her [Alice] for a moment like a wild beast, began
screaming, 'Off with her head! Off with –'
'Nonsense!' said Alice, and the Queen was silent.*

– Lewis Carroll
Alice in Wonderland

Being 'feminine' has often meant that a woman is submissive and
indecisive, and that when she says 'no' she *really* means 'yes!' It is
hardly surprising, therefore, that women find it very difficult to say
'no.' Since women continuously encounter requests from others to
do something for them or advertisements insisting that they buy
something, it is an enormous handicap for a woman not to be able to
say 'no.'

Yet, there is a good deal of resistance from women to learn how
to say 'no.' One of the biggest reasons for not saying 'no' is the
'Compassion Trap' – taking care of someone else's needs in spite of
your own, discussed in Chapter 7. For Doris, it is easier to say 'yes'
than to deal with the guilt she may feel after an assertive refusal. Or,
she may resist the fact that she has the right to evaluate a situation
herself and the right to disagree with the person who is making the
request of her. Doris lacks confidence in her own decision-making
power. She feels worthless in comparison to others and feels that
their needs are naturally more worthwhile than her own. Doris may
even believe that, because she is a woman, it is 'normal' to have
people take advantage of her. Like Doris, some women often say
'yes' to avoid any conflict or encounter with another person. Others

fear that refusal can lead to violence toward them or toward a loved one.

Our purpose in this chapter is to encourage every woman to feel free to say 'no' and to exercise her right of refusal. One can earn a great deal of respect and overcome feelings of powerlessness by exercising the right to refuse. Most negative repercussions can be avoided if the refusal is done assertively. In other words, what matters is *how* you say 'no' rather than the fact that you have said it. Here are some steps to help overcome the problem you may have of feeling guilty when you say 'no.'

Four Ways to Say 'No'
First of all, one of the most difficult hurdles to overcome is to decide whether or not the other person's request of you is reasonable or unreasonable. This can be tricky. Women must stop looking to the other person to find out if the request is reasonable. The mere fact that the request was made means that the person has decided that she/he wants something from you regardless of its reasonableness. Look inside yourself to find whether or not this is a reasonable request. If you find yourself hesitating or hedging, it may be a clue that you want to refuse. If you feel cornered, or trapped, or you notice a tightness or nervous reaction in your body, this may also mean that someone is requesting something unreasonable of you. Sometimes you may be genuinely confused or unsure because you just do not have enough information to know whether something unreasonable is being asked of you.

Second, assert your right to ask for more information and clarification. Many of us grew up under the influence of such dicta as 'Children should be seen and not heard,' or under religious demands that we accept what we have heard as the truth, that to doubt or question is sinful, or that to be submissive and unquestioning was 'ladylike.' Nevertheless, the first step in asserting yourself when a request is made of you is to make sure you have all the facts. April does not commit herself to a yes or no until she fully understands what is being asked of her.

Third, practise saying 'no.' Once you understand the request and decide you do not want to do it or buy it, say no firmly and calmly. It is crucial that you give a simple 'no' rather than a long-winded statement filled with excuses, justifications, and rationalisations about why you are saying 'no.' It is enough that you do not want to do this, simply because you do not want to do it. You can accompany your refusal with a simple, straightforward explanation of what you are feeling. A direct explanation is assertive, while many indirect and misleading excuses are non-assertive and can get you into a lot of trouble by leaving you open for further challenge.

Fourth, learn to say 'no' without saying 'I'm sorry, but . . .' Saying 'I'm sorry' frequently weakens your stand and the other person, especially Iris, may be tempted to play on your guilt. When you evaluate a situation carefully and decide the best thing is to say no, you have nothing to be sorry about. In fact, April feels strong and happy with her decisions to say no.

The Broken Record

Whenever a person like Agatha does not accept your assertive refusal and resorts to high-pressure tactics with you, you can use the 'broken record' method. In this technique, you simply become a 'broken record' and repeat your original assertive refusal each time the person tries another tactic to persuade you to change your mind. If you remain firm with your original statement, and resist the temptation to answer 'Why?,' or respond to possible insults, the person will soon run out of new materials and give up. If you tire before this happens, you can end the conversation or change it to another topic. *Watch out for this technique, however; it can be hard on relationships!*

'You Won't Mind, Will You?'

Imagine the following situation: You have a close friend who has three small children. She has frequently called on you to watch them for a couple of hours at a time, since she is a part-time estate agent and has to see potential customers at a minute's notice and at odd hours. You are home anyway, so she feels you will not mind watching them. However, she has been tied up lately and often her two hours drag on for six or seven. You are stuck without being able to reach her by phone; consequently you can't do what you have to do. She calls you on the day you have set aside to clean out your garage and prepare for a garage sale. What would you do? Let's see how April would handle this situation.

Jan: 'Oh, April, I really have a big buyer today. This one could get me out of debt. You won't mind watching my children for a while, would you?'

April: 'What do you mean by "a while"? How long will you be gone?'

Jan: 'Oh, I don't know exactly. This is a hot one though, and it shouldn't take more than an hour or two.'

April: 'Let me think a moment . . . Lately, Jan, when I have watched the kids, you have been tied up for longer than you expected and I have no way to phone you. So, I really cannot risk being tied up with the kids today, and I will have to say no.'

Jan: 'April, what can I say? I need your help so that I can make this sale.'

April: 'I really have to say no, Jan.'

Jan: 'Well, I suppose I could call a babysitter.'

April: 'That would be great! I'm glad you understand. Let me know whether or not you close the deal.'

Exercising your right to refuse and giving yourself time to evaluate requests made of you are both active ways to protect your resources. Any valuable resource, when drawn upon frequently, will become depleted within a short time. When that resource is your energy, time, or love, knowing how to protect it is vitally important to your happiness.

'Enough Is Enough'

Kim, a college student, was an active participant in several major campus organizations. She maintained a high scholastic average and spent several hours each day studying before attending one of her many meetings. Kim's reputation as a 'natural leader' grew along with her list of organization meetings and appointments. Kim was vitally interested and involved in all of her activities. She didn't want to drop any of them, even though she frequently felt too tired to enjoy an evening out with her friends. After one particularly exhausting week, Kim decided to see a doctor for a routine check-up. Kim was found to have mononucleosis, and as a result she was instructed to withdraw from college for the term to have complete rest. For Kim, trying to do too much resulted in not being able to do anything at all.

Beth is a talented photographer who enjoys her work. She encountered such an enthusiastic demand for her services that she spent every minute trying to satisfy all of the requests for her time. She didn't want to refuse anyone because she really loved photography, and enjoyed spending time on it. But Beth's talent also became her liability as her schedule became heavier and heavier, and her free time began to disappear. Beth wisely began to refuse some photography assignments, worked to stabilize her schedule, and successfully protected her talent and her enjoyment.

Giving yourself time to evaluate requests made of you will also protect your resources. You don't have to commit yourself to something as soon as you are asked to do it. 'Let me think it over and get back to you' is an important statement to make.
Before you make your decision, ask yourself:
- Do I want to do this, or am I trying to please someone else?
- What will I receive for my participation?
- If I decide to do this, will it continue to be rewarding or will it become oppressive?

'No' Without Guilt

For many women, saying no elicits an immediate feeling of guilt, regardless of the appropriateness of the refusal. The following situations show you how saying no can be an effective – and guilt-free – process. As you read them, look for the broken record technique as well as others we have mentioned. Imagine yourself in the situations as you read them, and practice feeling good about saying no. As we have noted before, real life situations will not always go this smoothly, but these examples help illustrate an assertive approach.

'My Car Is In the Garage'

Carol has taken her car into the garage to be repaired. The mechanic gave her an estimate of £25 for the repairs. When she returns to pick up her car, she is told that the repairs come to £50. Carol asks to see the manager, and tells him that the price is much higher than the estimate that she was given, and that she feels the higher charges are not justified. The manager begins a lengthy description of all repairs performed on her car. Carol listens carefully, and replies that she still believes the charges are much too high. She adds that she will contact the Consumers' Association to complain about the charges, and that she doesn't wish to bring her car to this garage in the future. The manager consults with the mechanic and upon his return, concedes that the mechanic had made an error in the computation, and the charges will be £25. Carol pays the charges and resolves to find a more trustworthy garage.

'It's Not Quite What I Want.'

Debbie has been shopping for a sturdy bookcase. She enters a department store and asks the salesperson to show her several bookcases. The salesperson shows her many different models, but none of them are quite suitable for Debbie's needs. Debbie tells the salesperson that she doesn't think any of them are, suitable and the salesperson takes her to another section of the store where there are several more models. After disassembling one of them to demonstrate how sturdily built it is, the salesperson asks Debbie if she doesn't think it would do. Debbie feels quite empathetic toward the salesperson because of all the time and effort he took to show her the bookcases, but she has not found what she wanted. She thanks the salesperson for all the help, and states that the bookcases aren't quite what she had in mind. She leaves the store, glad that she didn't buy something that she really didn't like, despite the salesperson's extra efforts.

'Would You Stay with the Kids Tonight?'

Kay's parents request that she do quite a bit of babysitting for her brothers and sisters. Her parents are very active, and Kay is often asked to babysit four or five nights a week. As a result, Kay is missing out on many social activities with her friends. Kay has tried sulking and moping around the house without any success. She decides to try to openly explain her feelings to her parents and reach some kind of compromise. When she does, her parents are surprised and indignant. Kay repeats her feelings calmly, explaining the situation and emphasizing that she would very much like to participate in some social acitivities of her own. She adds that she would be willing to babysit once or twice a week, but says that babysitting four or five times a week is really unreasonable. Her parents feel that her solution is a good one and they agree to get another babysitter for other times. Kay feels good about the outcome and does not feel that she has 'let her parents down.'

'But What About Grandfather?'

Suzanne's 80-year-old grandfather has been bedridden for several months. Suzanne is particularly fond of him, and she often seeks his opinion on matters that are very important to her. Recently, however, he has been demanding to see Suzanne more often and asking her to read to him for several hours at a time. Suzanne wants to comfort her grandfather in whatever ways she can, but his requests are interfering with her other activities. She doesn't want to hurt her grandfather's feelings, but she feels she must find a way to say no to his requests. Suzanne tells her grandfather that she would really like to help as much as possible, and explains her other responsibilities. She gently tells him that she doesn't have enough time to comply with all his requests, but that she will do whatever she is able to help him. Her grandfather says that he understands her situation, and that he is glad she didn't try to 'humour' him or treat him condescendingly. They both look forward to future happy visits.

A Resource Checklist

The first step in protecting your resources and making your strengths work *for* you is identifying what personal strengths *you* have and want to preserve. Check as many as apply to you.

● What do you spend a large part of your time doing?
—— cooking, laundry

—— studying, reading
—— working away from home
—— driving
—— attending school
—— caring for children, family members
—— pursuing hobby (photography, writing, etc.)
—— watching TV, movies
—— entertaining
—— other

● What specific requests are regularly made of you?
—— driving
—— doing errands
—— working overtime
—— attending meetings, accepting leadership positions
—— talking with friends, counselling friends
—— donating time or volunteering for worthy causes
—— travelling
—— other

● What tasks or situations do your family and friends frequently call on you to help with?
—— housecleaning
—— cooking
—— chauffeuring
—— watching the children
—— loaning money
—— visiting and caring for relatives
—— other

● If you feel proficient in certain areas, do you leave yourself enough time to enjoy 'doing your thing'?

Give some thought to these questions and try to identify the resources you have by looking closely at your answers. They will give you an idea of the resources you draw upon often and need to protect.

The assertive woman can say 'no' to requests when she is already busy, and she can give herself time to decide what she will do. By exercising these two options, she protects her strengths and prevents them from becoming her liabilities.

Chapter 14

Manipulation

*Women have the same desires as men, but do not have
the same right to express them.*
– Jean Jacques Rousseau

When women have been denied access to direct means to attain
their desired goals, they have had to rely on indirect, or manipulative, methods as their primary means to for power and control.
From childhood, many women learn to 'wrap him around her little
finger,' to 'play it cool,' or to 'play hard to get.'

The message on a 1987 glossy cover fashion magazine hailed 'The
Return of Hard-To-Get (Smart Girls Don't Phone First).' Are they
serious? Yes and no. While the author does not suggest that women
should trap unsuspecting males into making the first move, she does
base her argument on the notion that there is value in subtlety.
Extravagant gestures – sending a huge bouquet of flowers to a man
after the first date, or writing long letters or cute notes too early in
the relationship – should be used very carefully, if at all, cautions
this writer. So it's not that trickery is being recommended. The
message seems to be: a straightforward, assertive approach by a
woman eliminates the thrill of the chase. It's just not *fun* to be
assertive any more!

We agree that subtlety has a lot going for it – but ot take it a step
or two beyond, it's easy to see how women have become passive
targets for manipulative actions – motivated by guilt, shame, or a
sense of duty to do another's bidding. That is the key and important
distinction.

We define manipulation, then, as the conscious or unconscious use of *indirect* and *dishonest* means to achieve a desired goal. Still, persistent assertion is sometimes confused wtih manipulation. Acting in a persistent manner – using the 'broken record technique' to repeat a direct assertive message, for example – may be powerful (and potentially harmful to a relationship), but it is not manipulative.

Manipulation can be persistent and extremely persuasive, but it is characteristically indirect: *what is said is not necessarily what is meant*. Persistent assertions are honest and straightforward, and the assertive person will act for herself, but will not choose for others. Manipulation is deceptive, and the manipulator is acting through indirect means to get someone to do something. The manipulator will 'set it up' in such a way that you feel that you have no choice but to do as she wishes. There is just too much riding on it to refuse.

'I'll Try to Finish Everything'

To illustrate this difference, suppose two flatmates had planned to do some house cleaning together on a particular evening. Iris is just starting to assemble the vacuum cleaner when Doris says that she has to attend a very important meeting that same evening, and cannot help with the cleaning. Doris suggests that they postpone the cleaning until the following evening. If Iris responds in her usual non-assertive, manipulative manner, the situation will be something like this:

Iris: (sheepishly): 'Do you really have to go? I mean, we had planned to do it all tonight.'

Doris: (firmly) 'Yes, I really should go. I'd hate to miss the meeting, even though we had planned to clean the house (weakening). You don't mind, do you?'

Iris: (actually minding very much) 'Oh *no*, Doris. You go right ahead. I'll just do it all *somehow*' (sounding pained and overwhelmed).

Doris: (feeling guilty) 'Well, maybe I could miss the meeting to help you – are you sure we couldn't do it tomorrow night?'

Iris: 'No, I really couldn't. I promised to help with voter registration, and you know how important that is (sounding overburdened). But, you just go on. I'll try to finish everything.'

Doris: (feeling even guiltier and colluding with Iris) 'No, Iris, I'll stay and help you. It's really too big a job for one person anyway. I'll just skip the meeting.'

Iris succeeds in getting Doris to stay home and help her clean by playing on Doris's guilt. Iris felt that it would be too aggressive to state honestly that she wanted Doris to help her. Although she genuinely cares for Doris and didn't want to hurt her, Iris' manipulation is really destructive to honest, assertive communication. In this example, Doris is left feeling angry and resentful toward Iris.

'I Don't Want to Do It All Myself'

Suppose the same situation were handled assertively by both Iris and Doris. Notice the differences between our manipulative encounter and the use of persistent assertion:

Iris: 'I was counting on cleaning the house tonight, Doris, and I'm upset that you've made other plans' (honest, straightforward).

Doris: 'I can understand that you're upset, Iris. Cleaning is a big job, and both of us should try to share it. This meeting is really important to me, though, and I want to attend it tonight. Can we get together after the meeting to arrange another time to clean?'

Iris: Yes, that would make me feel better. But I'm still upset that we can't do it tonight, and I don't want to do it all myself' (takes responsibility for feelings).

Doris: 'I really do understand how you feel. It's frustrating to have plans changed at the last minute. The meeting is important to me. I really want to go to it' (persistent, honest assertion). 'I'll be home about nine; so let's talk then and arrange a time that's good for both of us.'

Iris: 'Okay, I'm glad you understand how I feel. See you later.'

In this example, Iris and Doris effectively and assertively communicated with each other. Both women are honest and take responsibility for their feelings, without resorting to indirectly aggressive or manipulative techniques. Their trust, and their friendship, remains strong and intact.

Emotional Blackmail

Emotional blackmail is manipulation at its most powerful. The emotional blackmailer, consciously or unconsciously, is able to coerce a victim into a particular action by playing on the victim's compassion, fear or guilt. Emotional blackmailers, as well as other manipulators, find ideal targets in women trapped by compassion. Because compulsively compassionate women place others' wishes and feelings ahead of their own, they are easily exploited, and can be made to feel guilty simply for thinking of their own feelings and needs.

Emotional blackmail can only take place under certain conditions. Typically, it involves two people who have established a close personal or intimate relationship (mother and daughter; husband and wife; sister and sister; two close friends). Note, however, that just because you have a close relationship with someone does not mean you will end up as a blackmailer or victim!

This is how it works: once a close relationship is established, the blackmailer will interact with the victim in the best, and sometimes the only way she/he knows: through indirect manipulation. The victim must care for or love the blackmailer. The blackmailer always has something the victim wants – usually love or attention – in return. The blackmailer can coerce the victim into a particular action (or prevent the victim from doing something) by capitalizing on the victim's emotions. The victim will remain blackmailed as long as she continues to fear the consequences of escaping the blackmail trap (which usually involves fear of losing the blackmailer's love). As with other manipulative actions, for the manipulation to be successful, the victim of emotional blackmail must be made to collude with the blackmailer.

The following examples of emotional blackmail illustrate the subtlety of the manipulative process.

'Women's Night Out'

Situation: A woman is getting ready to leave for her womens' group meeting one evening when her husband says to her: 'Well, a "woman's night out" with the girls is fine. I have my night out, too. But you share our personal intimate secrets with them! I am always the villain. How could you humiliate me like that? You must not value our relationship as much as I do if you are willing to make it common knowledge to all those women. I just don't know how long I can take this. If I leave you, you'll know it's not because *I* let *you* down.'

Result: The woman (victim) decides she'd rather cancel her meeting than feel guilty for causing her husband (blackmailer) so much pain.

A more assertive, honest message from the blackmailer might be: 'I'm upset about you going to your meeting because I'm afraid you'll become so independent that you won't need me for anything anymore.'

'Letter of Recommendation'

Situation: Two close friends are discussing the difficulty of getting a good job in their field. Iris has a lead on a job opening, and has asked April if she would submit a letter of recommendation to the prospective employer. April doesn't feel she can write an informative letter because she has never worked with Iris and knows nothing specific about Iris' skills. Iris pleads with April to write the letter anyway: 'Look, we've been friends for a long time. You know me better than anyone. If you were *really* my friend, you'd write the letter. If you really cared, you'd do it.'

Result: April (victim) decides to write the letter for Iris (blackmailer) to save the friendship.

A more honest and assertive message from Iris could be: 'I'm afraid you won't write the letter for me, and I really need your help.'

' Don't Be Too Friendly'

Situation: A man and a woman are on their way to a party where there will be many mutual friends. As they are driving, the man says, 'You know, it would be a good idea if you didn't talk to John too much tonight. I know he's a friend of mine, and I like him, but I worry about what people will think if they see you talking with him. His divorce hasn't been final very long, and if you talk to him alone, it would make people wonder what was wrong between us. What's more, you are wearing a very revealing dress.'

Result: The woman (victim) decides she'll avoid talking with John (collusion) because she certainly wouldn't want to give a poor impression of herself or worry the man (blackmailer) she's with.

A more direct message from the blackmailer might be: 'I'm feeling insecure and jealous, because I know other people find you attractive. I'm afraid you might leave me for someone else.'

All of us may be tempted to blackmail or manipulate someone close to us at some time. We also can be victims of emotional blackmail. The main thing to remember is that manipulative tactics are destructive for relationships and for you as a person. Learning to recognize and to counteract manipulative attempts will help you to be more assertive and honest in your dealings with others, without the potentially disastrous side effects of manipulation (distrust, resentment).

The Question Trap

Before you can deal effectively with manipulation, you have to be able to recognize it when it happens. One manipulative strategy is the use of questions. This can be a strong manipulative weapon against women, because we have been taught not only that we must answer all questions asked of us, but we must also answer immediately and truthfully. Manipulators rely on that when they use questions dishonestly.

One example of a manipulative 'trap' question is a 'why' question. Although 'why' questions can also be used appropriately, without hidden motives, more frequently 'why' questions are not questions at all, but disguised statements or accusations. Putting a statement in a 'why' question form evades responsibility for the statement. Typically the person asking already knows the answer, but is really trying to corner you or to start an argument. Other questions can be used in the same deceptive way as the chart indicates:

Why Question	*Really Means*
'Why were you so late?'	'I don't think you should have been so late.'
'Why can't you keep your room clean?'	'I don't think you should leave your room so messy.'

Additional Deceptive Questions	Really Means
'Why were you so rude with me?'	'I don't think you should be so rude with me.'
(A parent, knowing the daughter/son has *not* taken the rubbish out yet):	
'Have you taken out the rubbish?'	'I want you to take out the rubbish.'
(A spouse, knowing the other has *not* called the restaurant to make dinner reservations):	
'Have you called the restaurant for reservations?'	'I want you to call the restaurant to make dinner reservations.'

The peril in using questions manipulatively is that you teach others not to trust your questions. If asked a manipulative 'why' question, an assertive woman may decide not to answer. She knows she doesn't *have* to answer any question she's asked. An especially effective reply to the why question or deceptive question is, 'Why do you ask?' This usually causes the questioner to say what she/he really means.

Another manipulative approach is the use of particular phrases that actually mean the opposite of what they sound. These, again, are designed to allow the manipulator to avoid taking responsibility. Some common examples of these 'red flag' words and phrases are:

Red Flag Words	Often Really Means
'I don't know.'	'I really do know but I don't want to take responsibility for it.'

Red Flag Words	Often Really Means
'I can't.'	'I won't.'
'I'll try.'	'I won't.'
'I should.'	'I don't want to,' or 'I won't.'

When you hear these phrases, mentally send up a little red flag to signal you to be prepared for a deceptive statement. Unless you really mean it, avoid using these phrases yourself.

Deactivate Your Buttons

A third manipulative tactic is 'word loading.' Only people who know you fairly well can use this one to manipulate you, because it depends on being able to identify your vulnerabilities, or 'buttons.' The manipulator will try to get to you by pushing your button. If you are sensitive about your weight, a manipulator can push your 'weight' button by calling you a 'fat slob.' If you are sensitive about your intelligence, the manipulator can push your 'intelligence' button by calling you 'ignorant' or 'brainy.' If you hate to disappoint anyone, a manipulator can tell you that you have 'disappointed me.' The best protection against this kind of manipulation is to be able to identify what your 'buttons' are. Then you can practice 'deactivating' them by learning *not* to react automatically, so a would-be manipulator can't catch you off balance.

With a friend, make up your button list. Exchange lists, and read each vulnerability aloud as realistically as possible, while you practice *not* responding to them. Use the check list to identify the buttons that apply to you and include some of your own.

Button List

- Being told I disappoint someone.
- Being told I am unreliable or untrustworthy.
- Being told that I smoke too much, bite my nails, or some other bad habit.
- Being told that I am overweight (or underweight).
- Being teased about my freckles, new hair style, style of dress.

- Being ridiculed or teased about my sex, home town, accent, race, or income bracket.
- Other items that make you feel vulnerable:

Not responding will involve controlling your facial muscles so you don't automatically smile or laugh nervously. It will include controlling whatever anxiety responses you usually feel when someone has pushed your button.

Practise relaxation as you listen to your friend. What you are doing is exercising your choice not to react, and giving yourself a feeling of control. When you can go through all of your buttons on your lists without reacting with undue anxiety or hostility, you will have made it difficult for the buttons to control you, and you can thwart a button-pusher's attempts to manipulate you. This isn't as easy as it sounds. You may be unable to deactivate your buttons alone. Consulting a professional counsellor or therapist can provide you with the extra support you may need.

Counter-Manipulation
There are two major counter-manipulation techniques you can use when you feel you are being 'set up' as a victim. By using counter-manipulation, you refuse to be manipulated and you promote assertive communication. The first technique is to respond to what is said, not to what you know is meant. In our first example with the two flatmates, April could have responded only to what Iris actually *said*, instead of responding to what she knew Iris meant:

'You Go Right Ahead.'
Iris: (sheepishly) 'Do you really have to go? I mean, we had planned to do it all tonight.'

April: (firmly) 'Yes, I really want to go. I'd hate to miss the meeting even though we had planned to clean the house.'

Iris: 'Well, you go right ahead. I really don't mind at all. I'll do it all somehow. Really, April, it's fine with me' (meaning that it's not fine at all).

April: 'That's great, Iris. I'm glad you understand. I'll see you later.'

'Fighting fire with fire' as in this example, will not permanently solve the problem, but it will solve the immediate communication problem and keep you from being a victim. Using this counter-manipulation strategy will also discourage the manipulator from trying again.

'Reading Between the Lines'

The second strategy can help cut through manipulation to encourage assertive, honest communication. It involves 'reading between the lines' and getting the manipulator to be honest about what she/he really wants. There are three components of this process:

- *Parroting:* Repeating back exactly what was said to you.
- *Summarizing:* Verifying what was said to you by summarizing it and asking for acknowledgement.
- *Reflection:* Reading between the lines: 'You seem angry with me.'

To demonstrate how you can use these techniques to cut through manipulation, let's go back to our two flatmates again. This time, April will be able to get Iris to say what she really means, because she knows how to handle manipulation with the three techniques:

Iris: (sheepishly) 'Do you really have to go? I mean, we had planned to do the cleaning tonight.'

April: (firmly) 'Yes, I really want to go. I'd hate to miss the meeting, even though we had planned to clean house."

Iris: (actually very angry) "Well, I really don't mind. You go on ahead. I'll just try to do it somehow. Really, I don't mind."

April: (parroting) 'You don't mind that I'm going to the meeting tonight, Iris?'

Iris: (minding very much) 'No, I can understand (sounding terribly overburdened). You have to go to the meeting, and that's it. (Voice louder) I'll just stay here. I'm pretty tired – I've been busy – but you go ahead.'

April: (summarizing) 'Are you saying that you don't mind my going to the meeting, Iris? That means you would have to do the cleaning . . .'

Iris: (interrupting) 'Right – I don't mind. I can see why you don't want to do the cleaning.'

April: (reflection) 'You seem angry that I'm going to the meeting instead of helping you clean the house.'

Iris: (lying) (voice louder) 'Me? Of course not! Go ahead to your meeting.'

April: (reflection) (gently) 'Iris, you do seem upset to me.'

Iris: (beginning to say what she really feels) 'Well, I guess I am a little upset.'

April: (reflection) 'Yes – and I would be, too.'

Iris: 'You would?'

April: (reflection) 'Sure, I'd probably feel deserted and as if you didn't care about helping with the cleaning at all.'

Iris: (honest) 'Yes, that's really it. I don't want you to leave me with all the cleaning. I guess I'm pretty angry about it.'

April: 'I'm really glad I know how you feel now. I do have to attend the meeting, though. Why don't we get together after it's over and plan a time to do the cleaning together?'

Iris: 'Okay. I'd feel better then, and maybe we could figure out some way to plan the cleaning for a good time for both of us – so other things don't get in the way.'

April: 'That's a great idea. See you in a couple of hours' (supporting Iris for being honest).

This discussion resulted in assertive communication, with both April and Iris feeling good about the decision: April attended her meeting, Iris expressed how she *really* felt, and the cleaning remained a cooperative project.

When you try these strategies, keep in mind that it may take a little longer to accomplish than the others, but the results are worth the effort. Keep your voice even and well-modulated. It takes some self-control and patience, but if you do that, and learn to use the other counter-manipulation guidelines we've presented, you can be confident that you don't have to consent to being a helpless 'victim' of even an experienced 'set up operator's' plans to blackmail or manipulate you. You can be an assertive woman.

Summary

Manipulation is a matter of playing fast and loose with both circumstances and people until a desired goal is achieved: he feels so guilty that he won't play golf today and spend time with me instead; she's so uncomfortable and self-conscious after I asked her that question about her weight that she won't be able to upstage me for once. What is said produces anxiety, guilt, remorse, or some other uncomfortable reaction in another person, often resembling a jab at a particularly tender spot. And precisely because a manipulative exchange is indirect, a manipulator can always deny that she or he had any dishonourable or hidden intentions.

At the same time it's important to remember that manipulation is not always a conscious, deliberate, calculated strategy. The indirect approach, focused as it is on motivation through guilt or regret, is one way to get what you want if you don't have the courage or the skill to get it straightforwardly. It may have been the only way you could get what you wanted as a child in your family, for example, if direct, assertive approaches were thought rude or impolite.

In this chapter, we've defined manipulation and illustrated ways to recognize it and respond to it. We have also looked at some of the more persistent forms of manipulation that you may recognize in your own behaviour. Manipulation is directly opposite assertiveness in one key way: accepting responsibility for one's own feelings and decisions is a hallmark of assertiveness, while manipulative, indirect encounters are focused on avoiding or denying responsibility.

Although manipulation can sometimes be effective in the short run, the price is *very* high: when the manipulator's intentions are discovered, the relationship is diminished (or even finished), and the 'victim' thinks primarily of revenge.

Chapter 15

Asserting Your Sensuality

> *To look at me, you'd never suspect I was a semi-*
> *nonorgasmic woman. This means it was possible for me to*
> *have an orgasm – but highly unlikely.*
> *To me, the term 'sexual freedom' meant freedom from*
> *having to have sex. And then along came Good Vibrations.*
> *And was I surprised! Now I am a regular Cat on a Hot Tin*
> *Roof.*
> 'Trudy, the Bag Lady'
> – Lily Tomlin and Jane Wagner
> *The Search for Signs of*
> *Intelligent Life in the Universe*

In the mid-1970's, when *The Assertive Woman* was new, the United States was experiencing what has been called 'the sexual revolution.' A flood of 'how-to' books accompanied this rather sudden lifting of the veil of human sexuality. Some of this material was very helpful; some was destructive, inaccurate, and sexist. Psychologist and established author Albert Ellis clearly described what's wrong with many of the most popular books on sex in his excellent book, *The Sensuous Person: Critique and Corrections.* Masters and Johnson's extensive research on sexuality, widely reported, was also extremely helpful in dispelling sexual myths.

What progress have we made in matters sexual? After experiencing a 'sexual revolution,' dropping old taboos, and creating new ones, are we better off in the 1980's than we were in the 1970's? Or, have we regressed? What do the 1990's hold? . . . and after the year 2000?

A Historical Perspective

In 1972, the Boston Women's Health Book Collective published their first edition of *Our Bodies, Ourselves*, a breakthrough compendium of women's health information. A general guide to women's physical health issues, the book exhorted women to take responsibility for their well being. Not only did Barbach say women deserved as many orgasms as they wanted, she gave explicit exercises to assist them in reaching maximum orgasmic potential.

In 1975, in her book *For Yourself: The Fulfillment of Female Sexuality*, Lonnie Barbach advanced the concept of personal liberation for women as sexual human beings. She suggested that women could – and should – assume full responsibility for their sexuality.

Sexual liberation meant freedom to choose the kinds of sexual activities and stimulation that were most pleasurable. And it meant the freedom *not* to do what failed to meet your values or needs – freedom to be in control of the most intimate part of your life.

The decade of the 1980's brought a crescendo of exciting information about female sexuality. The 'G-spot,' named after German gynaecologist and sex researcher, Ernst Grafenberg, was rediscovered. His theory that there are two kinds of orgasms – clitoral and vaginal, including female ejaculation – resurrected an old controversy, and argued with Masters and Johnson's sex research.

Lonnie Barbach's second book, *For Each Other: Sharing Sexual Intimacy*, gave women a complete programme for dealing with the complex physical and psychological aspects of sexual satisfaction in relationships. And yes, it did include a G-Spot stimulation exercise, along with many other exercises to promote sexual expression.

Meanwhile, women felt stepped-up social pressure to enhance their sexuality. 'Satisfaction' was no longer enough. Only virtuoso sexual performances would do. Against this backdrop, Dr. Barbach and TV's 'Dr. Ruth' Westheimer offered frank, sensible guidance about sexual and sensual assertiveness.

In the mid-1980's the sexual revolution was declared 'over' by the media, and attention turned to some downside outcomes: an epidemic of AIDS, widespread herpes, battles over abortion rights, child sexual abuse, resistance to condom ads on TV.

Responses to the potential dangers have ranged from improved education and access to information to less noble, more controversial answers: newsagents pulled *Playboy*, *Penthouse*, and other adult magazines off their shelves; television networks refused to air advertising for condoms; the Pornography Commission, headed by Attorney General Edwin Meese in the U.S. published a compendium of graphic, detailed summaries of hundreds of X-rated films and videos.

Putting our heads in the sand even caught the talented eye of cartoonist Garry Trudeau, who featured condoms in a series of his immensely popular 'Doonesbury' strip. (Perhaps predictably, some major newspapers threatened to pull the offending strips.)

Social Attitudes Affect Sensuality

In the Victorian era, a hundred years ago, women believed that they were asexual; they denied or distorted authentic sensual sensations. Now, some women force themselves into unwanted sexual encounters or acrobatics, believing the modern message that women are tirelessly orgasmic and should pursue sexual pleasure at all costs.

These social attitudes affect men too. Society's expectation that men be amorous Don Juans pressured men into a mode of compulsive sex. Many men responded non-assertively, forcing themselves to be sexual because they thought it was expected of them.

In the early '80's *Playboy* magazine featured an article which attributed male sexual impotence to intimidating, overbearing feminist sexuality. It was completely untrue. Women certainly did not dream up aggressive sexual schemes to 'even the score' with men. Women were attempting, finally, to be assertive – to enjoy sex themselves.

Some Positive Changes

Although we are still grappling with conflicting societal messages, new taboos, and increasingly complex challenges to our sensual and sexual freedoms, there is a strong emerging commitment in women and in men to achieve balance and mutuality in sexual relationships. Old traditions are crumbling. We are beginning to see positive changes.

We have, fortunately, outgrown those traditions. In the 1986 edition of their assertiveness book, *Your Perfect Right*, psychologists Robert Alberti and Michael Emmons depict past and current sexual expectations for women and men. Here are a few ideas adapted from their list:

- Women expect equality today, rather than passivity.
- Women initiate and communicate their enjoyment rather than remaining silent.
- Women are becoming straightforward, honest and confident sexually.
- Men are becoming much more expressive emotionally – demonstrating a new openness.
- Macho male expectations are giving way to vulnerability, involvement, gentleness and patience.
- Equality and responsiveness in men is replacing exploitation and score keeping.

We cannot overstate the importance of mutuality; the sensually assertive woman shares much more sexual and sensual responsibility than did the docile doves of the past.

What is Sensuality?

Sensuality involves not only an appreciation of your bodily senses but also an ability to experience your environment through sight, sound, smell, taste, and touch in a direct, straightforward way. The assertive woman allows nothing to inhibit her from feeling alive, energetic, and sensitive to life.

April feels free to go to an art show and experience it in a completely visual way that is unique and personal for her, without feeling compelled to provide intellectual interpretations for those around her or to justify her likes and dislikes. She can be turned on to something she sees regardless of what others think. Similarly, her music, her enjoyment of the sounds of the natural outdoors, babies cooing, her own voice, even, are all open for her pleasure.

You need not be shy about your sense of taste. Allow yourself to explore different tastes whether they be food, drink, or the tastes of your lover. Keep your body clean, and do not be afraid of how you may taste to your lover. April does not feel obligated to buy products designed to make her taste or smell unlike her own clean, beautiful, natural self. An assertive woman need not live in paranoia about the way she tastes or smells.

Take full advantage of your sense of touch. Allow yourself to compare the softness of your own skin to the softness of a rose petal, or another woman's skin, or to the head of the male penis. April is not inhibited about sensing her environment through touch. This naturally extends, of course, into sexuality. Your sexuality can be expressed along with your sensual self. Sensuality is not limited to genital sex. It includes the pleasure derived from the use of all your senses, regardless of whether or not there is genital contact.

The Sensually Assertive Woman

The assertive woman becomes sensually assertive by getting to know herself better. She experiences herself and her environment freely and joyously through all of her senses – sight, taste, smell, sound, and touch. She explores her sexual attitudes to discover where she may be inhibited. She also explores her physical self through techniques that range from reading about female physiology to actually exploring her own body through masturbation, taking a look at another woman's body closely, or looking at herself with mirrors.

To believe that her own sensual and sexual needs and desires are legitimate, as real as any other feelings she has, is another important way a woman can be sensually assertive. The assertive woman knows that she has options about how she expresses her sensuality. Nothing is wrong if she chooses for her own pleasure something that is not destructive to another person.

The sensually assertive woman explores her environment with others. She feels free to discuss sexuality with other women and with men. She strives for mutuality in a sexual relationship; she knows that she and her partner can exchange roles, that they can experiment with various levels of passivity or assertiveness in lovemaking. She can do *anything* she wants to do as long as she isn't destructive to herself or her partner. Being open, honest, and direct about sexual expression is the key to enhancement of sensuality.

Know Thyself. Look at yourself to learn your own unique sensual/

sexual responses and patterns. This step is very active and may involve an exploration of your own fantasy life. You can learn a great deal from your fantasies, and come to a greater acceptance of your sensual/sexual preferences. Self-knowledge can liberate you from a passive, solely responsive sex life. Knowing your preferences may also include exploration of your body. It is important for you to know what feels good to you instead of passively expecting your partner to read your mind. You should not be afraid to explore your body's sensations and responses. The most personal and accurate way to learn about your own sexuality is through masturbation. This, of course, is a *choice* you have as a woman. We are not writing a defence of masturbation, but strongly suggest that you consider how masturbation may assist you in becoming a more sensually assertive woman. Perhaps you have not allowed yourself to consider the knowledge and research about masturbation which is available to you.

Your Needs Are Real. The next step in becoming sensually assertive is being able to see that your sensual/sexual needs and feelings are as real and legitimate as any other feelings you have. Once you accept the legitimacy of your own sensuality, you need to be able to express it directly and honestly. You can do this verbally as well as nonverbally. The important thing is that *you do it.* It's dishonest to pretend to be interested only in giving pleasure or in liking no more than what you get by chance!

Express Yourself. Along with honesty of expression, another aspect of becoming more sensually assertive is to allow yourself to open up to different kinds of sensual/sexual expression. This means looking at other possibilities besides the standard penis/vagina, man-on-top, male-initiated, orgasm-oriented sexuality. Being assertive means learning that you have choices and then feeling free to exercise these options.

A Sexual Look At April and Her Friends

We've outlined, in the chart on the next page, some of the ways the 'Four Women We All Know' might exercise their options; some of this material has been adapted (with permission) from Alberti and Emmons' sexual communication types.

	Characteristics	Thoughts	Expression	Feeling	Body Language	Her Options
DORIS DOORMAT	Hesitant Shy	He hurt my feelings by saying, "I'm not sexy tonight".	I'm sorry I'm not sexy	Hurt Irritated	Hidden	No way! I could **never** say anything.
AGATHA AGGRESSIVE	Demanding Pushy Insistent	He's got to change. He'd better learn some new techniques!	Can't you get with it? Everyone is into this.	Hostile	Confrontive	If he doesn't shape up, I'll have an affair.
IRIS INDIRECT	Devious Manipulative Sneaky	Ugh! sex tonight . . . I'll fake a headache	Takes some asprin, looks distressed, sighs & rubs her head.	Disgusted	Subversive	What else can I do to avoid him?
APRIL ASSERTIVE	Honest Open Straight-forward	There hasn't been enough foreplay for me to be ready for intercourse yet.	I'd like us to take a little more time tonight. I'd enjoy more foreplay before intercourse.	Positive Bright	Open Forthright	I feel closer when I exercise the option to express my needs in a caring way.

Exploring Your Sensual Environment
The sensually assertive woman appreciates the many influences that
shape her sensuality, whether they be biological socio-political,
intellectual, or emotional. To know what factors you want to
change and then learning how to control them yourself only en-
hances sensual assertiveness. You can't just do this in your head – it
requires both full exploration of all your senses, and open discussion with others. Achieving *mutuality* in a relationship is the final
hallmark for those who are assertive, and is a beautiful reward for
those who are willing to risk being open, honest, and direct.

'Dr. Truth's' Personal Sensuality Survey

The following questions are designed to be a beginning toward
getting to know yourself – the first step in becoming sensually
assertive. Answer honestly in your journal.

- Have you ever indulged yourself in looking at a person or a thing
  that you found beautiful or interesting?
- How do you feel about smelling your natural body odours and
  those of your lover?
- Have you ever explored anything besides food with your tongue
  and let yourself really taste it?
- Under what circumstances do you let yourself sing out loud?
- How do you feel about making sounds or talking during lovemak-
  ing?
- Are there taboo words that you don't dare utter aloud to your
  lover?
- Why do you make love?
- Do you feel guilty when you masturbate?
- When you have sexual intercourse, do you always expect to have
  an orgasm? If not, where does this leave you and how do you feel?

- Do you always expect the same level or orgasmic response?
- Have you ever experienced sexual or sensual attraction toward
  another woman?
- If you are already committed to one person, how do you handle
  your sexual attraction toward others?
- If there is no lover in your life presently, do you feel worthless?

- Does your self-image depend more on what you think and feel about yourself or upon what you believe others feel and think about you?
- How do you communicate to your love what you expect in your love-making?
- Do you have fantasies that you would like to actualize?
- How do you share these fantasies with your lover?
- Who initiates experimentation in your lovemaking?

Sensual Fantasy

In your journal, write down, in as much detail as possible, your favourite sensual fantasy. Then share this fantasy with your sexual partner or someone to whom you feel close. Remember, sensuality includes more than sex. Decide how this fantasy can have any bearing on your ability to be a sensually assertive woman.

Exchanging Sexual Roles

This next exercise involves making a sincere effort toward acting out a role as honestly as you possibly can. Try switching roles for five minutes with your sexual partner, taking on each other's behaviour. If one of you is more passive or assertive, be sure to emphasise this when you switch. Exchange names, clothes, or any other props that will best help you to re-enact the other person. You can try this on three different levels:

a) centered on a domestic, routine situation you two usually get into around the house.

b) giving each other a massage, taking turns, and being sure to role-play how you see your partner giving the massage.

c) switch roles in your actual love-making situation, including verbal as well as non-verbal actions. This one may take more than five minutes!

After you have tried this role-reversal, discuss with each other how you felt about it, using the following questions as a guide:

Were you surprised at what your partner did or said?

How did you 'read' certain things?

What did you learn that was new?

Were you able to laugh with each other about things that appeared humourous?

If not, how can you best deal with each other's preferences?

Sexuality and Safety

In this day and age it doesn't pay to have a passive attitude about sex. Just as we have learned to manage time, communications, or a career, it is now in our best interests to learn about 'sexual management.'

Sexual abuse is a relatively new area of concern and study. There are many forms of sexual abuse, from obscene telephone calls to rape. Until recently, most information on avoiding sexual assault has focused on the most obvious – rape by a stranger. However, statistics show that most assaults occur in situations that are supposedly safe. For example, acquaintance or 'date rape' occurs where there is familiarity and trust – a seemingly safe relationship. In the book *No is Not Enough: Helping Teenagers Avoid Sexual Assault,* authors Caren Adams, Jennifer Fay, and Jan Loreen-Martin present a continuum of 'force,' a valuable framework which makes clear that the difference between consenting sex and sexual assault is not the *sex*, but the degree of *force* used. There is no force in freely consenting sex between two partners, but there are subtle increases in force that escalate from seduction, silent rape, bribery or coercion, acquaintance rape, to maximum-force stranger rape. Avoiding sexual assault is not merely a matter of staying away from dark alleys. It is the ability to read and respond to the more subtle, and dangerous, sexual signals – without hesitation or apology.

Harrassment. Sexual harrassment is difficult to define and respond to without guilt or fear. Adams, Fay, and Loreen-Martin define it as 'any repeated and unwanted sexual attention (verbal or physical) ranging from advances, suggestive looks, jokes, innuendos to explicit propositions and assaults which cause discomfort to a woman and interfere with her job or school performance.' Men can be harrassed too, but women are harrassed three times as often and suffer more serious negative results: inability to concentrate, anger, diminished self-confidence, sharply reduced job effectiveness.

Abusive Relationships. Sexual battering within families is a devastating form of physical violence that victimizes even those who merely observe it: children. It teaches childhood victims to become adult victimizers.

Whose Fault Is It, Anyway? Taking responsibility for oneself is generally agreed to be a quality of maturity. However, taking responsibility for what other people say or do is a trap. Too often women believe that if they 'had only tried harder' they could have avoided becoming targets for sexual abuse. Courts and other institutions often foster blame-the-victim thinking, colluding with men in rape cases by inferring that if the woman hadn't looked so sexy or in some other way led the rapist on, he wouldn't have reached the point of no return. How unfair it has been to blame women for inciting 'uncontrollable passions' in men! Rape is an issue of power, not sexuality. Women must be aware that their powerlessness is much more an incentive to male attackers than is their sexuality.

How Does An Assertive Woman Avoid Abuse? An assertive style is one of the best defences against sexual assault. Silent, trembling, pleas, or tears demonstrate to a would-be attacker that a woman is indeed helpless.

Healthy self-esteem and an assertive attitude may be your greatest sources of safety. People who are confident can identify unreasonable pressures and manipulations that might lead to abuse and assault. They invite respect.

Future Forecasts
As we have pointed out in this chapter, 'the sexual revolution' was only a beginning step in advancing the full expression of human sexuality. Researchers uncovered new data that dispelled old myths. Yet, as traditional obstacles crumbled, there were new hurdles to overcome.

One of the many paradoxes still unresolved is that we don't really know how to use all this 'freedom' and sexual information. Just because the media have kept information flowing about G-spots, AIDS, abortion, impotence, orgasms, condoms and pornography doesn't mean that everyone understands or is even willing to read or listen. And little of the information is directed toward open, frank discussions of people's fears and feelings. (Certainly a mixed message is television's explicit sexuality in programming and simultaneous refusal to air condom commercials. The broadcast industry is missing a major opportunity to contribute to the critical fight against AIDS with its concern for 'offending' a few viewers.)

There is still a sexual cover-up in our society: sexual issues are not addressed directly in public. We can meet the challenge *individually* as we approach the 21st century, however. Let's break open the communication barriers. Develop your skills at negotiating with your romantic partner for safe sex. Free yourself to discuss personal issues about everything from body odours, AIDS, and contraception to sexual preferences.

For you, asserting your sensuality may mean tuning in to the 'Dr. Ruth' show and discussing your reactions. It may be reading this chapter with your partner and completing the exercises together.

Chapter 16

The Anger in You

Twenty-Mile Zone

i was riding in my car
screaming at the night
screaming at the dark
screaming at fright
i wasn't doing nothing
just driving about
screaming at the dark
letting it out
that's all i was doing
just
letting it out

well along comes a motorcycle
very much to my surprise
i said officer was i speeding
i couldn't see his eyes
he said no you weren't speeding
and he felt where his gun was hung
he said lady you were screaming
at the top of your lung
and you were
doing it alone
you were doing it alone
you were screaming in your car
in a twenty-mile zone
you were doing it alone
you were doing it alone

i said i'll roll up all my windows
don't want to disturb the peace
i'm just a creature
who is looking
for a little release
i said
and what's so wrong with screaming
don't you do it at your games
when the quarterback
breaks an elbow
when the boxer beats and maims

but you were
doing it alone
you were doing it alone
you were screaming in your car
in a twenty-mile zone
you were doing it alone
you were doing it alone
you were screaming

i said animals roar
when they feel like
why can't we do that too
instead of screaming
banzai baby
in the war in the human zoo

you were screaming

he said i got to take you in now
follow me right behind
and let's have no more screaming
like you're out of your mind
so he climbed aboard his cycle
and his red-eyed headlight beamed
and his motor started spinning
and his siren screamed

he was doing it alone
he was doing it alone
he was screaming on his bike
in a twenty-mile zone
i was doing it alone
i was doing it alone
i was screaming in my car
in a twenty-mile zone
we were doing it together
we were doing it together
we were screaming at the dark
in a twenty-mile zone
we were doing it together
alone
in a twenty-mile zone

– Dory Previn

Dory Previn's lyrics poignantly illustrate the taboo that women have endured against overt expression of anger. Women have been taught that it is not 'lady-like' or feminine to show that they are angry. They have been intimidated by the threat of being called 'bitchy,' 'castrating,' 'nagging,' 'aggressive,' or 'masculine.' The Compassion Trap further prevents women from expressing negatives by making us feel guilty for even thinking of expressing anger or displeasure. After all, 'someone has to keep peace in the family.' Guess who that someone is? Women smile sweetly and grit their teeth hoping that no hint of their anger or hostility will be exposed.

Because anger is a powerful emotion, it is difficult for many women – who already feel a sense of powerlessness – to express. It is frightening for these women to 'play around with anger,' since they view it almost as a deadly weapon. To them, anger can only lead to violence. Actually, an assertive expression of anger has much more potential to *prevent* violence. Research shows that much domestic violence, even murder, is caused by people who could not express their anger in honest, non-destructive ways.

We can learn about anger, accept it, and learn to express it assertively. We need no longer deny that very real part of ourselves.

Anger Is Not Aggression!
Anger may be defined as an emotional reaction to feeling used or put down. There are many forms of anger, as well as aggression, including hostility and violence. However, some authors and anger theorists put assertion and aggression on the same continuum as though aggression were just an intensified form of assertion.

But assertion and aggression are completely different, as we've seen. Moreover, *anger is not aggression*. Anger is a legitimate *feeling* that may be *expressed* in passive, aggressive, indirect, or assertive ways. The following examples and discussion will help to sort out these often-confused concepts.

Modified Anger
'Modified anger' is a label given to expressing annoyance or irritation without really admitting that you are feeling angry: 'I'm fed up with this job. No, I'm not angry. I'm just sick and tired. That's all.

This type of anger is most often expressed by Doris, who mistakenly thinks that she is being assertive by complaining. Unfortunately, however, she usually complains to the wrong source, as in the following situation:

'Mirror, Mirror on the Wall . . .'
Doris: 'I bought this face cream to tighten my pores and clear up my complexion. Instead my face is covered with a rash, and now I look awful. This cream is useless and a total waste of money.'

April: 'You sound pretty cross about it. Why don't you return it and get your money back?'

Doris: 'Oh, I couldn't do that. I'm not really angry. I'm just disgusted with my skin problems. I should try something else.'

Indirect Anger

Another form of anger is 'indirect anger.' This is Iris' forte. She denies angry feelings and attempts to make the other person feel guilty. Here is an example of Iris being angry with her friend in an indirect way:

'*Leave Me*'

John: 'I'm leaving now, and won't see you until next week.'

Iris: 'Of course, I don't mind. Go right ahead. It doesn't bother me, I've been lonely before. I'm just disappointed that you want to leave me at a time like this. But, go right ahead anyway.'

It is important to mention that women also express anger indirectly through their sexuality. Sometimes 'holding out' sexually, seems the only way a woman who feels powerless communicates her resentment. If you find yourself holding back sexually, ask yourself why you're feeling distant. Is it because you're angry? What about? Are you frustrated because you did not handle another situation assertively? Also, if you find yourself being 'overly sweet' in a situation, look inside yourself to see if you are compensating for some residue of anger that you have not confronted.

Sometimes when Iris is 'overly sweet' (or even condescending and patronising), she is expressing hostility indirectly. This strategy often elicits a reciprocal indirect expression of anger also.

'*Some of My Best Friends Are Black*'

Iris: 'Just because you're black doesn't make any difference to me. I don't even notice that your hair is frizzy and all that stuff. I really like you. You're just like anybody else. It doesn't bother me the way you talk. I'm sure glad you joined our group.'

Angela: 'I'm really glad you let me into your group. I'll try not to notice that the rest of you are white. Some of my sisters think your group is racist because of the way you talk to us, like we were to be pitied because we don't look and talk like you. But, that doesn't make me angry. I just feel weird and left out sometimes.'

Iris may not recognize that Angela and others are repaying her for her insults. Iris will not change until she is directly confronted with her put-downs and how they affect others.

Violence

Although violence may be an overt, direct expression of anger, it usually is an overreaction. For example, Agatha often feels that she can only express her anger with insults, even physical abuse. You need not use violence to convince people that you mean business. Being assertive is enough to get this point across. However, when people have been frustrated in their attempt to express anger assertively, they may see violence as the only option left.

'Cry Rape'

Let's look at a situation which ignites so much anger that it can easily result in violence. Agatha's friend Joyce has been raped. She asks Agatha to help her go to the police. When Joyce and Agatha arrive, they are both treated disrespectfully. A police officer asks Joyce what she did to seduce the guy into going after her. Then he insinuates that she probably enjoyed it, or that she may be lying just to get some poor guy into trouble. Of course, this makes both women furious. Agatha calls the officer a 'sexist pig.' She threatens the officer, saying that he probably rapes women whenever he has the chance, that women have no rights when it comes to law enforcement, that all men are pigs and back each other up in doing violence to women. She is ready to spit on him, when he grabs her arm and shakes her. They get into a tussle and Agatha is arrested for assaulting a police officer.

In a situation like this, Agatha's anger is controlling her. She has a legitimate reason to be angered by the officer's humiliating remarks and behaviour, but her behaviour only escalates the tension and provides no support for Joyce.

Assertive Anger

It is easy to recognize assertive anger because it is expressed clearly and directly. It is not physically or verbally abusive. April, in Agatha's situation, would let the officer know that she is angry by stating her feelings this way:

April: 'I have accompanied my friend because she has been raped. This is not a joke. I am angry when I see you refuse to take her seriously. She has been humiliated once, and there is no need

for her to be humiliated again. I would appreciate it if you treated
her with kindness and respect.'

Recognizing your anger is the first step toward learning how to
deal with it. Once you notice the feeling, it is important to admit it to
yourself as real. Women deny their anger even after they recognise
it because they don't believe they have a valid reason for it. They
may feel it is aggressive, or unreasonable. Recognizing anger is not
just an intellectual exercise; it is actually being in touch with the
emotional feeling of anger.

Once you accept your angry feelings, identify the source of your
anger. *Where* is it coming from? It is easy to blame somebody else
for your anger either out of guilt or perhaps to save face in an
embarrassing situation. Be sure that you identify the real source.

Next, look at *why* you are angry. It may be more convenient to
get angry over something small and irritating rather than face the
real cause of your anger, which may be a major disappointment or
unfulfilled expectation.

Many women have lived through years of unexpressed anger. It
seems a woman in this position must, when first she becomes aware
of her anger, go through an 'angry phase,' in which she is angry a
great deal of the time. This phase usually lasts a few months, until
she begins to deal with her anger *appropriately* and *realistically*.
This last step can be called assertive use of anger.

It's Your Choice

When you express anger assertively, the person with whom you are
angry may respond with backbiting, aggression, temper tantrums,
over-apologizing or revenge. The assertive woman may choose *not*
to assert herself when she is dealing with overly sensitive individuals, or if speaking up would be redundant. If she is appropriately understanding when another person is having difficulty, she may
decide not to assert herself at that moment – but the assertive
woman knows the difference between appropriate understanding
and the Compassion Trap. Last, she may choose not to assert
herself when she discovers that she is wrong.

Action Exercises

We started out this chapter with Dory Previn screaming on the roadway. Now we are going to ask you to do some 'screaming' too, but perhaps in your own home or another comfortable spot. Once you have found a room of your own, get together with a friend and try these exercises:

'X-Y-Z-1-2-3'

Sit facing another person. One of you choose 'letters' and the other 'numbers' to shout randomly at each other. Before you start, think of a situation or person with whom you are angry and get in touch with those feelings. When you are ready, begin shouting simultaneously for at least two minutes. Be aware of whether or not you begin with a bang and soon fade; note if you try to understand what the other person is shouting. This happens regularly with women: if they started with letters they suddenly find themselves shouting their partner's numbers. Practice until you feel that you can stick with your own anger consistently. (Another valuable part of this exercise is to get used to how to make angry sounds and to desensitize you to fears of hearing these sounds from others.)

The Silent Movie Technique

Next, allow your body to express anger nonverbally. In a film on individual assertiveness training, the late behavioural psychiatrist Michael Serber demonstrated this effective technique. Facing your partner, pretend that you are both in silent movies and that you are trying to communicate to one another how angry you are. Use facial expressions, gestures, and your body to convey angry feelings *without* talking.

Getting Into the 'Talkies'

Now that you have practiced the verbal and nonverbal parts of anger, put them together in this next exercise: Repeat these phrases, using good eye contact, appropriate body language, and varied voice volume and tone:

'I feel angry right now.'
'I do not like it when you ignore me.'
'I am very upset about what you said/did.'
'Stop that!'

Make up other phrases too. Give each other honest feedback on how well you communicated.

Disarming an Angry Person

When someone is very angry at you and is screaming and shouting at you, try the following exercise to disarm the anger. First, acknowledge with an assertive message that you definitely hear her/him. You can say, 'I hear you,' or perhaps 'I know you're angry at me.' Often this acknowledgement will calm the person enough to enable you both to discuss the issue. If not, in a calm, assertive manner say something such as, 'I really want to talk to you, but I cannot talk to you when you're shouting. As soon as you're calm, I will be happy to talk to you.'

You can repeat this until the person calms down. Then *listen*. However, if the screaming continues, you have the right to leave the situation. You can say that you are leaving until such time that you both can hear each other out. Or, you can just leave! Women are notorious for 'hanging in there' in an argument and often feel compelled to hold out until the 'bitter end.' This is masochistic and totally unnecessary.

Before you try to disarm an angry person in a real life situation, try to role-play this procedure with a friend until you feel sure about what you are doing. Ask for positive feedback and suggestions. Remember it is very important to support one another when dealing with situations that in the past have caused you anxiety and pain.

Don't Get Even, Get Angry!

If you can see from our brief exploration of anger in this chapter that this is especially difficult for you, we encourage you to read more about the subject in one of the resources listed below. Consider carefully your responses to anger – your own and that of others – and seek the help of a qualified professional therapist if you find yourself:

   . . . totally unable to express anger.

   . . . unaware of any feelings you'd label as 'angry.'

   . . . bursting into tears whenever you feel angry.

   . . . reacting aggressively or even violently to minor annoyances.

. . . often depressed about your life and relationships.

. . . experiencing frequent violent or destructive thoughts about others or yourself.

If you do seek to work seriously on your anger, don't be satisfied with 'treatments' – self-help *or* from a therapist – which merely teach you to *vent* your feelings by pounding a pillow, shouting epithets, or hitting another person with a 'harmless' foam bat. While such approaches can help you get in touch with anger you have denied, at best they only open the door to effective *resolution* of your anger. At worst, they teach you inappropriate, aggressive methods for expressing anger.

A sensitive, complete approach to learning to express anger should include ways to:

● *become aware* of your angry feelings (including steps for strongly and emotionally venting angry feelings in non-destructive ways – this is where pillow-pounding can come in.)
● *develop greater tolerance* for situations which have sparked anger.
● *change attitudes* which lead you to believe that life 'should' be fair, non-hurtful.
● *relax* in the face of minor annoyances.
● *learn new, assertive methods* to express your anger.
● *practice new, assertive methods* to express your anger.

Your anger is a healthy and natural part of you. Listen to it, treat it with respect, express it assertively when it's appropriate – but don't let it control your life!

Chapter 17

Humour – We Need More of It!

Feminist cartoonist Nicole Hollander, in one of her infamous 'Sylvia' strips, captures the attitude of many women: panel 1 shows Sylvia listening to the unforgettable Enjoli perfume commercial, 'I bring home the bacon, fry it up in a pan . . . and never let you forget you're a man . . .' In panel 2, Sylvia responds, 'That woman must be on drugs.'

Humour can be used to express love, affection, and caring, and to spotlight your 'quick wit.' It can also be devastating when used as a weapon to stab others in their Achilles heel – where it hurts most. Women have experienced humour largely as victims, mainly as targets for countless bad jokes – 'Did you hear the one about the mother-in-law . . .?' – and we have laughed because we were expected to laugh.

As for expressing our own humour, it simply was not part of being a woman. Like anger, humour was not to be displayed freely by any woman who would remain a 'lady': passive, reserved, demure, and quiet, seen but not heard.

Women find it hard to trust humour – including their own – because it has so frequently been used against them. There's the woman who's elected treasurer for an organization, saying she'd be pleased to take on the job as long as the books don't have to balance to the penny; the woman librarian who misplaces the dictionaries; and the ever present dumb-but-sexy-girl-after-a-man jokes. We've learned to laugh, yes, but not at what was really very funny to us. We've been expected to grin and bear it.

While the tide has turned against many comic portrayals, women are still subject to ridicule both for their traditional feminine traits, and for new liberated attitudes. Jokes about Poles, Chinese, Blacks, and other minorities, about the handicapped or the poor or the downtrodden are strenuously avoided, but women are fair game for cartoonists and comics, television writers and comedians and businessmen who want a snappy opening for a speech.

We have all heard jokes like the following, which are 'funny' at the expense of women:

- 'Who was that lady I saw you with last night?'
  'That was no lady, that was my wife!'
- Happiness is . . . discovering at the school play that when your son said his teacher was 42, he didn't mean her age.
- 'You gave your mother-in-law a plant for her birthday?'
  'Yeah, poison ivy.'
- 'Look at that fender; were you in a crash, Joe?'
  'No, this is my wife's car. You should see our garage door!'
- 'Honey, we never seem to have any more conversations together.'
  'O.K., so lie down and I'll talk to you.'

As women begin to express their anger openly and assertively, they no longer want to laugh at unfunny jokes. They have the freedom and the opportunity to develop and to use their own sense of humour, and to refuse to be passive victims of its misuse.

Sarcastic Humour

Using humour assertively takes practice, and involves knowing the difference between its use and abuse. Sarcasm, considered a form of humour, is a powerful tool that can be particularly hostile, and is usually safest in the hands of experienced comedians such as Don Rickles or Joan Rivers. If you have been the recipient of sarcasm, you probably sensed anger and hostility passing for 'humour.'

Sarcasm and caustic wit are Iris Indirect's' favourite ways to be 'funny.' She is, of course, actually hostile and is attempting to upset you with her remarks. Iris may say to a neighbour who was late for a morning meeting: 'Late again, Ethel? You better cut out all that late-night drinking!' – or to an overweight friend who is struggling with a diet – 'Sure, Mary, have some cake – you are looking a little underweight today.' Obviously, Iris uses 'humour' as a vehicle for her insults and hostilities. Don't use sarcasm and 'humorous insults' to express anger. It is better communicated assertively, directly and honestly.

The 'Achilles Heel' humorist attacks others where it hurts most. Consider how April handles the Achilles Heel humorist in the following situations:

'You're Not One of Those Women . . .?'

Achilles: 'April, when are you going to do something with your life instead of just being a housewife?'

April: 'You obviously have never met a Domestic Goddess before!'

Achilles: 'Hey, April! Let's see what you're reading. Oh, no! You're not one of *those* women who read silly romance novels!'

April: 'Did you know that *those* women have more satisfying sex lives than non-readers? There's research to prove it!'

This style of 'humour' is directed at a personal characteristic, habit, favourite pastime, or lifestyle of the victim. To the victim, of course, it is not funny at all. April responds to an Achilles Heel attack effectively with a quick retort, or by telling the attacker to stop. If you don't feel as confident with your 'comebacks' as you do with telling the attacker to stop, give it a little practice. You don't have to make a witty remark at all if you don't want to. Directly expressing your annoyance is equally effective in stopping an Achilles Heel attacker. The important thing to remember is to *act*, not to be the quiet, passive victim.

Teasing

Teasing is another form of humour which involves 'poking fun' at someone. Sometimes the use of subtle affectionate teasing can help someone overcome anxiety. Usually, however, teasing serves to alienate others instead. Taken to its extreme, teasing can be a form of attack. At this point, teasing is an expression of aggression, not affection. Consider the following situation, for example:

'Violets Are Red, Roses Are Blue . . .'

April is enrolled in a poetry class. Agatha Aggressive has persuaded April to let her read some of her poems. Agatha thinks that April's poems are the funniest things she's ever read, and asks April if she has considered doing comedy writing. Another friend, Iris, enters the room. Agatha reads some poems aloud and asks if April's poems aren't absolutely hysterical. Iris joins Agatha in laughing at April's work. April had been spending a good deal of time with her poetry, and she is hurt and angered by Agatha's 'teasing.' Agatha and Iris have alienated April with their 'humour.'

April has the option to put up with the teasing or to demand that it stop: 'Come on, cut it out. I don't like to be teased about that.'

If April chooses to assert herself and ask that the teasing stop, she will likely be teased a little more: 'What's wrong with you, can't you take a joke?' She can respond with the same request again, using the 'broken record' technique. This should be enough to stop her friends' unfair teasing.

We suggest that you review your use of teasing. Is it affectionate or aggressive and alienating? How have you felt when you've been teased to the point that it's not funny anymore? Try to be aware of how you use teasing, and beware of launching aggressive attacks. Tease sparingly and affectionately.

Humour – A Weapon Against Yourself

As you grow to understand the importance of the labels you attach to your behaviour, you will be more aware of how women have also used humour against themselves in the form of 'humorous' self labels: Doris Doormat says, 'I forgot my chequebook – isn't that just like a woman?' or 'You know how I am – I'm just *lost* without my husband (ha ha).' In the guise of gentle humour, Doris makes herself the target for attention that is not funny at all.

We are not suggesting that being an assertive woman means that you must be humourless, or that you cannot 'laugh at yourself' every once in a while. But you can use humour assertively by declining to use it as a weapon against yourself or others.

Happily, you can learn to use humour actively and assertively to express yourself uniquely and positively with no residue of anger or negative feelings. Giving yourself permission to *respond* to humorous situations, to laugh at things that make you want to laugh, is the other component of assertive humour. How do you respond to situations you find humorous?

Doris doesn't respond with spontaneous laughter. She waits to see how others respond. If they laugh, she will, but she is careful to stop laughing before everyone else does, so she isn't 'caught' laughing too much. Doris may also not laugh at all, fearing rejection if she does laugh. She may also feel guilty because she is enjoying herself.

Agatha, by contrast, laughs uproariously with little provocation. Agatha laughs the loudest and longest. It gives her a chance to 'steal the show' and call attention to herself, but other people find her laughter overpowering.

Iris, like Doris, may laugh to hide nervousness or insecurity, but often her laughter is a subtle mask for her hostility.

April will laugh when she finds humour in a particular situation. She won't use her laughter to dominate others, and she doesn't feel guilty or anxious about laughing at something that is funny to her. She is aware of others' feelings and rights, and she will not 'laugh in someone's face.'

Healing Humour

'Laughter is the best medicine,' as they say at *Reader's Digest*. Humour can be healing. It eases tensions when no other strategies work. It can melt an impossible conflict, by-pass an impasse, soothe hurt feelings, and promote a sense of well-being.

One of our favourite healing humorists is Lily Tomlin. She has blended laughter with compassion ever since her earlier TV days with the 'Laugh-In' series. Most recently, Tomlin's healing and hilarious humour has reached thousands of people through her one-woman show, 'The Search for Signs of Intelligent Life in the Universe,' which first opened on Broadway in 1984. The script, written by her longtime collaborator, Jane Wagner, focuses on the female perspective of the latter part of the 20th century. The commentary is narrated by Tomlin as 'Trudy,' an outrageous bag lady who communicates with outer space aliens who are studying

our planet and who uses 'awe-robics' every day. Tomlin's interpretation of Wagner's clever monologues brings out the funny side
of the struggles and dilemmas experienced by contemporary
women. Here are some examples:
On knowing what you want and being assertive –
   'Yes, I am having an affair. But not for long, I think. It's one thing
to tolerate a boring marriage, but a boring affair does *not* make
sense.'
On rejecting a date at his place –
   'He invited me to his place. I told him I'd love to another time,
but that I had my shift on the Rape Crisis Hot Line.'
On being a pregnant woman in management –
   'No, I haven't told the office, it might affect my job. This morning
I threw up at a board meeting. I was sure the cat was out of the bag,
but no one seemed to think anything about it; apparently it's quite
common for people to throw up at board meetings.'
On the androgynous male –
   'I worry sometimes, maybe Bob has got too much in touch with
his feminine side. Last night, I'm pretty sure, he faked an orgasm.'

   Cathy Guisewite, another healing humourist, has been showing
us how to laugh at ourselves through her popular 'Cathy' cartoon
strips. In Guisewite's book, *Another Saturday Night of Wild and
Reckless Abandon*, Cathy spends a good deal of time in restaurants,
alone and with friends. In one sequence, dining alone and noticing
an attractive man across the room, Cathy summons the waitress –
and her courage. She requests that 'a dish of macaroni salad' be
delivered to the man's table with her compliments. When the
waitress hesitates, she exclaims, 'Why are you looking at me like
that? Haven't you ever seen an assertive woman in action before?'
In the last panel, the waitress points Cathy out to the man; Cathy,
meanwhile, has pulled the tablecloth over her head.
   In another strip, Cathy and her friend Andrea are shown leaving
a restaurant when Cathy decides to go back and complain about the
food. Noting to Andrea that 'women have to learn to stand up for
themselves,' she announces 'You are about to witness the assertive
woman in a restaurant!!' A defeated Cathy returns, in the final

frame, telling Andrea of the outcome: 'The waitress demanded a bigger tip.'

Laughing at Myself – A True Story – by Stanlee

A funny thing happened today. I've been a little uptight lately – writing, not getting enough sleep, taking it all too seriously!

I went out for a short errand to photocopy some material for this chapter on Humour [no joke!]. I was in a hurry and feeling that I didn't have enough time.

When I arrived back home, I found the flight of stairs and banister leading up to my front door covered with what looked like 200 doughnuts! Yes, they were assorted and the aroma was maddening. Flowers and other little surprises had been artfully arranged amidst the doughnuts as well.

As my eyes scanned the stairs, focusing on all the sprinkles, sugar, drippy frosting and crumbs that would need to be cleaned up, I was furious. In thinking about the mess, I was so frustrated I actually considered sitting down and eating as many as I could!

While I was carting it all to the bin, sweeping and hosing away the remains, I recognized how upset I had become. My neighbours all came out to watch and thought it was terribly funny.

I asked myself what went wrong. Why didn't I think it was funny?

It had taken my friend a lot more time to put everything together than it took me to disassemble. I was tired but I was smiling.

The whole thing seemed so silly . . . me cleaning up all those doughnuts as if my life depended on it.

I laughed out loud at myself and wanted to share this story with you.

Express Your Humour

To express your sense of humour assertively, accept the idea that it's OK to express it.

- Doris Doormat would not risk sharing something she found funny with anyone. She fears rejection and needs approval: 'What if they don't think it's funny?' She may also feel anxious and guilty about finding humour in a serious situation, and would not joke about it.
- Iris Indirect uses humour as a vehicle for her insults and hostilities. She often is an Achilles Heel humorist, who uses humour to attack others. Sometimes she uses humour to put herself down, to bait the Compassion Trap for others.
- Agatha Aggressive, on the other hand, is a regular comedian – she uses humour aggressively, whenever she can. Others feel that to Agatha everything is a joke, and their own interests will not receive serious attention from her.
- April Assertive knows that it's OK to express her sense of humour. She can say something funny without feeling unduly anxious or guilty, and without fear of rejection. April knows that some people will laugh and others won't, but exercising her right to say something she thinks is funny without harming others is most important to her.

Actively expressing your sense of humour means saying whatever is funny to *you*, so long as you aren't hard on yourself or someone else. It doesn't matter if someone else doesn't think it's as funny as you do, or if you inject humour into a serious conversation or situation.

Humour Yourself

The first tender years of the Women's Movement were singularly devoid of any humour; the issues were deadly serious. Gradually, as the years went by, jokes sprouted here and there, most of the best conceived by women themselves (Question: How many feminists does it take to change a lightbulb? Answer: Five. One to change the bulb and four to form a support group). The difference, of course, was that now women were kidding themselves. We had enough perspective to find the humour in our achievements and our pitfalls.

Like any other skill, humour can be cultivated. Consider trying the following to strengthen your own humour power:

- Collect funny cartoons and jokes in a 'Humour File.' Refer to it frequently.
- Post funny stories, anecdotes, pictures, even fortunes from Chinese cookies on a bulletin board so you can get a chuckle every time you look at it. This has worked well for both authors. For example, Nancy's last three fortune cookies advised: 1) 'For better luck, you have to wait until autumn.' 2) 'For better luck, you have to wait until winter.' 3) For better luck, you have to wait until spring.' No kidding.
- Don't be afraid to inject a little levity into business presentations. You don't want to be outrageous, but you can lighten your style enough to keep your audience attentive.
- Think of your own experiences, and try recasting them as short anecdotes or amusing stories. You might be surprised to discover that what was mortifying at the time is very funny later. A friend learned this when her intelligent young son, then eight, got bored and wanted to leave school one day at about noon, instead of the usual 2:30. He quickly wrote the following note to his teacher: 'Please excuse Jeremy at noon today. He has to visit his aunt.' He signed it, 'Jeremy's Mother,' in his eight-year-old's idea of her handwriting. Jeremy's mother received a call from the teacher, and after a few minutes, they were both laughing about it!
- Come up with your own 'code words' that you can use when you feel under pressure and need to step back from a situation. Repeat them whenever you feel a downward, anxiety-driven spiral beginning, or to relieve tension.
- Build a video library of your favourite funny films. Do the same with books.
- Smile. It sounds trite, but research has shown that if you smile when you don't really feel like it, your emotions get the message and start to adapt to what's on your face! Conversely, if you frown, you actually spark the emotions commonly associated with frowning: worry, depression, frustration.
- Pick a funny role model and watch how she or he handles problems or crises. What would Dawn French do? How about Lucille Ball? Victoria Wood? Maureen Lipman?
- Every day make a conscious effort to look for something funny in

your own behaviour, in a situation, or in another person's behaviour. Describe, through your own eyes, what tickles your funny bone about this. Share your perception with someone else without *trying* to be a comedian. Instead focus on expressing the humour in such a way that you are inviting the other person to delight in your perception and laugh with you. Laughter is contagious. It's also healing, helpful and playful.

To respond assertively to something that you find humorous is to laugh, or smile, or chuckle about it. The important thing to remember is to express your humour, honestly and spontaneously, without feeling guilty or anxious about it, and without aggressively 'taking over' every humorous situation.

Go ahead; express your own unique sense of humour – as long as you remember it can be a 'lethal weapon' if misused. Your sense of humour is part of who you are; expressing it is part of being an assertive woman.

Smile!

Chapter 18

Friends and Lovers

. . . I met this guy at college. I wasn't assertive when we met and we discussed the issue. He went to the campus bookshop and looked and looked until he said he found the perfect book for me – The Assertive Woman. *We did the exercises as we read it together.*

– a 22-year-old college student.

Becoming assertive, many readers of this book have told us in conversations and letters, has had an astounding effect on their relationships with family, romantic partners, and friends. As one person becomes more assertive, the balance of a relationship shifts – sometimes a threatening change. Can we restore balance in our lives, without reverting to the false security of the old ways of relating? How are women to reconcile the old with the new? What can we discard in order to make room to embrace new standards? Do we push ahead and rock the boat? How can we work through the guilt when we let go of relationships that aren't working? How can we maintain love and trust while nurturing changes? What tools can we use to break through our histories and create relationships that work? Can the men in our lives participate in this process of liberation for both sexes? How do *they* feel about it?

Being Assertive with Yourself
It starts with you. Being assertive with yourself may be the most difficult relationship of all. You must be comfortable being *alone* with yourself and making your own decisions. As we discussed in earlier chapters, an assertive woman trusts her inner wisdom and bases her assertions on this understanding. Inner wisdom can blossom if you give yourself time and space alone.

Can you see assertiveness as a way to make room for new choices and possibilities in your life? This is taking a chance on really feeling and being alive! It is the difference between settling for past options that leave boredom or depression in their wake, and waking up to new choices that spark a sense of adventure and aliveness.

To begin opening up to new possibilities, be truly honest with yourself about any pretences that you are living. Many women have become masters of deception and have used assertive skills only to further sabotage themselves or others. An assertive woman answers these questions honestly: what am I really committed to? What is my payoff or reward for this commitment? Is the reward also a punishment, paradoxically? Or, does my commitment give me a sense of exhilaration and joy?

If your answers reveal that you are using assertive tools to punish yourself, it is time to let go and make new choices. It is time to become assertive with yourself, to experience your power.

The chart below contrasts ways assertive skills can be used for self-sabotage, or for aliveness and power.

WANTED: DEAD OR ALIVE!!

DEAD	ALIVE
Having an assertive discussion with your parents on world affairs while suppressing your feelings about their constant disapproval of you.	Confronting in a loving way your parents' disapproval and your hurt feelings.
Assertively requesting that your mate correct your child's behaviour, while you still feel helpless and powerless to stop the child's manipulations.	Negotiating with your mate how to mutually share the discipline of your child and empower one another to do so.
Telling your date where you'd like to go for dinner and what film you'd like to see, then feeling obliged to have sex to show your appreciation.	Showing appreciation for your date's cooperation in going along with your plans by inviting him to choose the restaurant and theatre next time.
Asserting yourself with a co-worker, but remaining in a job you hate.	Examining your real feelings of dissatisfaction on the job and doing something positive to make a change — perhaps a new job.
Assertively, yet ruthlessly, completing your TO DO list(s) while ignoring messages from your body to slow down, rest, or take a "sanity break"; you are exhausted, irritable or ill.	Being assertive with yourself by listening to your inner wisdom which is guiding you towards balance and harmony in your daily activities.

Approaching Mates and Lovers Assertively
While reading The Assertive Woman *I have been using the exercises to better myself and my personal life. I still find myself in the Compassion Trap with my ex-husband. I'm not going back. I'm going forward to make a better life for me and my children. I'm trying to be assertive, but it doesn't always work and I get depressed. What can I do?*

– a data transcriber
divorced and in her 30's

Everywhere women look there are books, magazine articles, advice columns, and talk shows expounding on the do's and don'ts of romantic relationships. The topics range from 'how to be a better flirt' by using subtle communication, to the 'unconscious attitudes' that separate women and men as two alien cultures.

Other popular subjects: the pluses and minuses of dual career relationships (especially the clash between the executive woman and her equally high-powered man); the new 'aggressive woman,' who asks dinner guests to leave early so that she and her lover have time to make love; the single woman over 30 who lives with the realities of feminism and the sexual revolution and asks, 'Why am I still single?'; the Superwoman who desperately searches for Superman, and for ways to put a little nurturing back into her relationships; the divorcee who wonders how to choose a mate the second or third time around; the partners who wonder how to go from 'his' to 'hers' to ours in a fresh, new way.

How can you make sense out of all of this and make new information work in your own intimate relationships? Recognize that there is no end point where two people can claim that they now 'have a relationship,' as if it were a goal fulfilled and time to move to the next goal. Relating is a *process* – of discovery, of learning and teaching, of giving and receiving, of growing and being, of accepting and challenging. To be assertive with your partner is to live the daily experience of commitment to that process.

Assertiveness in intimate relationships means risking rejection, feeling foolish and expanding into unknown territory. Afraid of losing your own identity in love? Working through such fear and conflict can give you the best of both worlds – personal freedom *plus* intimacy with a partner.

From a Man's Point of View
We asked a few men to respond to the question, 'What's it like, dating, interacting with, being friends with or living with an assertive woman?' We think their answers provide an inside look at men's current attitudes about assertive women.

● Peter Hof, Computer Specialist and Engineer
Amsterdam, The Netherlands
I have just met my first assertive woman – you! – and just completed reading The Assertive Woman. *In reading it, I noticed that I already knew about many of the things you wrote, but I haven't acted like it! I realized that it is time for me to make some changes and learn to understand how women feel. Men have similar shame that maybe a lot of men would find it difficult to read a book called* The Assertive Woman.

● Greg Klock, Real Estate Broker
Menlo Park, California
There's a unique quality of partnership in a relationship built on assertiveness, honesty and openness. One of the things about living with an assertive woman, is rather than dealing with what you think *she wants to do, she literally tells you what it is that will please her, what she wants from you, what she wants from the relationship, what she wants to do tonight, what she wants in bed, etc. It creates an enormous amount of freedom for a man who is interested in being a partner, because he no longer needs to second guess or be the one responsible for figuring out what she wants. Clearly, he can rely on the fact that she'll tell him. It also creates an arena for him to express what he wants, how he feels, and what he wants from her.*

● John Yacenda, Ph.D., Writer, College Instructor
Truckee, California
The assertive woman – what species of creature is she? A lot of

*men have different ideas about assertive women – so do
women. To me, she's free to be whoever: to seek the most
creative expression of herself through her art, music, imagination, loving and sexuality, and through her anger, fear, and all
that is reflective of her very being. I find this freedom appealing;
how about you? Wouldn't you like to be friends, good, good
friends with this kind of woman. I would, and am.*

*The assertive women with whom I share friendship or whom
I love, are not threatening, not demanding, not defiant – all
misconceptions of years gone by. Rather, they are beautiful in
spirit, in heart, in mind. They infuse my life with realities I
cannot find anywhere – anyplace, but with them, often through
them, because they bring all of themselves to our friendship.*

Approaching Friendships Assertively

*A friend is the highest sense of security one person can experi-
ence. With a friend, I can travel the countries of possibility,
exploring the limitless boundaries of hope and destination,
speaking in only truth: the ultimate language of friends.'*

A young woman answered a survey on friendship with this poetic
response. The survey was part of a project conducted by colleague
Dr. John Yacenda, the writer and college instructor whom you met
on the previous page.

How would you describe your feelings about friendship? Perhaps
you view friendship as appropriate with members of your own sex
only. An assertive woman has the freedom to enjoy friendships with
men as well. The same dimensions of friendship can be shared with
them in a non-sexual way.

What about friendships that don't work out? In her book, *Smart
Cookies Don't Crumble*, Sonya Friedman describes a young married woman with children who, in an honest effort to be 'true to
herself,' builds an interior design business. Her friends watch with
dismay, anxious that they'll be left out of her life entirely. As a
result, they express neither interest nor support: 'Their apathy
brings tears to your eyes; they make you feel *bad* for feeling good

about yourself.' Friedman's suggestion is not to *expect* total support when making changes which may be threatening to friends. Instead, control your need for approval and emphasize the ways in which your friendships provide a connection.

Confronting their lack of support may terminate or enhance the friendship. In a rapidly changing world, it is common to see friends come and go, to have many acquaintances, and to need close friends more than ever.

A Note on Best Friends
by Nancy

In a time when 'networking' and 'power' meals are the preferred means to meet people who presumably can help advance one's career, I long for the fine, out-of-fashion notion of the 'best friend.' Networks and friendships do sometimes coexist, but the connection to a best friend isn't made because of what may come your way as a result. Best friendships may be downright quirky. But what sweet relief to have a friend who doesn't promise anything more than . . . well, friendship. With a best friend, you don't have to guess, you know you [and your mistakes and triumphs] are accepted. It's comfortable. It's stimulating.

I've been thinking lately about my best friend when I was nine. Wendy. We went to school together, played together, devised appropriate torments for our respective brothers, wrote a nine-year-old's version of the ideal cookbook [heavy on hamburgers, desserts, and carrots], shared a passion for building snow-women in the winters, taught each other our first ballroom dance steps, stood up for each other, defended each other's characters. For all that, we weren't anything alike: school came easy for me, Wendy had to work hard to get by – and she didn't particularly like it. I was tall and skinny; she was shorter and stockier. I bit my fingernails; Wendy had the most beautiful hands I'd ever seen. And she was left-handed, a constant fascination to me.

I was allowed to accompany her family on summer vacations to the lake – a time I still recall as enchanted. During one such summer at the lake, I found a tiny baby mouse and pleaded to bring it home. Wendy tried to talk me out of it, I remember, saying something about nature and that she didn't think the mouse would survive. I didn't listen; I lined a small box with pink Kleenex and took my mouse home, where it lived for a day. I was heartbroken, and I learned something from Wendy: I might be good at school, but Wendy was wise.

Disaster struck some three years into our inseparable best friendship. I moved. We wrote, arranged special and eagerly anticipated long distance calls, sent photos and Christmas cards. After a while, the letters dwindled to a couple each year. I didn't see Wendy again until I was at college, some ten years later. It was affectionate and awkward meeting that day, and I think we were both a little relieved when it was time for her to go back to her world and I to mine. We no longer shared a world that belonged to both of us.

But I miss Wendy still, and I think of her often.

Though women are advised to build all sorts of productive relationships – from career networks to marriages – a 'best' friendship carries its own unique rewards. A best friend can get you through ups and downs the way no one or nothing else can. The term itself – best friend – may sound clumsy or out of date, but that's a charming dilemma. The effort it takes to kindle and sustain a best friendship is entirely worth your best efforts. If Wendy were here, I'd tell her that.

When to Let Go

Several years ago, a best-selling poster showed a cat hanging onto a rail, barely keeping itself from falling: the caption read, 'Hang in there, baby!' – a virtue women are expected to possess. We noticed that women all over the country were congratulating each other for staying in impossible, destructive relationships and situations. Whoever endured the worst for the longest time was admired.

That's not assertive behaviour – it's the newest form of relationship macho.

An assertive woman knows that making a clean break may be the most assertive act of all. Often, we have little choice about the occurrence of an actual loss: divorce, separation, geographical moves, being fired or laid off from a job, financial losses, or other estrangements are often beyond our control. However, an assertive woman can gain control of her feelings, thoughts and reactions. She believes that for every loss, there can be a gain. She embraces the letting go process.

The choice to let go of an unhappy relationship is a vital assertive skill. If you need support in letting go, you'll find some help in the reading list at the end of this chapter.

The Bottom Line

All relationships – romantic, friendship, family, or professional involve human actions and reactions. They are constantly reverberating to changes in the individuals and their perceptions of themselves and one another. They will never be entirely predictable, measurable or even practical.

The relationship and the people who compromise it cannot be controlled or managed; what is manageable is how you interpret what is going on in the relationship. As we've seen, sometimes it is a choice between 'dead' and 'alive.' Take the time to give your relationships your best – and learn to go easy on yourself if it doesn't work out. When you accept yourself, you build the best foundation for lasting relationships.

Chapter 19

Assertive Family Relationships

My adventures with being assertive are bewildering my husband of 29 years. My parents are very traditional and I was raised to leave everything to the men and not bother my head, and I found as I raised my five children I was quite capable of taking care of things myself.

I am a farm wife and they, traditionally, are the helpmates and take care of the house, plus garden the yard to leave the man of the house to his important work. My parents aren't farmers, so I didn't know some things were my job. Being a farm wife has its rewards, but it's a job you don't understand unless you've experienced it. His work is always more important than yours, but you're expected to have a spotless house, plus always be available for what he wants you to do.

My girls are grown and married. I have one son who I'm trying to teach respect for female ambitions.

I have never gone to college – but I will!

All my children are supporting me when I take college courses. My husband says he does, but he sure makes it difficult when I have classes. He gets upset at the money going out and wants to know when he's going to get a return on his money.

I'm sure there are more frustrated farm wives out there. There are more and more farm wives working off the farm.

Asserting myself is becoming much easier.

– letter from a reader in the USA

To make room for assertiveness in important relationships, take a fresh look at the state of your relationships now and understand how they got to be as they are. The way we approach relationships as adults was seeded by our interactions with our parents and other authority figures; non-assertive patterns and guilt may have been planted and reinforced early.

When adult difficulties can be traced back to childhood, it's easy to be bitter. Nursing an old grudge, however, prevents us from moving on to discover joy in relationships. To laugh at ourselves and our awkward beginnings, to move forward, we must forgive those who've hurt us.

Mum, Dad and Me
There are hundreds of resources available to help women understand their relationships with their parents. How we've interacted with our own mothers and fathers determines in great part how we choose our mates and how we treat children – ours or others'.

Linda Hagood describes three common categories of father/daughter relationships: 'Daddy's Girl,' 'Hands Off,' or 'Can't Measure Up:'

> The 'Daddy's Girl' will remember a father that gave in to her against mum (often not openly, though), and generally treated her as a very special little girl (even after she grew up). Women who experienced 'Hands Off' primarily express a sense of their father's absence – either physically or emotionally. They related to and through their mothers because they were a mystery to their fathers. Women who couldn't 'Measure Up' often feel competitive with males. Their fathers expected very little success from them because of their sex and yet, they feel a drive to redeem females in the eyes of their fathers.

In her role as director of a Southern California counselling centre, Hagood counsels to parents and children, urging them to work on their relationships as adults. She believes it's possible to complete 'unfinished dances' with each parent and move on to assertive ways of relating.

'Who's Assertive?' – A Checklist
Use the following checklist to discover how assertive you can allow your children to be, and how assertive you are with them. Each item

requires only a 'yes' or 'no' answer.

If you are a parent, be aware of the choices you make with regard to your children. As you answer the following questions, give some thought to the underlying choices you've made.

- Do I demand from my children only what they can realistically complete at one time?
- When I make requests of my children, do I provide follow-through help?
- In most situations, do my children understand what I expect from them? Are my requests specific as to time, place, and other requirements?
- When I make requests or demands of my children, do I also specify how the demands can be met?
- Do I provide my child with some privacy, or do I feel threatened when I am not in direct control (eg., talking on the telephone without my knowing to whom she is talking)?
- Do I treat my child as though he has personal rights (eg., privacy in his own room)?
- Do I set realistic limits for my child (curfew, TV time, household chores)?
- Do I encourage my child to handle some situations independently but with my support (helping with homework, letting her resolve difficulties with friends)?
- Do I allow my child to disagree openly with my judgment (allowing him to choose his own friends)?
- Do I encourage my child to stand up for her rights with others as well as with me?
- When unable to control my child, do I resort to threats, shouting, or physical punishment?
- Do I listen to my child's point of view?
- Does my view always prevail, or do I also let my child 'win' sometimes?
- Do I over-protect my child (not wanting him to be involved in any sports activities for fear of injury)?
- Do I allow my child to state how she feels, without *telling* her how she feels?

After you have completed the checklist, review your responses. Your answers may reflect particular areas that could be handled in a more assertive, less controlling way.

Stepping Out?
An expanding area of concern for women today is how to be an assertive woman within a blended family, one in which there are children from a former marriage. Step-parenting is a unique and challenging role in which you're an authority figure one minute (with support and power assists from your spouse) and an interloper the next! On top of that, stepchildren often exercise considerable power of their own by driving a wedge between the natural parent and step-parent in hopes of keeping the natural parent to themselves and sending the step-parent packing!

The only way to get around this mess is for both parents to decide how to discipline the children, including specific responses to specific problems and what to do if one parent doesn't live up to the deal. Since each parent's wishes are susceptible to manipulation and sabotage by the children, discuss how you can quickly regroup and get back on track. A united partnership which has assertively chosen to be together doesn't merely limp along as a 'broken' family.'

Assertive Parenting
When you are in the midst of cleaning up spilled milk, officiating whose favourite TV programme will be watched, bandaging scraped knees, getting youngsters dressed and undressed, into bed and out of bed – acting 'assertively' with them may well be the last thing on your agenda! But if you often feel put upon by your children, you may have brought it on yourself by not acting assertively with them and by not allowing them to learn to act assertively themselves.

We have emphasized that as you become more assertive, you will experience the rewards that go along with it. One of those rewards is seeing those around you become more assertive also. As an assertive woman, you are a 'model' for others. Your children, through watching you, can learn to be independent people, and go on to become models for families of their own.

Children, of course, also watch and learn from you when you act nonassertively, and they will learn those behaviours as well. This can have unpleasant results, as it could for Iris Indirect or Agatha. Iris's children may learn from her example how to be expert manipulators. Agatha's children may adopt her loud, bossy, and bullying ways to get what they want. And Doris' children may learn to be helpless and passive.

Fortunately, children succeed very well in learning to be assertive – and they can learn most of it from you. They will receive the same benefits when they assert themselves as you do when you assert yourself: a feeling of personal worth, strength, and independence.

What attitudes are you teaching your child? Answer the following questions as 'True' or 'False.'

True False

—— —— Children should be seen and not heard.

—— —— I spend a good deal of time doing things for my child.

—— —— I am frequently angry with my child's behaviour.

—— —— My child needs to be protected.

—— —— My child can make many decisions with my guidance.

—— —— I encourage my child to do things 'for her own good.'

—— —— I feel that my child takes me for granted.

—— —— My child depends on me for everything.

—— —— I encourage my child to be independent.

—— —— I respect my child's feelings and opinions.

You may find that in some situations, you treat your child as a 'kid.' At other times, you probably see your child as a person, although someone with perhaps less personal power than you have. The first step in learning to behave assertively with your child is to recognize her as someone with certain personal rights. It is true that you do have to make some decisions for your child's own welfare, but you can also help a child to be assertive and to stand up for herself.

Start by observing what your child actually does and what you *expect* her to do. Usually this means distinguishing between appropriate child-as-child behaviours and child-as-adult behaviours. In some situations, do you expect your child to behave as you would rather than as a child? Although you probably wouldn't play in the mud, your child may, and to expect otherwise is probably unrealistic. If you provide your child with spending money or an allowance, it may be unrealistic to expect her to spend the money (or save it) as you would. Part of helping your child to be assertive, then, is to try to avoid expecting her to function as an adult in all situations. You can then provide support and guidance when it is needed and allow the child to tackle other situations independently.

'The Rock Concert'

Cindy, your 13-year-old daughter, wants to go to a rock concert in a city 25 miles away. It is a week night, and Cindy has school the next day. Several of her friends are going, and one of the parents will drive. You don't want Cindy to go to the concert on a week night, and you are also uncomfortable with the 25-mile distance. Which approach would you be likely to take?

Passive: After listening to her daughter's pleas to go to the concert, Doris says: 'Oh, I don't know, Cindy. Who is going to the concert? Who is performing?'

Cindy: 'All of my friends are going, and there will be lots of bands there – I can't remember all of them. Mum, can I go to the concert or not?'

Doris: 'Well, I don't know; why don't you ask your father?'

Aggressive: Before Cindy is halfway through her request, Agatha interrupts:

Agatha: 'Are you crazy? Going to a silly concert on a school night? what's got into you?'

Cindy: 'But, Mum –'

Agatha: 'No *buts* about it! Absolutely not! And don't talk back to me like that. If you keep making these ridiculous requests – a girl of your age – I'll take away your allowance for a week!'

Cindy: 'Mum, you didn't even let me explain . . .'

Agatha: 'I said forget it. Don't you argue with me, young lady. You're not going to be there with all those punks and who knows what!'

Indirectly Aggressive: Iris listens to Cindy's request attentively, and then says.

Iris: 'Cindy, you disappoint me. I thought you had better sense. No, not tonight. It's really for your own good. I'm older and I know about the world.'

Cindy: 'But Mum, everyone's going. It will be fun.'

Iris: 'When you're older, you'll see that I'm doing you a favour. It's only that I care about you. Those other parents must not care at all to let their children go. I wish someone had cared more about me when I was a child. You'll be a better person for it, Cindy.'

Assertive: April listens to Cindy's request attentively, and then replies:

April: 'Well, Cindy, it does sound like a good concert, and I can see you really want to go, but I'll have to say "no" this time.'

Cindy: 'But Mum, all my friends are going! I'll be the only one who will miss it!'

April: 'I know several of your friends are going. But tonight is a school night and you have to get up early tomorrow morning. I really have to say no. Concerts are fun to go to, and if you were going to a Friday or Saturday night concert it would be OK, but I must say no under these circumstances.'

(Or, had April not felt ready to let Cindy go to such events at all, her last sentence might have been, 'Concerts are fun to go to, but I don't think you are quite ready to deal with such a large event at night just yet. Let's limit it to daytime activities until you are fourteen.')

In this situation, *Doris* is tentative with her 'no,' and ultimately passes the decision on to someone else. Doris is more concerned about not displeasing her daughter by saying 'no.' On the other hand, *Agatha* doesn't even allow Cindy to finish her request. Agatha gives excessive orders and commands and behaves like a dictator. In this case, Agatha's daughter only had the right to obey her mother's commands. The manipulative *Iris* uses an indirect approach with her daughter, by making Cindy feel guilty for making her request. It is difficult to see how this experience would make her daughter 'a better person,' as Iris says.

April handles the situation assertively and communicates to her daughter that she has the right to disagree and to bring the subject up again later. April doesn't precede her 'no' with a lecture, nor does she overload Cindy with commands and punishments. April encourages assertive communication.

Generally, we suggest you approach acting assertively with children in the same way you do with adults. We have labelled two particular communication traps to beware of when interacting with children: as the 'Aggression Trap' and the 'Slavery Trap.' Each can get in the way.

The Aggression Trap

This trap short-circuits assertive communication because you are practically forced into 'exploding' at your children. It generally occurs when you have put off asserting yourself, hoping that the situation would change without your intervention.

'It's Marijuana'

Situation: You suspect that your 14-year-old son, Gordon, has been experimenting with marijuana. You haven't mentioned anything to him about it, hoping that it was only temporary. You are hanging up Gordon's jacket one day when a marijuana cigarette falls out of the pocket. You approach Gordon, waving the cigarette in front of him: 'I knew it! I knew it all along! Next thing I know you'll be hooked on something stronger! Have you lost your mind? What are you trying to do, land in jail? I can't believe you'd do anything so stupid! Can't you see how silly you've been? You'll turn into a real addict!'

If you have been in the Aggression Trap, you know you are left feeling shaky and angry at yourself for exploding. The trap can be avoided by dealing honestly and assertively with your problems when they appear. Hoping the situation will improve, or ignoring it, can build you up for a headlong plunge into an aggressive, irrational encounter.

An assertive approach with the same situation would occur as soon as you sense there might be a problem or something to talk about. It might go like this: 'Gordon, I want to talk to you about something that's been bothering me lately. I think you might be smoking marijuana, and I'm concerned about it. I'd like to hear your side of it.'

The assertive parent acknowledges the child's feelings, and then states clear expectations for the child's behaviour. Here's one way to do that:

'I know you want to try marijuana; it's exciting at your age to do something that's "against the rules." *I don't want you to smoke marijuana*, and I won't allow you to have it or smoke it here in the house. You're aware of the risks involved, and you'll have to accept the responsibility and the risks if you do use it. You'll be breaking my rules for you, and you'll be breaking the law. I can't support you in that choice; I'd really prefer you didn't use it at all. I know that sounds pretty strong, but that's the way I feel . . . Now that you know my point of view, I'd really like to hear yours. It's important to me, and I have as much time as you'd like to talk about it.'

In this approach, the expectations, the parent's rules, and the consequences are clear to the child. It is a strong statement, but it allows room for the child to respond.

(Please note that we are not trying to tell you *what* to say in such a situation – indeed, you may think marijuana use is fine; our purpose is to urge you to give your children clear assertive messages, and encourage them to respond the same way.)

The Slavery Trap

When you perform an excessive number of tasks for your children, most of them unnecessary, you are in the Slavery Trap. This trap encourages your children to be too dependent on you.

For example, a typical morning finds Doris awakening her children for school, bathing and dressing them, preparing breakfast, packing lunches, and driving them to school (only a short distance away). Realistically, all of these tasks could be performed independently by the children. Doris is actually doing her children a disservice by not allowing them to manage their own behaviours. Because they have learned to be too dependent, they won't have the confidence to stand up for themselves when necessary. Parents permit the Slavery Trap at the cost of their child's independence and assertiveness – a high price. Doris may also pay a high price as a result of the Slavery Trap. She may grow to resent her children, find that she has little time for herself, and worst of all, once her children are grown, she may realize that her 'slavery' was more of a burden than a benefit.

Inheriting the Compassion Trap

Parents can pull their children into the Compassion Trap by making them responsible for taking care of the parents' needs. This happens frequently with single parents, who often refer to their child as the new 'man' or 'woman' of the house. Children may resent being placed in this position, but usually do not complain too much because they would feel guilty for saying anything.

A parent who feels helpless can engender a feeling of super-responsibility in a child by forcing him to make decisions or take on adult responsibilities prematurely. The parent may foster guilt in the child as well as excessive compassion. The parent's message is 'Care about your parent! Feel sorry for me!'

You know your child is in the Compassion Trap is he is frequently saying: 'Don't worry, I'll take care of you; I'll do that for you, you're too sick; I won't leave you alone.' It is understandable that children in the Compassion Trap experience tremendous guilt feelings for pursuing their own interests. They may also develop an attitude of parental over-protectiveness that can stay with them well into adulthood, something they may pass on to their own children.

Forcing your children to be your 'parent' deprives them of their right to choose how they will live. Since the average lifespan is 75 years, it isn't too much to allow children to be children for a decade or two.

In the Land of Giants

How you assert yourself is important. The physical components of assertive behaviour are a key element when you are asserting yourself with your children.

Getting your child's attention so you can talk with her is a necessary part of acting assertively with her. Combining several techniques is most effective, particularly with younger children.

- Since you are much taller than your (young) child, try bending down so that your child looks down at *you* while you are talking. You can also do this by squatting or sitting on the floor while your child is seated. The goal is to avoid looking like a giant to your child, and to help maintain eye contact, just as you would with an adult.

- Touching your child gently – holding her hand, touching her shoulder – while you are talking will help keep your child's attention directed toward you.

- You can also get your child's attention by saying, 'Listen to what I'm going to say, because it's important.' Be sure that your voice is loud enough to be heard, but don't unduly raise your voice, or sound threatening. Experiment with your voice volume to find what works best for you. Sometimes keeping your voice lower than normal is an effective attention-getter also.

Combining these techniques also serves to give you the appearance of being an 'equal' who will talk *with*, not yell *at*, your child.

Role-playing with Your Child

We believe that the best way to teach your children to be assertive is to act assertively yourself. Since you cannot be with your children all the time, you can also teach your children to be assertive by giving them specific instructions, and by 'role-playing' – rehearsing common life-situations – with them.

Suppose your seven-year-old son, Sean, has a friend who likes to play with matches. Your son tells you that his friend, Tommy, was playing with some matches one day after school, and that he wanted Sean to play with them, too. Your son doesn't want his friend to play with the matches, but he doesn't know how to tell him that. You decide to help Sean handle the situation assertively. To do it, you pretend to be Tommy, and have Sean practice telling you assertively he doesn't want you to play with the matches ('Tommy, I don't want you to play with matches while you're with me!'). You can give your son encouragement and support for being appropriately assertive ('That's right!' 'That's good.'), and add any suggestions you may have for improvement ('Try saying that again in a louder voice.'). You may also switch roles: you pretend to be Sean, and your son takes the role of Tommy.

You can use role-playing with your child very successfully to teach assertion. Young children particularly like this approach because of its 'game' nature. The advantage of this approach is that by watching you, your son can see an example of how he could handle the situation.

Keep switching roles, and have your child practice a few times more before trying to be assertive with a real friend.

Behaviour Contracting
Another effective approach to encourage assertive behaviour patterns with your children is to agree on a 'contract.' If both parent and child abide by the terms of the contract, aggressive outbursts and mismanaged communication can be considerably reduced.

A contract has the advantage of clearly specifying what is expected of both parties. Also specified is what each party will receive for keeping up the agreement. Some families prefer to have loosely structured, verbal agreements, while others may choose to write down the terms of the contract. A rough idea of a sample contract is shown on the following page.

Child	*Parents*
Complete homework	Allow child to watch TV after homework.
Do home chores.	Provide pocket money.
Tell parents where she is going, when she will be back.	Avoid 'nagging.'
Do not scatter clothes, possessions around the house.	Allow child to keep his room in any condition he wants. Room is the child's personal territory.

Contractual agreements work well for some families, and others prefer not to use them at all. The choice is up to you and your children. If you do decide to try a contract, remember the importance of following through with the terms.

Exercises for Assertive Parents and Children
The following exercises will help assertive parents (and those who are developing assertiveness) to help children grow toward becoming mature, assertive adults.

'King and Queen' Exercise
This exercise works best with a group of children (at least four and at most ten), approximately seven to ten years old. We designed this exercise to teach children how to give and receive compliments assertively, one of the first steps in learning to be assertive.

The girls and boys in the group take turns being the King or Queen, sitting on the 'throne' (a chair placed in the room). The other children and the adult group leader sit in front of the King or Queen as 'subjects.' The King or Queen calls on the subjects individually, and each comes to the throne bearing a 'gift' in the form of a sincere compliment for the King or Queen. The children are encouraged to let their imaginations run, and to imagine that the

King or Queen is wearing a royal robe, a jewelled crown, and is holding a sceptre. As subjects, the children can bow down in front of the throne and present their 'gifts,' saying, for example, 'Queen Susie, I have brought you this compliment: you are fun to be with.' The children are expected to make eye contact with the King or Queen when they are bestowing their compliments. The King or Queen must acknowledge the compliment in some way, e.g. 'Thank you,' 'I agree with you,' 'You have pleased me.'

The rest of the subjects and the group leader monitor the sincerity of the compliments by cheering or saying 'that's good,' or by saying 'keep trying' or 'try again.' The children are encouraged to give personal, rather than superficial, compliments. If the compliment is judged by the subjects and adult to be personal ('I like the way you haven't been hitting everyone lately'), the subject receives a reward (fruit, small toy, etc.). If the compliment was thought to be superficial or false flattery ('You're wearing green – that's my favourite colour'), the child is encouraged to try again.

The children will lend a great deal of support to each other in this exercise and will offer to help each other out, particularly when a child is having difficulty. (However, you should be prepared to help out if they do not.) This game is really an enjoyable one for children to try.

The Rights of Small People
The assertive woman recognizes that her children are also people, with rights of their own. She encourages her children to act independently, but also provides specific guidelines for them. When the assertive woman makes a demand or request of her child, she specifies clearly what she expects, and how her child can meet her expectations. In return for the child's respect for the home in which she lives, the assertive woman also respects the child's territory. By assertive communication and behaviour, the assertive woman avoids the 'Aggression' and 'Slavery' traps, and avoids passing the 'Compassion Trap' on to the child.

If you apply the principles and suggestions offered in this chapter to your interactions with your children, you will be less likely to terrorize – or be terrorized by – them. If your home has been a constant battlefield, you can look forward to improved communication and possibly increased peace.

There is no fool-proof formula for living with children or anyone else, but the assertive woman is headed in the right direction.

We hope you will include children among the people with whom you will behave assertively. If you'll teach them to be assertive as well, you will be giving them something they can rely on all their lives – a sense of personal worth, strength, and independence.

Chapter 20

Assertiveness on the Job

1986 was an historic year for United States business and industry: that was the year that the number of working women topped 50%.

Women hold jobs in virtually all corners of the economy, from the traditional strongholds of retailing, financial services, education, and health care, to newer playing fields – old line manufacturing plants, engineering, aeronautics. And from Debbi Fields' cookie empire to Sandy Kurtzig's ASK Computer Company, women are starting – and running – their own business enterprises at a rate three times that of men.

Whether they own their own companies, occupy management positions, or pound the pavement selling everything from computer parts to cosmetics – working women agree on one thing: assertiveness is a career asset.

Building a Successful Career
So what's an aspiring career woman to do? You can't afford to be passive and you can't afford to be aggressive – unless your first name is Chairman. You can, however, make a lot of mistakes in your career and survive: Mary Kay Ash, founder of Mary Kay Cosmetics, has remarked 'I failed my way to success.' She's in excellent company; Thomas Edison was quoted as saying the same thing! But how do you manage your working life so that your mistakes won't derail you permanently? A study conducted several years ago by three colleagues offers a useful model to understand how successful people look at their jobs.

Our friends looked at the way successful careers progress. They discovered that high performance is a matter of performing well within four successive working roles: *newcomer* (Stage I), *colleague* (Stage II), *mentor* (Stage III), and *sponsor* (Stage IV). Performance in each stage is keynoted by a different set of tasks to perform, different relationships to establish, and different emotional adjustments to make. Their research showed that the people who received the highest performance ratings were the ones who were moving through each of these four stages successfully, while those who remained in the early stages were more likely to receive lower performance ratings. Their work is a helpful framework for an assertive working woman interested in building a successful career.

Stage I: The Newcomer
As the new kid in the firm, you may be dismayed to learn that management thinks of you as an apprentice, not an authority – even though you may have years of prior experience (and perhaps an excellent degree to boot). Your employer is interested in learning whether your judgement can be trusted, observing how well you can perform the basic responsibilities of your new job, and seeing how well you can 'get things done' in the organization. Your performance along those lines will be closely watched. Assertiveness aimed at enhancing your own position is likely to be interpreted as premature, naive recklessness now.

Beginnings are delicate times. Maintaining a balance between accepting guidance and demonstrating initiative in your new role is usually the most difficult challenge for the newcomer. The biggest problem you're likely to encounter is the temptation to *oversell yourself*. It's understandable: you want to show you're smart, capable, innovative – in fact, all the things success is made of – but there is one drawback. If you overfocus on selling your contributions, 'you're asking for an audit,' as one friend put it. And if you get that audit too soon, you are more likely to fail in a big way, and, even worse, not be given a second chance.

The thing to keep in mind is that you have a job to perform first, and a career to manage (if you want one) second. If you don't do the job well, you won't have a shot at that career. Just 'doing the job' can be extremely frustrating, since at this point the work is more detailed and mundane than you probably imagined. Higher-ups expect to guide and direct your work until they feel you are ready for more responsibility and more independence. Personal initiative is welcome, but within clear boundaries established by your supervisor.

This situation irritated a friend who had just been hired into a staff position by a large electronics firm. Convinced she was 'management material,' she constantly searched for opportunities to demonstrate her organisational skills. Unfortunately, what she didn't take seriously was the way her behaviour looked to her peers and to management. So determined was she to showcase her talent that she neglected the nuts and bolts of the job she was hired to do. Higher-ups got the impression that she cared more about moving up than doing her job well. She approached every meeting as an opportunity to assertively state her position, when she should have been listening to what others had to say. As a result, she soon developed a reputation for not being a 'team player.'

The good news is that she also had a boss who, over several months, took the time to give her feedback about how she was being perceived by those around her. The bad news is that she wanted executive status more: she suspected her boss was simply trying to blunt her otherwise bright career prospects. Eventually, she had alienated too many of the existing management team. The damage was too extensive to repair, and she left the company.

What happened here? The irony is that our friend was doing what women in business have been advised to do – look for ways to stand out, hold your ground, shoot for the top. The problem was that she tried to do all that *too early in her career*. When she should have been learning about her new organization and how things get done there, she overfocused on projecting a 'professional' image. She should have listened more and projected less.

Although the emphasis during your first few weeks or months on the job should be on listening and learning, we don't mean to suggest that you should never take an assertive stand when it is called for. The trick, however, is to choose those times very carefully. It is not as simple as some authorities would have you believe.

A recent sampling of popular advice yielded this example: You suggest that new product innovations are needed in your company, but the chairman of the planning committee rejects the idea as 'blue-sky' and 'unrealistic.' (Your position relative to the chairman is not clear, but the assumption is that you are subordinate.) The test then offers you three possible responses: 1) lash back at the chairman, citing evidence which supports your case; 2) feel foolish and withdraw from the discussion; or 3) make it clear to the chairman that you expect your ideas and proposals to be given adequate consideration, not be summarily dismissed. The 'correct' answer, according to the creators, is the last one – supposedly the 'assertive' response (as opposed to aggressive and passive).

The problem, however, is that such a recommendation assumes that the organisational landscape is pretty much the same from place to place, and that assertion is assertion is assertion, no matter when, no matter who is sticking up for what they want. The fact, of course, is that assertiveness is a meaningful choice only relative to a particular time and place. What worked in your last job may not fare so well here; what was just right for one organization is foolishness (or worse) in another. Your personal style of assertiveness must be adapted to the situation!

During the early days on the job (and later, too), there is no absolute assertive standard to live up to. Just because you *can be* assertive in a given circumstance doesn't mean you *should be*. If most of the working men and women we know took as gospel the advice handed out in the quiz we described earlier, they would seriously undercut their own credibility. Instead, the best option is – usually – to learn as much as you can from other's reactions, such as the chairman's pre-emptive response in our earlier example. What could be learned from this outburst? What does it tell you about the organization you have joined? What kind of approach might have been welcomed? How do you feel about your answers to these questions? That's the value in listening to and learning about your organization, your peers, your boss. In the end, only you will be able to judge whether assertiveness was worth it, even whether you have chosen the right company, for the right reasons.

Appropriate and effective assertiveness on the job isn't always easy to come by. Consider the following experiences:

- You have just taken a job as a sales representative for a hospital supply manufacturer. You have completed the extensive product training courses and know your products – and your company's top fifty customers – by heart. As you make sales calls, your previous nursing training serves you well. You find you can easily answer customers' questions about how one of your company's products might meet their needs, since your own medical background adds credibility and informed experience to your presentations. You speak with the authority of someone who knows what she's talking about, and your employer has responded enthusiastically to the equipment orders you have worked hard to get.

  During the past few weeks, three different customers have described special problems with wound-healing which you feel could be met if your company modifies one of its best selling pieces of equipment. Your experience tells you that their request is not only valid, but could probably be achieved with minor production and design changes. However, when you describe what you see as a new sales opportunity to your boss, she remarks that 'All new sales reps want to go along with every customer whim,' and she advises you not to pursue the matter further. 'You have to do a better job selling what you already have,' she says. Should you press for the changes, or sit tight, as your boss advises?

- You are a single parent who joined a large insurance company as an executive secretary six months ago. During coffee breaks and casual conversations with other secretaries, you discover there are quite a few other single parents in your division. You have recently spoken with several who complained about your company's lack of support for day care facilities and flexible working hours. You feel strongly that flex time particularly would be a step into the twentieth century for your company, and you are thinking about forming a task force to begin discussions about flex time and day care. You are aware that the cost of employee benefits and insurance has skyrocketed, but you think you have enough data to show that flex time will actually reduce absenteeism and sick days taken. There are also several firms in your city which have introduced day care on an experimental basis, and have expressed interest in sharing their data with your company. While you believe your case is a strong one, and you have the support and co-operation of half a dozen peers, you are uneasy about how to proceed. You want to handle this situation assertively, and not cave in at the first sign of resistance or become angry and impatient. What steps do you take?

- You are the newest member of the quality control department in your manufacturing company, which makes moulded plastic and metal dashboards for automobiles. You care a great deal about your work, and it bothers you to see less-than-perfect parts shipped to customers. Since joining the company, you have noticed a disturbing pattern. Although your boss has stated repeatedly that quality is the most important goal and cannot be compromised, when shipping deadlines are imminent his primary interest is getting the most product out the door as fast as possible. You can understand the pressure to show a healthy number of units shipped at month-end, but you are concerned about the potential for below-par products being built into cars, which seems to you a defeating strategy in the long run. You are sufficiently disturbed by this turn of events to consider taking it up with your supervisor's boss. What is the assertive thing to do? Each of the three situations might sound familiar to you. In every case, you are faced with a somewhat ambiguous situation in which there may be more than one assertive course: what is appropriately assertive conduct in one organization may be disaster in another!

OK, Experts, What Are The 'Right Answers?'
1. The sales rep who wants to make product modifications according to customer specifications faces an interesting dilemma. She could decide to 'take the party line,' go along with her boss, and offer what sympathy she can to her frustrated customers, stopping short of a further push for the requested changes. If her customers ask her why no product changes are forthcoming, she could rationalize the outcome by blaming it on the slowly-moving 'bureaucracy.' This is not an assertive choice, and does not resolve the situation at hand, but is certainly a popular one in many

companies! In some organizations, the sales rep could very easily and appropriately go around her boss and take her customers' requests to higher-ups, where they might stand a better chance of being heard and acted upon. This strategy, however, depends on the nature of the organization itself, and won't work everywhere.

Probably the best strategy for the sales rep in this case is to convince her boss to meet directly with a customer or two. The purpose of such a meeting, however, is *not* to sandbag the reluctant boss, but to promote a genuine opportunity to discuss customer service in general. She must also ready both her boss and the customer for such a meeting by speaking with each individually beforehand, when she can answer questions either may have and prepare them for what the discussion might cover. If, however, the boss is still unwilling to meet, the problem extends beyond what the sales rep's assertiveness can accomplish. It will require pressure from senior management to get the boss to take the first step – and that's a long way from taking customer suggestions seriously as a way of doing business. The sales rep might be better off finding a company with a clear commitment to customer responsiveness. Going out on a limb to assertively press for more customer contact in the face of such resistance is futile. If she persists, the sales rep will be accused of not being a 'team player,' and not understanding 'how we do things around here.'

2. The newly-hired secretary who wants to convince her employer to introduce flexible working hours and to consider day care services is in a sensitive position. The first thing she should do is get more information. Are the expectations of her peers realistic? Have similar proposals been introduced before? With what results? Is everyone committed to a careful investigation of the possible alternatives, or is this an opportunity to 'take a stand?' How willing are the others to be openly identified with the issue? Once she has answered these questions (and it may take some time), she is ready to approach her boss. The object of such a discussion is to briefly summarize the group's position and to obtain feedback that will help put the issue in proper perspective. The secretary herself doesn't want to get stuck as the sole standard bearer in a hot situation: she wants to develop a workable solution that will serve

both the company's and the employees' needs. She understands that having her boss's support will be critical. In this case, going to her boss is not giving away her autonomy or power; it's gathering information that is critical to success, and getting it early in the process.

3. The newcomer to the quality control department should first collect information, based on her private observation, of the times in which she believes product quality has been compromised for the sake of expediency. This initial data-collection period will strengthen her point of view when she sits down with her boss to express her understandable confusion about the situation. She should *not* use the information she's gathered as an indictment of her boss's conduct, but as a way to explain why what she sees, on the one hand, and what she hears, on the other, don't fit together. Her next step depends on the results of that discussion. Based on one meeting with her boss and the limited amount of data she's collected, she probably won't have enough information to allow her to take it convincingly to higher-ups. She could instead discuss her concerns with a peer whom she trusts. If she finds agreement, she can raise the issue once again. She shouldn't assume that her boss is acting deliberately; she may discover that her boss is actually unaware of the inconsistency and appreciates the opportunity to do something about it.

The assertive choice is to take it a step at a time, and to make clear that her discomfort arises out of loyalty to her employer, and not from a desire to make her boss look bad. There may, of course, come a time when she realizes that her company attaches less weight to the problem than she does. Indeed, the policy may come from higher up. If that happens, and she feels her own ethics are being compromised, it's time to consider finding a company which demonstrates a consistent commitment to quality.

The Later Stages: Colleague, Mentor, Sponsor
Once you have completed your career apprenticeship, assertiveness becomes less 'loaded,' more appropriate, and more productive. Now you'll be expected to show sound, independent judgement, to have an interest in developing others' abilities, and to exercise

power and authority directly to influence the overall direction of your company. It's easy to see why assertiveness is so often cited as a leadership characteristic!

Probably the most difficult transition is moving from a dependent position as a newcomer to taking confident independent action as a full-scale team member. There's a great difference in how much power and influence you use in each case. Nothing new there. What may come as a surprise is that leadership is as much a game of inches as your apprenticeship was. Leading means you can mobilize support for a worthwhile goal and sustain it over time. And assertiveness helps not because it will make you a brilliant strategist, but because achieving distinction is a nuts and bolts game.

What's the difference between successful leaders and also-rans? It's not that one has a more brilliantly designed plan than the other. People don't fail because their plans are faulty; they fail because the plans aren't carried out with the same kind of attention that was used to create them in the first place. In the real world, what counts is doing the tiny things very, very well.

A friend runs a little candy company in Eugene, Oregon. Janele's competitive edge against the mammoth chains (who supposedly have the advantage of sheer size) is the superb quality of her products. Fenton & Lee candies are beautiful and original, made with fruits and nuts grown in the Pacific Northwest. Janele would never dream of selling anything but the very best, and she lives that dedication every day so that it is crystal clear to each employee – even the newest. She's nothing short of a broken record when it comes to making the best hand-dipped chocolates around. A less-than-perfect confection has no place in her operation. Janele's strategic secret isn't found in her plans or budgets – it's in her memorable, assertive leadership and skillful, meticulous execution.

Assertiveness on the job, then, is standing up for your department, your product, your company, your reputation, your ideas. There is a certain stubbornness at the heart of really good leadership – and followership – which comes from the same place as self-confidence, self-respect, and a feeling of power.

Does Your Company Encourage Assertiveness?
We have noted repeatedly in this chapter that assertiveness on the
job is, to some extent, in the eye of the beholder. That is, assertiveness will be welcomed in one company and discouraged in another.
How can you tell which kind of company you work in? The list of
indicators below is intended to give you a head start. Add your own
unique observations to it!

Encouraging Signs	*Discouraging Signs*
Employee suggestions are actively sought in all parts of the operation.	Employee participation in policy setting is unheard of.
Communication flows openly up, down, and across organizational levels.	There are stories about past employees who were fired on the spot for 'insubordination.'
Assertiveness is literally rewarded: prizes or other forms or recognition are given for independent action.	Your boss does not seem interested in hearing your ideas for improving your department's performance; that's management's job.
More emphasis is placed on performance than on status.	You get the impression that employees should be seen but not heard.
People who speak up are considered imaginative innovators.	Your boss's decisions are capricious and unpredictable.
Management maintains an 'open door policy'; employees need not fear retribution for voicing their concerns or complaints	Morale is low in your department; people feel powerless to make even the smallest change.

Encouraging Signs	*Discouraging Signs*
Your boss takes the time to listen when you have something to say.	People who even gently criticize company policy are called 'troublemakers.'
Non-supervisory employees sit on decision-making committees.	The motto of your group is 'Don't rock the boat.'
Your company or department sponsors regular employee forums where any question is OK.	The most frequent words from your boss are 'We tried that last year,' or 'I'll have to get back to you.'
Your boss regularly asks for your opinion on work-related decisions or issues.	Managers stay in their offices with their doors closed; the only way you can see your boss is if you make an appointment.
Employees' ideas for new products or services are eagerly sought and the most successful acted upon.	Yours is a rigid, structured environment in which the newest members are expected to work 60 or 70 hour weeks.
Informed risk-taking (testing a new billing system, streamlining the accounts payable process, modifying an existing product) is the norm.	There seems to be an excessive amount of office politics and back-stabbing going on.
Being called 'outspoken' is a compliment.	Most of what you know about your company's plans you learn from the rumours you hear.

Encouraging Signs	*Discouraging Signs*
Mistakes are regarded as learning experiences.	
Your company is fun to work for.	
Disagreements are aired openly.	Outstanding contributions are not formally recognized.
There are five or fewer layers of management in your company.	Your boss won't back your judgement.
There is a profit or gain-sharing programme in effect in your company.	There is no profit or gain-sharing programme in which all participate.
Employees' ideas for new products or services are eagerly sought and the most successful acted upon.	There are more than five layers of management.
Management works to rid the company of excessive rules and regulations, and stresses using common sense in your work.	There is an executive room and reserved parking spaces for executives only.
You see your boss and other managers frequently because they make it a habit to stay in touch with all parts of the organization.	Management writes frequent memos to announce bad news or make new rules.

Chapter 21

The Mythology of the Working Woman

Although such a large proportion of women work, there are few companies – from health care provider to manufacturing firms to universities to restaurants – in which women feel truly welcome. Even when she is fully qualified for the job she holds, a working woman soon discovers that there's an invisible job description, one that warns against making an emotional 'scene,' one that suggests she lacks the confidence to perform as well as men, one that insinuates she really doesn't belong: it's the persistent mythology of the working woman.

Whether she's a senior member of management or the newest teacher's aide, no working woman is completely immune to the sting of these particular slings and arrows. We describe five hallmark myths: *the Too-Emotional Woman; the Insecure Woman; the Workhouse Woman; the Unprofessional Woman*; and *the Superwoman*. They are unique to working women and have nothing at all to do with fairness or observable job performance; nonetheless, each of the myths has the power to derail a career or short-circuit a job well done.

The presence of women in increasing numbers is still a new development in business, even in fields which traditionally have attracted them: public relations, personnel, fashion, retailing,

---

This chapter was adapted from an article by Nancy Austin, titled 'Goodbye to All That: The Mythology of the Professional Woman,' in the January–February 1986 issue of Healthcare Forum Magazine.

---

education (teachers more often than administration), health care (nurses more often than doctors). Yet women are expected to prove themselves worthy of their job responsibilities in ways not demanded of men. It's even harder on women who have broken into exclusively male conclaves – airline pilots, scientists, high-flying financiers, dentists. Women must prove, among other things, that their 'raging hormones' will not cloud their decision-making ability, that they will not crumble in the face of criticism, that they can handle adult responsibility, that self-confidence and strength are not uniquely masculine characteristics.

We describe each myth, show how it can affect the way a woman is perceived in her job, and then debunk it! Part of being assertive on the job involves doing much the same thing – learning to spot the myths that affect your job performance and progress, and assertively sweeping them away. Don't assume that every roadblock in your job is your fault, or that any difficulties you encounter are of your own making, or that everyone is against you personally. We think the five myths bring some perspective to a hotly debated issue.

The Myth of the Too-Emotional Woman

Those with a hankering for this ubiquitous myth contend that a woman is poorly suited for positions of significant responsibility (power) because she will panic under pressure (and therefore cannot be counted on in a crisis), will crumble or explode if criticized, cannot stomach confrontation, and generally allows her heart to overrule her head. The old logic is inescapable. To hold on to her career she must exercise judicious control over her nine-to-five emotions (to do less, of course, would be reacting like a woman instead of thinking like a man).

But the office, argues Dr. Irene Pierce Stiver, director of psychology at Boston's Maclean Hospital, has always been emotional territory. 'Women give men permission to be intensely emotional. Men can be angry, vengeful, fiercely competitive – these are all emotions.' But giving men the go-ahead to rant and rave doesn't guarantee women the same privilege. The woman who shows anger or admits she has career plans is scorned – a barracuda, something predatory, with teeth. She is admitted to 'people' functions, owing to her more sensitive nature, but barred from others for the same reason.

Emotional Management Works

When learning the ropes of corporate politics, maintaining professional reserve and keeping a lid on one's emotional life may be well-spoken advice. But when the issue is productivity, distinguished performance, and extraordinary leadership, the operative words are ownership, commitment, and caring – conspicuous in all corners of exceptional organizations, sadly lacking in the also-rans, and emotional as all get out.

Traditionally, women employees have been regarded as the 'keepers of the emotional flame' in their companies. When found in men, that emotionalism is often respected as 'company spirit,' but in women, it's a sign of weakness. It's still the department secretaries who make sure birthday cards to out, one of the few 'approved' emotional expressions for many working women. At the same time, what might be the assertive expression of frustration with friends doesn't translate as such in the office. The secretary who complains to her associate that 'I can't stand it when Ms. Jones gives incomplete directions,' or 'It drives me crazy when Mr. Thompson wants me to tell callers he isn't in the office when he is,' is clearly communicating her frustration, but such commonplace expressions only diminish her effectiveness. When an emotional response is sparked by impatience, for example, it is usually read as weakness, not strength – in both women and men.

But when emotion accompanies strength – rallying support to meet a deadline; expressing clear, firm support for a desired change; mobilising a group to improve their work performance – the emotional component is not only helpful, it is essential.

The irony, of course, is that this new approach requires the very characteristics that women have been advised to abandon for the sake of their careers. But old myths die hard. In many work environments, emotional responses serve to undermine the value of a woman's contributions. Women must adapt, they believe, to the environment and let traditional masculine values go unchallenged. When a woman gets to the top, she'll change things. In her useful book *Feminine Leadership,* Marilyn Loden observes:

Although adaptation offers women managers the possibility of some measure of business success, it requires them to repress and essentially deny much of their natural identity and many of their most useful skills. Some are willing to pay this price, others are not.

That the workplace benefits from an infusion of skills other than the purely rational and analytical is an idea whose time is overdue. Patricia Aburdene, co-author of *Reinventing the Corporation,* described a Dartmouth College study in which women's negotiating and deal-making skill outpaced that of their male counterparts in videotaped simulations. 'Women wanted to forge a solution that worked for everyone, whereas the men just wanted to score and were less successful as a result.' Aburdene also believes that 'we are so inundated in our data-drenched society that we're being forced to rely more on gut and intuition, the way entrepreneurs have always done. Women better start to claim these abilities, or pretty soon we'll be hearing about men's intuition!'

The Myth of the Insecure Woman

Women have been told that they lack the confidence they need to perform successfully on the job. 'She's insecure.' 'She waffles on decisions.' 'She doesn't trust her own judgement.' 'She's not tough enough.' This is the stuff the myth is made of; its corollary is that women believe it. Convinced we are our own worst enemies – and finding ready agreement on the part of some male bosses or peers – we invest countless hours and a good deal of money to make ourselves over into worthy competitors for better jobs.

When *The Assertive Woman* was first published, it spawned some 40 books on the same subject; assertiveness training seminars appeared in the course catalogues of almost every university, community college, or women's resource centre in any city you could name. Believing that the reason for our dismal prospects 'lay in (our) own psychology,' according to Rosabeth Moss Kanter, women literally flocked to the programmes in hopes that our underlying deficiencies would be fixed.

Later, women were advised how to dress for success, and, most recently, how to dress in our most becoming colours. When management's doors failed to open for assertive, well-dressed women, it was taken as proof of our persistent personal shortcomings.

We were too busy learning how to pull ourselves up by our own bootstraps to notice the inherent fallacy in such an endeavour. Organizations seemed no more receptive – and perhaps less so – to self-improved women than they were to the original variety! If women are to have a real shot at the jobs and careers they want, it is the organization – not its women – that could use the overhaul.

New Environments for Women – and for Men

The tight managerial control typical of rigid, centralized, bureaucratic organizations is giving way to 'hands-off management,' which carries the expectation that creative contributions can and will be made by all, and grants the elbow room needed to do it. Instead of the all-powerful headquarters staff whose regulations and reporting structures cripple the productive power of the people in the operating divisions or sales regions, some of the best (and top performing) companies are trying out totally new forms of organizing.

Quarter-billion dollar W.L. Gore & Associates in Newark, Delaware, has created what founders Bill and Vieve Gore called a 'lattice organization' (like the lattice structure of a crystal molecule). It means that there is no fixed authority in the traditional sense; the company is run on the basis of fairness, freedom, commitment, and something called 'waterline' – a concept that spells out the responsibility of each associate to consult and share responsibility with other associates when addressing an issue critical to the company's overall health. Having said that, we probably don't need to mention that there are no titles at Gore, other than 'Associate,' except for 'Supreme Commander' – conferred on one woman who wanted that title and who held it until she retired.

You could well argue that women have a built-in upper hand in these places. The feeling is less 'clubby;' there is less emphasis on politics and more on performance; more concern with tangible and often nontraditional measures – such as the degree to which the manager contributes to the development of others, creativity, teamwork, and perseverance.

Women who work in health care fields – especially nurses – have long been expected to serve not only their patients, but the doctors as well. Doing their jobs well often meant doing the work that the doctors regarded as unworthy of their superior skill. But when the escalating cost of medical care forced hospitals to come up with ways to cut back and do more with what they had, it also led to a rediscovery of a most underused asset: the nurses. Goodbye menial worker, hello health care professional! The change was more than semantic. A 'professional' is capable of independent decision-making. A 'professional' is accorded respect consistent with that status. Hospital administrations now depended on nurses to do what the nurses always knew they could do, namely a lot more than change beds. When the stifling restrictions of the past were removed, an entire force of confident professionals was born.

Wendy Reid Crisp, former magazine editor and now founder of her own publishing firm, offers the last word on the myth of the insecure woman. Observes Crisp: 'It's the constant looking over a woman's shoulder that's the real problem. If you just leave her alone, you'd be surprised how much more confident she gets!'

The Myth of the Workhorse Woman (or, 'Women must work twice as hard as men to be thought half as good)' Author Marilyn Loden in her book *Feminine Leadership* recounts this tale: 'At a mock graduation ceremony for 20 women in training to become service technicians, certificates of achievement were awarded to everyone who had completed the rigourous ten-week course. The inscription on the award read: "Whatever women do, they must do twice as well as men to be thought half as good. Fortunately, this is not difficult." ' Working women in every industry agree with Loden when she asserts that they must work harder than men to succeed.

Because there are still relatively few women in corporate managerial ranks, those who hold high-level positions are public figures; every action sticks out. These women work hard to avoid making career mistakes they can ill afford – even a small mistake can provoke a highly visible fall from grace. After the fall, the rest of the organization's members conclude that women just can't cope.

One popular explanation for this pattern has been that women are stymied by their own fear of success. Once more, women's career disappointments are attributed to their own psyches, when in fact, thanks to their extremely high organization profiles, it is the added *visibility*, not success, that they fear.

Added to that is the fact that many prominent women feel it's not only their careers but those of the other women in their organizations that are at stake, and whose interests they must protect. The combination of endless scrutiny and the responsibility to represent an entire class adds up to a lot more work.

Exploiting the 'Worker Bee' Syndrome
There are, of course, organizations which ferociously exploit women's willingness to work hard. They use women to get the job done, because they know we are great worker bees. There may be no money and no recognition in it, but women do it to prove we're capable and independent. Sometimes, what we're really showing is that we can be intimidated.

What we believe we are doing with our overachieving ways is putting to rest the belief that women aren't tough enough to handle a job. The strategy is only partly successful. Plain hard work is seldom recognized, earning women no more than 'assistant vice president' or 'acting vice president' titles – but no shortage of responsibility or extra hours.

Can working harder ever be a successful, constructive, and healthy strategy? In environments where a quality effort is recognized and rewarded, and where management doesn't ride roughshod over employees, dedicated contributions are the source from which extraordinary performance springs. But these remain the exception. That imbalance has beckoned many women veterans of 'worker bee' structures to strike out on their own in entrepreneurial ventures, where they can 'go public' with the skills that their former employer took for granted.

Mary Kay Ash, whose Mary Kay Cosmetics brings in about $275 million each year, told *Inc.* magazine in July, 1985: 'Twenty-two years ago, a woman walked two paces behind the boss. Anytime I made a suggestion, my boss would say, "Mary Kay, you think like a woman." I had this terrible burning inside that said women deserve more than they're getting.' Some may dismiss Ash's success as a fluke, as tacky even – those pink Cadillacs! But, as the cover of *Savvy* queried, 'What colour was the car your company gave *you*?'

Thousands of women have resolved the work-till-you-drop dilemma by learning which environments to avoid, what they do best, and what they're willing to give up for the sake of their careers. Some have found their niches by starting their own enterprises or by contributing their time and talent to employers which value – not exploit – their efforts. It takes guts to do what you know in your heart and soul you can do, whether it's refusing to be overworked and undervalued by your current employer, or going out and building a business on your own terms. Take care with the choice!

The Myth of the Unprofessional Woman
Wendy Reid Crisp described an encounter on a rainy Monday morning as she attempted to hail a taxi: competition for a ride is especially fierce. Loaded down with overstuffed briefcase and bulky manuscripts, she cannot gracefully assert her place in the taxi queue outside King's Cross Station. After several others push and shove their way past her, Crisp realises she'll have to give this competiton all she's got. Deciding that 'total imperialistic aggression is called for,' she dashes at a vacant cab just as a man in a Burberry raincoat makes his approach. She gets there first. She clings to the door handle, won't give it up. Crisp recounts his response: 'Oh, very nice. Very ladylike.' And then, he adds a final insult. '*Very professional.*'

The title of the *Savvy* column in which Crisp offered this report was 'That Was No Lady,' and there's something here for any woman who has ever bumped into the limits of professional behaviour. 'What is "professional" conduct keeps you in your place. "Unprofessional" used to be called "immature." But if a woman – say a director of marketing – does things differently from the man who had the job before her, she's unprofessional. If I did the same things as my male counterpart might – he's an "outrageous genius," but I'm unprofessional.'

The rather Victorian 'unladylike' has been replaced by the modern 'unprofessional,' but the song, as they say, remains the same: It means she's stepped outside traditional, acceptable bounds; she's forgotten her proper place.

For Ladies Only?

Judging from an article that appeared in *USA Today*, perhaps a seminar on 'professionalism in the English language' is needed. The article reported on a study that found the term 'woman' to be 'used in practice for the most respect-worthy woman.' Here's the twist: 'Women are significantly more likely than men to use the term "woman"; men are more apt to refer to "ladies." '

Professional conduct has to do with honourable behaviour, treating people with respect, not going back on your word, doing the best you can, refusing to sell trade secrets on the other side – but it is not necessarily unprofessional to exhibit poor judgement ('That's what people do when they're not 40 years old yet,' says Crisp); to make a mistake; to expect others to honour the terms of a deal; and it is not unprofessional to violate some 'mythical pecking order,' in Crisp's words. But to be summarily dismissed with a hissed 'how unprofessional' – now that's low.

A Woman's Proper Place

But even twentieth century professional women are expected to remember their proper place – which, according to some, is limited to service businesses and 'people functions,' areas where they can make full use of their feminine intuition, sensitivity, and desire to nurture others. People functions, and the jobs within them, however, are not accorded the same respect as line or operating jobs, where the emphasis is placed on the task, the bottom line, and profit and loss.

Crisps warms to this subject. 'Women are regarded as intuitive right-brainers who cannot deal with hard data or acute analysis,' she declares. 'Intuition is neither accepted nor admired in business. The dominant belief is that women are too emotionally attached to people to function objectively; they're afraid to deal with budgets or numbers.' The World of Business has acknowledged women as good nurturers. At least they told us we were good at something! Yet women are still the ones – regardless of the seniority of their positions, in many cases – who are expected to order the office birthday cakes and keep track of births and anniversaries.

Women, in other words, have their own special slots in which they must demonstrate competence and comfort, and which are far removed from the mainstream of the business. Those who succeeded in non-traditional areas did so by proving their 'bottom line orientation.'

This is an area in which educational programmes designed for women can provide a needed service. But ask a professional woman if she participates in all-women educational or special interest groups today and she'll likely tell you, 'Oh no. I outgrew all that years ago. Women's groups are passe.' Women's groups may be good for an evening's entertainment, but we reserve our respect for the co-ed variety. In our haste to avoid being labelled 'troublemakers' or 'radical feminists' we have cut ourselves off from a powerful source of information and support, from organizations and programmes that have moved mountains for many.

The nature of women's groups and programmes has changed over the last decade; they offer positive solutions, not a chance for catharsis. They provide the chance to learn some new skills without an unwanted, judgemental audience; they also teach concrete, useful skills in financial management or planning that some women prefer to learn outside their own organizations, on their own time. It's a lot easier to relax and not worry about asking a 'stupid' question when you are among friends.

The Myth of the Superwoman
Some time in the late Seventies, there was a television commercial aimed at the new woman who does it all. Even now, we can't get its cloying jingle out of her mind:
 I can bring home the bacon
 Fry it up in a pan
 And never ever let you forget
 You're a man . . .

The product is Enjoli perfume. Why we should unwillingly recall the words and music to a commercial for a fragrance we have never sniffed, let alone purchased, who can say. Surely product recall is exactly the point of advertising? But we don't buy the perfume, and the reason has less to do with scent than with that 30-second crash course on how Today's Woman handles at least half a dozen full-time roles, who reduces our mountains into her molehills, and smells great at the same time.

We will admit to an inchoate sense of longing as we viewed that commercial the first time. There, we thought, is the woman who has it all; a great job, a nice house, husband, glamorous evenings, polished kitchen floors. It is not too far a leap to conclude that there's a woman who has not squandered her options, not settled for second best. Buy this perfume and you too can be happy doing it all.

'Doing it all' is a very pretty image, the super-successful woman with the Midas touch, whose responsibilities to employer, family, friends, children, and car pools exhilarate rather than exhaust. What we didn't notice was that the image sold us out: Doing it all is as easy as walking and chewing gum at the same time, croons that commercial, if you're a real woman who has her life together. Lesser vessels need not apply.

To protest that it's not easy, that it's extremely difficult to make compatible professional and personal commitments is to miss the point entirely: Most of us work because our families depend on our income and not out of a desire to prove there's nothing we can't do. And there's the rub. Thanks in part to the elite successful-women-only Enjoli image, we renewed our membership in a club we thought was gone forever. We felt inadequate. But we took the cure and strode purposefully off in hot pursuit of added responsibility. If having it all made women happy, then we just didn't have enough. Soon, we had a name. We were Superwomen.

Fulfilment or Booby Prize?
Enter Carol Orsborn, founder of Superwoman's Anonymous, an organization dedicated to the proposition that 'Not only can you not have it all, but you don't *want* it all.' In 1986, Orsborn's philosophy

was published in her book, *Enough is Enough*. She's onto something here. Consider the opening page: 'Superwomen's Anonymous Handbook Pledge. Raise your right hand and repeat after me: I pledge to read only as much of this as I want, when I want, even if it means stopping in the middle of the sentence.' She knows, from her own fast-track experience, what life is like when coping is the best you can hope for.

'Superwomen's Anonymous produced a sigh of relief in women who suddenly realized they weren't alone,' says Orsborn. 'It doesn't mean they're dropping out; my members are people who have achieved enough to know they can't do any more.' Orsborn wants women to accept themselves as they are, whether they have careers, kids, families, or all three. 'Let's cry over the tough decisions we've had to make, the roads not taken – but this time, not with bitterness, but with the kind of sweet melancholy that reminds us that greatness is a path for the courageous,' writes Orsborn in her book's Epilogue. 'It is time to honour ourselves, to recognize our vulnerability and our limitations, to celebrate the nobility of our own choices . . . Time to appreciate the results when decisions work out – and to offer compassion when they do not.'

That's quite a different picture (and an assertive one) than the image of the working woman enslaved by her job and the demands of her friends and family. The Superwoman's got options, all right, but the price paid just to keep them all open is the problem. Has the media begun to recognize that the Superwoman expectation was misplaced? Enjoli has just launched a new version of that commercial:

I can bring home the bacon
Fry it up in a pan
But sometimes
You've got to give me a hand . . .
Stay tuned!

Chapter 22

The Hardy Spirit

Be nice, girl
You have to pay a price, girl
They like to give advice, girl
Don't think about it twice, girl
It's time to get to work . . .

. . . A vision's just a vision if it's
only in your head . . .
If no one gets to hear it, it's as
good as dead.
It has to come to life!

Bit by bit, putting it together . . .
Piece by piece, only way to
make a work of art.
Every moment makes a
contribution,
Every little detail plays a part,
Having just the vision's no
solution,
Everything depends on
execution
Putting it together, that's what
counts.

Ounce by ounce, putting
it together:
Small amounts, adding up to
make a work of art,
First of all, you need a good
foundation,
Otherwise it's risky from
the start.
Takes a little cocktail
conversation
But without the proper
preparation,
Having just the vision's no
solution,
Everything depends on
execution . . .

. . . Every minor detail is a major
decision.
Have to keep things in scale,
Have to hold to your vision . . .

. . . All they ever want is repetition,
All they really like is what they
know.
Got to keep a link with your
tradition
Got to learn to trust your
intuition
While you re-establish your
position,
So that you can be on exhibit . . .
So that your work can be on
exhibition!

  Bit by bit, putting it together,
Piece by piece, working out the
vision night and day.
All it takes is time and
perseverance
With a little luck along the way,
Putting in a personal
appearance
Gathering supporters and
adherents . . .

Mapping out the songs but in
addition,
Harmonizing each negotiation,
Balancing the part that's all
musician
With the part that's strictly
presentation,
Balancing the money with the
mission
Till you have the perfect
orchestration
Even if you do have the
suspicion
That it's taking all your
concentration.

The art of making art . . .
is putting it together
Bit by bit, beat by beat, part
by part . . .

Barbra Streisand: legendary performer, producer, arranger. Winnie Mandela: South African civil rights activist. Debbi Fields: President of Mrs. Fields Cookies, a $60 million company in 1986, up 140% from the previous year. Lieng Nhan: Vietnamese immigrant and creator of Tru Nails, a $4 million enterprise. A working mother of three in the midwest on a school morning in January. What do these women share? We call them 'hardy spirits': examples of those who keep going in spite of fatigue, fear, disappointments, tough times, even danger. They are women who, given the chance, we would want to know better.

Whether in Calcutta or Des Moines or a thousand places in between, these are women who count on themselves, who have learned to listen to and respect their own opinions; women who stand by their own perceptions and who are willing to act on them. They aren't always cheerful, but they are, somehow, optimistic. They expect good things from themselves. They believe they can handle what life gives them, and they know they can make the kind of life they want. They will take a few chances.

The pessimistically inclined, on the other hand, have no more faith in themselves than they have in anyone else. When the spouse does not run off with the neighbour, they are amazed. If the new venture fails, or every day is not a holiday, the cynic cannot be accused of lack of faith, but merely of realism when she says she told you so.

But let's make this clear at the beginning: a hardy spirit is not necessarily the one smiling out from the cover of *Time*, the one who takes such bold, audacious steps that you cannot imagine yourself doing the same in a million years. To cultivate a hardy spirit is not to aim for flashy, eye-catching gestures of bravery. It is not grandstanding or making bet-your-career decisions, nor is it aiming to please. The hardy spirit begins with a certain calm determination, a vision of where you are heading, bolstered by the faith that you can get there. The rest is accomplished in tiny, tiny ways: taking advantage of the opportunities you see, making the most of the skill you have, discovering that you can tolerate (and learn from) the unpleasant or uncomfortable, that disappointments can be bridged, and never, ever giving up.

Streisand and Sondheim are right: what counts is execution – the doing of the thing, little by little, and piece by piece, putting it together. It's an old idea, eloquently articulated by architect Mies van der Rohe: 'The spirit of the thing lives in the details.'

We could each make our own lists: 'Hardy Spirits I Have Known (or Wish I Knew).' Women who, from Kansas City to Hollywood to Johannesburg, share that same quality of rootedness, bravery – even boldness – in the face of difficulty. It is impossible to imagine such women scurrying away from trouble or challenge. We admire them partly because they're nobody's fool, and partly because they have done what the song describes. They take things as they come, bit by bit, step by step, even when a single step seems more like a leap off the edge, when safety or common sense might dictate hanging back.

Such is the case with Winnie Mandela in South Africa. Her hardy spirit leads her to stand against apartheid, under conditions so inhospitable as to be unthinkable to those who take freedom for granted. Her husband, Nelson Mandela, has been imprisoned for the last twenty-five years in Pollsmoor Prison, where he is serving a life sentence for sabotage. Winnie herself has been routinely exiled, imprisoned, and restricted by the South African government over the years for speaking out. Although she believes that this injustice cannot last forever, she lives in a place where official policies grind relentlessly to the contrary.

In a different realm but no less energetic is the comeback of Lieng Nhan, a woman wanted in her native country for spying for the Americans, and who was finally forced to leave Vietnam in the late '60s. She landed in Nevada, USA, attended beauty school, and set about improving on the design of the acrylic false fingernails she saw so many women wearing. Five years later, Nhan had perfected her design, and sales reps couldn't wait to start selling. Her company now spans nine beauty salons, staffed by thirty-plus family members whom she brought to the United States. But as she told *Success!* magazine last year, triumph was not without cost: 'I saved every penny for my shop. I lived in a $132-a-month apartment, ate nothing but fried rice, and never even went to the cinema.' Through it all, she put her fears behind her and headed toward the future:

'The last time I saw my mother before I fled Vietnam I told her, "Don't worry – I know how to survive." She's beginning to believe me now.'

The young woman who is responsible for everybody's favourite cookies took her company public in 1986 on the London Stock Exchange Unlisted Securities Market. Twenty-nine million shares went for \$62 million. Pretty good for a former housewife who borrowed \$50,000 from her husband to start her own cookie company. Now practically an institution in the United States, Mrs. Fields Cookies was born in 1977 because, as Debbi Fields has explained, 'I am a cookie person.' She's turned that passion into an enormously successful business, one that many have tried to copy.

And what more can be said about Barbra Streisand, the woman who proves again and again that she's full of surprises. Known best as a multi-faceted performer and producer, she got her start in New York City in 1961, when she won \$50 in a talent contest sponsored by a local bar. From there it was Broadway appearances, motion pictures, and then producing and arranging movies and albums. There was 'Yentl,' the movie she wrote, directed, produced, and starred in. There was 'The Broadway Album,' the collection of music classics which gave new meaning to the word perseverance. Finding little encouragement for the project, she doggedly pursued her vision until it was real; she even found a song which captured the whole process for her, and persuaded Stephen Sondheim to write additional lyrics to more accurately fit her experience. We keynoted this chapter with an excerpt from it.

Streisand has been described as one of the 'new breed' of Hollywood women – among them Jessica Lange, Sally Field, Goldie Hawn, and Jane Fonda – who have broken out of their starlet beginnings with gusto. It's a long way from the perky purity of 'The Flying Nun,' the sex kitten adventuress in 'Barbarella,' the lush and lovely object of King Kong's affections, or the dizzy, endearing blonde.

And it's not just the successful and famous. All across the country there are women who are up with the sun every day, getting little fingers into mittens, dishing out breakfast, holding down jobs, making house payments, contributing to their communities. They may be the hardiest of spirits: the women who will never have public accolades, but who deserve them nonetheless.

It would be easy to get the impression that the hardy spirit takes a highly public stand against things as they are – Winnie Mandela for one – but it would not be complete. The same nobility marks the determined efforts of unsung, unseen women who work just as hard to change things as they are in some of the world's factories, hospitals and schools. All around us are women who bring their intelligence and their stamina to strengthen themselves, their families, companies, or communities. And most important, inside each of us is kindling to spark the hardy spirit, just waiting for a reason to show.

That's the heart of the matter. The hardy spirit can be encouraged, coaxed forth. You don't need a happy childhood (some would argue that overcoming a painful one forges the *hardier* spirit). You don't need a certain kind of education. You don't have to be a daredevil. The sort of equipment you do need you can't buy anywhere: courage, and a sense of humour. The essence of a hardy spirit is some measure of each.

Courage: Where would the hardy spirit be without it? Every day we're handed dozens of chances to step out and see what we're made of – courage or cowardice? Paul Tillich in 1952 wrote that 'courage is the knowledge of what to avoid and what to dare.' The operative word is 'knowledge,' and the key idea is *choice*. Accepting blindly every dare that comes your way isn't courage, it's recklessness. By contrast, people who could be called 'courageous' are informed risk-takers. They are alert to the possibility that marriage may become divorce, but they know themselves and their partners well enough to believe that's a risk worth taking. What bolsters their confidence even further is the conviction that if they do meet trouble in the future, they have what it takes to get through it; they won't fall apart under its weight.

They actually *practise* taking manageable risks, to learn how it feels, to get acquainted with danger signals, to become familiar with early warning signs. The courageous can visualize themselves bouncing back from disappointment or failure; the timid, once burned, resolve never to try again. A mixture of ingenuity and action – resourcefulness – marks the courageous individual.

'Hardy Spirit Power'

The longest journey begins with a single step, as the saying goes. Below we offer a collection of tiny steps which together contribute to the makings of the 'hardy spirit.' Each suggestion involves a degree of risk (we draw the line at skydiving) on the assumption that if you can do what you are afraid to do, some measure of courage results. Bon voyage!

1. Follow the example of our friend Dee, who, in her early 40's, determined it was now or never for the piano lessons (and that first public recital!) she didn't have time for when her two children were underfoot.

2. Face the British number-one fear head on: Enrol in a public speaking course.

3. If you are feeling adventurous, watch a scary movie all the way through. (We offer this seriously but advisedly. Nancy still refuses to watch 'Psycho.')

4. Volunteer several hours a week at your local hospital, youth centre, community hospice, drug rehabilitation centre – any public agency whose work you respect.

5. Become a 'Big Sister' and devote time each week or month to an underprivileged child.

6. The next time you experience a disappointment or letdown (even crushing defeat), stop yourself from whining or complaining excessively about it. Imagine how Katharine Hepburn would handle it. Do likewise.

7. Enrol in the 'Outward Bound' programme or another wilderness survival group experience. Graduates swear there's nothing more exhilarating!

8. Pack yourself off to the nearest health spa. Or, just go to the Y or your local health club and pretent it's a spa!

9. Audition for your community theatre group.

10. Learn to swim.

11. Watch yourself on videotape or film.

12. Listen to your own voice on audiotape.

13. Give a speech.

14. Write a letter to the editor of your local newspaper on a topic which is important to you and about which you have an opinion. Take a stand.

15. Learn more about the lives of this country's 'farm wives,' those women who work as hard as their spouses, but whose accomplishments go unheralded.

16. Join an exercise class and attend regularly!

17. Get serious about that hobby you have always been too busy to begin.

18. Keep a written journal to record your private thoughts and feelings. Set aside a few minutes each morning or evening to make new entries.

19. Ask a friend out to dinner.

20. Spend an uninterrupted hour with your kids – no flashy diversions, just listening and enjoying their company.

21. Enrol for further education, college degree, or post-graduate work.

22. Adopt a new puppy or kitten, or a sweet older animal who needs a home.

23. Take a holiday by yourself – even if it's only a day or two.

24. Be the first one in a group to laugh at a funny story or joke. Don't wait to see if anyone else is laughing first!

25. Play a game of 'Scruples' with your children. (Scruples is a game that zeroes in on how players would handle a variety of ethical dilemmas.)

26. Get up early and go for an energizing walk or run (this, too, is passed along with all due respect for the task).

27. The next time you feel anger or frustration, admit it and express it. Don't talk yourself out of it by pretending your feelings aren't important enough to express.

28. Ride your local funfair's most extravagant thrill ride!

29. If you're a manager and supervise others, ask them what three things you do that they like, and what three things you do that really drive them crazy. Listen! Take the responses seriously as valuable feedback. Begin to mend your ways. Then, repeat the process at least every month.

30. To a good friend, admit the truth.

31. Tell your boss when you think he or she has done a good job.

32. Start to read those books you thought were nonsense when you were at school.

33. Indulge your passion for romance novels (or science fiction, mystery, short story collections).

34. Forgive the one who done you wrong.

35. A funny movie with two very funny stars is 'Outrageous Fortune,' starring Shelley Long and Bette Midler. The first film in which two women co-starred in a big-screen comedy, there are priceless moments in this one! Rent and watch it.

36. Enrol in a foreign language course to learn Spanish, or French, or Italian, or Chinese – that language you have always wished you could speak and understand better than you do now.

37. How long has it been since you had a complete medical check-up?

38. Not for the faint of heart: Take flying lessons.

39. Attend your school class reunion.

41. Take the time to recognize (and respect) the first signs of stress, discomfort, or danger in yourself. Push yourself a little to reach an important goal, but honour your limits.

Every step toward becoming an assertive woman is also a step toward courage: the courage to say no, to offer a compliment, to declare your love, to make a mistake, to visit the dentist, to change your mind. Each step is underpinned by the faith that you can live with the consequences. Think of each entry in your own 'Assertive Behaviour Hierarchy' as a courageous step, and you've got a tailormade course in developing courage. It isn't that you will feel no fear or anxiety in the process, it's that you will take each step knowing that you might feel uncomfortable at first. With practice, it gets easier.

It also gets funnier. The hardy spirit has that marvellous ability to laugh at herself and her trials and tribulations. Humour can reconcile otherwise impossible situations and is probably the only thing that keeps life's disappointments from overwhelming us.

The hardy spirit – a unique blend of strength, vulnerability, and fun – resides in us all. Take the time to get to know her. She's worth it!

Chapter 23

Most-Often-Asked Questions About the Assertive Woman

To some people in 1975, *The Assertive Woman* was a controversial book. It was certainly the sort of book that made people ask questions.

We received hundreds of letters from readers of *The Assertive Woman* over the last dozen years, and we have worked directly with hundreds more women (and men!) who were attracted enough to the idea of assertiveness to find ways to make room for it in their own worlds.

The people who wrote to us certainly did have interesting lives! We heard from data processors, physicians, students, teachers, mothers, daughters, grandmothers, business executives, small business owners, sales reps, estate agents, farmers, consultants, travel agents, convicts, administrative assistants, school superintendents, librarians, chefs, soldiers, sailors, art critics, clergy, and mechanics.

In spite of remarkable differences in our readers and seminar participants, we discovered that their questions were quite similar and sometimes identical. We attempt here to respond to the most frequent questions about *The Assertive Woman*, with heartfelt thanks to so many who took the time to ask.

- *In your book, you describe four categories of behaviour: passive, aggressive, indirectly aggressive, and assertive. I get the impression, though, that the only 'correct' answer is assertive. Is that true?*
  Before *The Assertive Woman* was published, we spent several years working with women who wanted to improve their self-confidence and exercise more control over their lives. Regardless of their economic standing, age, occupation, or marital status, there

was a striking consistency in what these women had to say. They felt powerless – some said 'invisible' – and they were looking for self-respect, independence, and the courage to make their own choices, which might differ from the ones they were expected to make. They wanted to learn to say 'no,' to stop apologizing every time they turned around. They wanted to be comfortable taking the lead in new situations.

This added up to a pattern of passive, self-denying behaviour which women seemed to have been brought up to accept as synonymous with femininity. When assertiveness became popular in the early 'seventies, it was hailed as the most effective way to express oneself: for the first time, someone was saying that women could communicate without apology and without being called bitchy. No wonder it was so enthusiastically embraced by so many!

But the reason assertiveness seems the only 'right' answer may lie in its singular ability to promote self-respect. When you think about it, assertiveness practised over the years has more going for it than, say, a lifetime of battles that aggressiveness might bring, or a life that is spent wondering 'what would have happened if . . .?' that is the lot of the passive.

That's a big advantage. But there are good reasons why passive, aggressive, or indirect behaviour might, in fact, be more effective in some specific instance: you decide not to send your burned steak back to the restaurant kitchen when you learn it's the new chef's first night on the job; your assertive efforts to hail a cab on a crowded streetcorner fail miserably; you have a legitimate complain about your spouse's conduct, but decide to table it because he's had a disastrous day at work. Every day you have choices about how a given situation might best be met, and the answer won't always be the assertive one.

But here's the point to remember about making choices other than so-called 'assertive' ones: when *you* decide not to voice a justified complaint, or when *you* realize that the only way to get that taxi is to beat out the competition and stop worrying about being 'nice,' making those choices is, in itself, an assertive response, as long as you are willing to stand by the results. If you can't live with the consequences of your action (or lack of it), don't lose sleep wondering if what you did was 'truly assertive.' If you came by that choice honestly and can live comfortably with its costs or rewards, then you've done the best you can.

Ultimately, it's always up to you to decide whether or not to 'assert yourself' in a given situation. As assertiveness becomes 'second nature' to you, it has a unique fit with the way you are, with your own likes and dislikes, and with your own environment. What's assertive for you may not be for your best friend. What you're aiming for is not identical, word-for-word responses, but authentic behaviours that reflect your own thoughts, feelings, and preferences – and that respect the rights of others.

● *Are you saying there are times when aggressive, passive, or indirectly aggressive approaches work better than assertive ones?*

Assertiveness, as a life-long process, promotes equality in relationships and preserves self-respect. Along the way, however, there will undoubtedly be particular situations which cannot be resolved quickly or easily. Any complex negotiation, for example, involves extensive give-and-take – sometimes more give and sometimes more take – but eventually it can be resolved to everyone's satisfaction. In the same way, you will find that the assertive thing to do on certain occasions is to be more passive or aggressive than you might otherwise.

A passive approach might be best when you have a legitimate point or complaint, but decide not to bring it up because the timing is poor. For example, the person you want to speak with is clearly having a rotten day, or is so preoccupied with something else that any comment from you – regardless of how assertive or justified – will be unsuccessful. A better choice is to wait until he or she can give you full attention.

Aggression may be called for when you face a clear and present danger or threat. Crisis situations fall into this category. There is no time for discussion; action is what's needed. When you must protect yourself, either physically or emotionally or both, a rapid, aggressive response is appropriate.

The appropriate uses of an indirect aggression, usually some form of manipulation, are tricky. As short-run strategies only, some people have found them helpful in dealing with organizational politics – when what you want cannot be stated directly and must be 'finessed.' The problem here, however, is the tremendous potential for reprisal and revenge once the indirect strategy is found out. A less potent form of indirect aggression is volunteering to serve on a friend's pet committee because you want her help on a favourite project of yours. (The assertive choice would be to simply ask for your friend's help directly.)

The decision to approach a situation non-assertively must always be carefully considered. We think there are serious drawbacks and can't recommend the approach wholeheartedly, except under exceptional conditions.

● *In the beginning, assertiveness meant certain behaviours or ways to express what I wanted or felt in particular situations. Now I'm hearing about 'an assertive lifestyle.' What's the difference?*

Assertiveness started as a collection of skills and behaviours intended to help people who felt inadequate or uneasy in social and interpersonal situations. People felt too passive (apologetic) or too aggressive (hostile) in dealing with certain of these situations. As people started to change their less successful or productive behaviours and learned to be more direct, straightforward, and expressive, they found that loneliness and depression gave way to a sense of confidence and self-assurance. They realized they didn't want to go back to their old ways of behaving.

The term 'assertive lifestyle' really means a life-long commitment to behaving in ways that strengthen your own self-respect. Rather than spending years suffering in silence, it means being able to choose how you want your life to look. Assertiveness is much more, we have learned, than learning how to accomplish an immediate objective, such as getting the raise you want at work, or expressing anger. We now think of it as a process – one that grows over a long period of time.

This means, of course, that there are no 'magic answers' that fit everyone. The important point is that *you* take the time to focus on what feels right for *you*, and act in your own best interests. Viewed that way, assertiveness is much more than developing some new skills. It's something that starts inside you (see Chapter 5, 'The Inner Game of Assertion') and progresses from there.

● *You write about 'The Compassion Trap.' I am uncomfortable with it. Do you mean feeling compassion for someone else is a problem? Since when is compassion a trap?*

Though we didn't coin the term (Margaret Adams did, in an article she wrote in 1971), when we first heard about 'The Compassion Trap,' we recognized it. Since then, there has been a great deal of controversy and misunderstanding about exactly what it does mean.

The Compassion Trap describes the woman who believes she exists to provide compassionate support for others at all times. Compassion is only a trap when it *enslaves*: when a woman believes that the only way she can legitimately express herself is through serving the needs of others. Her own needs, feelings, desires, or ambitions are not respected or taken seriously – by herself or by others. A woman 'trapped' by compassion will not honour her own legitimate rights or needs. She 'gives up' on herself, comes to resent it, and then finds she is depressed or bitter as a result.

To be able to feel compassion is one of the hallmarks of being human. We certainly do not suggest that part of becoming assertive is to feel less empathy for others. We have found, instead, that real compassion for others depends on a healthy sense of self-respect first. Compassion is being *sensitive to, but not enslaved by,* others' demands and expectations. We've found that it's a subtle, but critical, difference.

● *The management in the company I work for seems to discourage assertiveness in their employees. Even when I have a good point to make, my boss just tell me not to rock the boat. This is getting frustrating. What can I do?*

If only we had a penny for every time we've heard this one! There are a few things you might try. First, keep in mind that your boss has a different perspective on the company. You can learn something about 'the way we do things around here' from the way your boss responds to your ideas. If, however, your suggestions are consistently ignored, you may have to consider other alternatives.

It is so easy to blame one's difficulties on the boss. While we don't suggest that you ought to stick it out in a job that makes you miserable, the first requirement is to be sure you have done *what you can* to make the situation work. Since managers want to see some tangible results, can you gather enough information to indicate that your idea is worth pursuing further? Can you, for instance, show how your suggestion would lead to improved efficiency or reduced costs? Have you done your homework before you present your idea? Or is it likely to be perceived as unrealistic or incomplete?

If you've done your homework and collected enough information to suggest that your idea has merit and you still can't interest your boss in your proposal, a slightly riskier strategy is to take your idea (if it's important enough to you) to someone else in the company who might be willing to back it. The risk here is going above your supervisor, who may resent that approach. In other companies, such a strategy is actually encouraged, on the theory that if you can sell it to a higher-up, you can sell it to anyone.

But if you still encounter resistance to your input, you may find that the only solution is to find a department or a company that appreciates you. It is always a hard decision, but in this situation, you may find it preferable to fighting a losing battle.

- *We hear a lot about how assertiveness is an advantage, both personally and professionally. Are there disadvantages as well? What about the cost of assertiveness?*

This is an intriguing question, one that could only be answered several years after the first blush of assertiveness had deepened and women and men had been living with the results for a while. There is no question that assertiveness carries a price-tag, although it's not as high as many predicted it would be. Ten years ago, there were those who said assertive women would mean the destruction of the family and of all the traditions our society holds dear. That, of course, has not happened. What has occurred is that women have begun to test themselves in new arenas. A very large percentage of women now hold jobs outside their homes. Relatively fewer women are having children, and when they do, they're having them later than they used to.

Assertiveness had something to do with these changes. Women discovered that they felt better about themselves and their surroundings when they exercised control over what they did, and when. But the piper must be paid: having more freedom of choice also meant adding responsibility to live with the outcomes, which was not always easy or comfortable. Deciding to delay having a family may be good for the career, but physically riskier as the biological clock keeps on ticking. Once you decide to assert yourself, it's only the beginning. The real challenge comes later, when you come face to face with the impact of the decision you've made; that's the time the cost, if any, will be clearer.

There's another facet to the cost of assertiveness, and it has to do with perception. It's still a fact of life that assertiveness in women is perceived differently than assertiveness in men. Although assertiveness is increasingly rewarded in women, there remains that not-so-subtle expectation that she should remember her proper – usually submissive – 'place' nonetheless. When she asserts herself, then, she is to some extent stepping out from the norm, which may not be wholly welcomed or respected. If this happens in important relationships, they must be rebuilt on more equitable footing to last; otherwise, the cost may be the relationships itself.

We hasten to add that most of the time, the benefits of assertiveness – enhanced self-esteem, confidence, enthusiasm, energy – do outweigh the costs. Most of us find a way to integrate assertive responses into our lives without causing tumultuous change, and in such a way that those we care about back us up. In other words, it's an evolution, not a revolution. We choose as thoughtfully as we can what our commitments will be, and we stand by our decisions. The outcomes may sometimes surprise, frighten, or anger us, but we still manage to feel it's worth the trouble, that there is more to be gained from acting directly in our own interests.

● *Assertiveness isn't just for women, is it? Don't men need to learn how to become assertive, too?*

Many people have asked us why we didn't call our book *The Assertive Person* instead of *The Assertive Woman*. The ability to assert oneself is a basic human skill and a positive characteristic for both men and women. But in 1975, we addressed an enormous social gap. If a man wanted to become more assertive, his interest was much easier to support and encourage than was that of a woman who expressed the same desire. Assertiveness was regarded as an essential component of masculinity, and could therefore be respected in men. Observed in women, assertiveness was very often threatening. It meant that traditional submissive, eager-to-please girlishness would be thrown over in favour of adult femininity, to reveal a woman who was fully capable of making her own choices and who did not feel compelled to secure anyone's approval first. A woman who could look you in the eye and tell you she liked you – highly attractive in a man, but when found in a woman, disconcerting in the extreme.

It's still a little easier, a decade later, to accept assertiveness as an essentially masculine quality – there's still room for a book called *The Assertive Woman*! And men, of course, can still get something from learning to be assertive. (Several other books on assertiveness are written for both sexes.) We have received many letters from men first drawn to the book to help their wives 'learn to speak her mind.' Later, perhaps, they wanted to be 'assertive, not so aggressive' in their own lives.

Because women had denied the validity of their own thoughts, feelings, and talents for so long, we wrote for them. We hoped they would react as we did, that it was such a *relief* to feel that you weren't alone, that your feelings were important and deserved respect, that you didn't have to go through life as somebody's doormat, that asserting yourself didn't mean locking the people you cared about out of your life.

It was more than a personal awakening, it was political and sociological. Although we concur that the world could use more assertiveness from men *and* from women, our special bond is with women. Their experiences, after all, mirrored our own.

Chapter 24

Freedom

As it has over the last decade, we hope *The Assertive Woman* continues to encourage self-respect and respect for others. The best way to protect your rights it to use them – honestly, often, sensitively, and well. Your enhanced sense of strength and worth will rub off on your friends and family, as thousands of newly assertive women have discovered for themselves. Yet you may be worried about negative or painful results: 'What if my family doesn't like the assertive new me? What if my husband leaves me? What if my parents kick me out of the house? Could I get fired for insubordination? Is assertiveness really worth it?'

There is no question that becoming assertive is not always a bed of roses – there are those thorns! If you face substantial resistance and cannot count on support at home, we encourage you to seek the help of a professional counsellor or an assertiveness training seminar (conducted by a qualified professional) that you and your family and friends as well as possible for your new assertive behaviours.

Even in less difficult situations, where the thorns are mere irritations, you will doubtless encounter some uncomfortable consequences of your assertive behaviours. Some people will misinterpret your behaviours; others will resent it; and still others may like what they see but will not know how to support you. If you are reluctant to assert yourself because you are afraid of the consequences, think about the legacy of passive or aggressive responses: you likely felt hurt, anxious, helpless, depressed, guilty, or ignored; you were taken advantage of more than once; though you wanted to, you couldn't find a way to change things; friends dwindled because they grew weary of yet another argument with you, or because they gave up.

Now consider the positive benefits that prompted you to seek a change: a greater sense of well-being, self-respect, control, and enthusiasm; less time spent complaining or suffering. Ask yourself whether it is the *fear* of being lonely (as opposed to actually *feeling* lonely) that is holding you back. Temporary discomfort can be tolerated and survived, and can even be *expected* to occur on the way to building enhanced self-confidence – as much as muscle aches or cramps occur when you start to exercise again.

If you are concerned about unpleasant consequences of assertion, or if you think your friends and family are not on your side when it comes to assertiveness, take the time to talk it over with them. Are there special circumstances which might account for the lack of support you feel? Is it temporary? Can you compromise or accommodate others' feelings? Just talking about the problem will help to reduce anxiety about what to expect.

Asserting yourself in your own life carried personal rewards; you can also work to bring those benefits to a wider circle of people. Here are a few suggestions about how one person can make a difference:

Business. The lack of employer backed day-care for children of employees is a national disgrace. A persistent, assertive approach is essential if we want child care programmes for working parents' children. It is not a 'woman's issue.' It is a *work* issue and it must be addressed as such. Without child care support, working parents experience undue hardship in simply meeting the basic employment contract – not to mention turning in an excellent performance! There is mounting evidence to suggest that having good, solid day care programmes available decreases absenteeism and improves morale in the working parent. As more parents work, reliable day care is a simple necessity, not a luxury. This is an issue which can be influenced by steady, collective assertiveness – meaning you'll have to be willing to break a little bureaucratic china in the process!

Other structural changes include alternative work schedules and flexible working hours to accommodate the lives of the women and men employees; an increase in 'cafeteria style' benefits packages, in which employees are allotted certain individual benefits such as pensions, or private health care; an increase in the number of company-sponsored health and fitness programmes open to all employees; the growing number of women who are leaving the corporate world to start their own businesses on their own terms. Each of these developments has been aided by an assertive approach.

A related area is employee participation in profit-sharing programmes. The first such approach, called The Scanlon Plan, was inaugurated in the 1930's. Giving every employee a 'piece of the rock' is an idea whose time is overdue. Either we deal people in and facilitate full participation in the success of the enterprise, or we don't. If we don't, we will not be able to compete. Period. Employees can and do make a difference in their organizations. If your employer does not offer profit sharing or gain sharing, do a little homework to find out what other local companies have such a programme. Research the successes and failures. When you have collected data that will show that you have given careful consideration to all sides of the issue, present it to your boss or to someone else in management.

Government. Under the strongly-felt influence of the National Business and Professional Women's Organization and other special interest groups, many laws relating to women's issues are being changed in the US. Women have successfully asserted themselves to bring women's issues more clearly into focus in the eyes of politicians who are sensitive to the power of women's votes. The most powerful and emotional issues concerning women are legal abortion and the complex issue of comparable worth. If the Equal Rights Amendment resurfaces during the next several years, both issues will receive enormous attention. An assertive response in each case it to dig into the issues and to become involved in some way that will be challenging. Don't wait for someone else to cast the deciding vote.

Society, Geopolitics, and the Environment. There are other compelling issues which deserve careful, assertive attention: the dilemma of South Africa's apartheid system of government and its connection to the rest of the world; the proliferation of nuclear arms; protection of the environment in which we live; protection of the world's wildlife, and particularly its endangered species; the growing number of homeless people in this country. These are only a few of the issues which can only be changed when people together work to turn them around.

Education. There is a revolution afoot in Western countries' educational systems. School administrators and teachers face new and controversial social issues: increasing evidence that drug use and abuse begins at an alarmingly young age; the frightening proliferation of AIDS and other sexually-transmitted diseases; the growing numbers of children having children; the sad fact that an alarming number are functionally illiterate; and the evidence of declining schooleavers standards in examination results. In most communities, pressure is brought to bear on the educational system to provide information and answers, a positive but incomplete step.

This is a time when parents and citizens must take an active part in their own communities to chip away at ossified educational institutions. Simply volunteering at the school library a few hours a week may be enough to start. The point is to beef up the attention you give to your own schools. How does your community rank in your town? What is most urgently needed in your local schools? Is your local PTA in good shape?

Running a Home. For the first time, running a home has begun to receive a little bit of what it always lacked: respect. That women can delay having children until after their jobs or careers are established has been the most significant change over the last ten years. It means that women hold down jobs and run households, and it changed the old idea of being a 'housewife' for good.

Whether the term is 'Domestic Engineer' or 'Domestic Goddess,' the role of the keeper of the hearth has undergone profound changes. In hundreds of homes across the country, women and men have forged working partnerships to handle the responsibilities of running the household. The one who cooks well prepares meals; the one who manages money well takes care of the books; chores that either could do are divided or accomplished on an ad hoc basis. Traditional roles have been reversed: it's a subject Hollywood dramatized with the wildly successful movie 'Mr. Mom,' in which she headed out to the office each morning and he ran the house and took care of the kids. One thing seems clear. All bets are off where running a household is concerned; it is something that is being invented on a day to day basis by the millions of people who do it. No two solutions look alike.

These are only a few of the broad scale social issues that can be influenced with assertive attention. Pick an issue or development that you genuinely care about. Then consider the varied ways you can become involved:

● Write letters; send telegrams.
● Form or join local community action groups.
● Attend local council meetings; PTA meetings, planning commission hearings.
● Write articles; write a letter to the editor of your local newspaper; take a public stand about an important issue.
● Volunteer your time to work on a political campaign.
● Participate on church, civic, or government committees or task forces.
● Don't buy furs if you object to cruelty to animals; don't consume goods or services if they support a cause you cannot stand behind.
● Organize a fund raiser for a cause you believe in.
● Get involved with The Samaritans, Riding for the Disabled, your local charity shop or any worthwhile organization needing help.
● Donate your time to a special organization you want to. Support: women's counselling centres; 'safe houses' for battered women; day care centres; women's health care programmes.

Public and social issues are amenable to change through assertive action. It's also important not to regard assertion as a cure-all for every social ill or as a simplistic way to achieve personal strength and self-worth. Real problems are stubborn and significant change requires patience and power. Speaking out on a subject you believe in will invite criticism or even censure – it is not easy. But until a better solution comes along, there is no substitute for that leap of faith that begins by taking the first small step.

Beyond Assertiveness

Assertiveness is much more than a strategy for self-defence. The assertive woman can use her assertive skills to reach out in a warm, humorous, expressive way, as a very positive, human communication. There is no 'standard' or single correct way to be an assertive woman. We have seen many women develop an assertive style that works for them, bringing to it their own personal touch, and we support this individualism for each reader.

Finally, we'd like to leave you with the same thought with which we began this edition: becoming an assertive woman is a giant step toward personal freedom and growth. We urge you to take this first step and let us hear from you. Good luck, patience, perseverance, assertiveness – and love.